THE CATHOLIC UNIVERSITY OF AMERICA
CANON LAW STUDIES

No. 183

COMMUNICATION—A SOURCE OF PRIVILEGES

AN HISTORICAL SYNOPSIS AND COMMENTARY

A DISSERTATION

Submitted to the Faculty of the School of Canon Law of the Catholic University of America in partial fulfillment of the requirements for the degree of Doctor of Canon Law

By

REV. RAYMOND ANTHONY MATULENAS, O.S.B., J.C.L.
Priest of St. Bede Abbey, Peru, Illinois

THE CATHOLIC UNIVERSITY OF AMERICA PRESS
WASHINGTON, D. C.
1943

NIHIL OBSTAT:

EDUARDUS G. ROELKER, S.T.D., J.C.D.
Censor Deputatus

IMPRIMI POTEST

LAURENTIUS A. VOHS, O.S.B.
Abbas Monasterii Sancti Bedae

IMPRIMATUR

JOSEPH H. SCHLARMAN, D.D.
Episcopus Peoriensis
Peoriae, Ill., die 22 iun. 1943

Printed By
THE WAYSIDE PRESS
MENDOTA, ILLINOIS

Ut in Omnibus Glorificetur Deus

TABLE OF CONTENTS

INTRODUCTION

The Catholic Church, which has been commissioned by Christ to direct the faithful to their supernatural, eternal end, accomplishes its mission here upon earth through the exercise of a threefold power: the legislative, judicial, and executive. She uses her legislative power by enacting laws which are necessary and useful for the attainment of her final purpose.[1] In order that the Church might attain her final end in conformity with the demands of justice, she must enact laws which impose uniform obligations upon her members, and she must secure the rights of her members in a uniform way, for the very nature of law demands that the common, rather than the particular good be promoted.[2]

Holy Mother Church has always complied with this cardinal principle of jurisprudence, but, at the same time, she has recognized the need, in exceptional circumstances, of deviating from the common law in order to foster the common good.

In a society as universal as the Church, circumstances are bound to arise in which exceptions to the common law or concessions beyond its provisions are deemed necessary. Recognizing this need, the Church has, since earliest times, provided for such contingencies of time, place, and person, by granting dispensations[3] and privileges.[4] By doing so, she has not exceeded the limits of her legislative power,

[1]Ottaviani, *Institutiones Iuris Publici Ecclesiastici* (2 vols. Typis Polyglottis Vaticanis, 1935) I, n. 42.

[2]Thomas Aquinas, St. *Summa Theologica* (6 vols. Parisiis: Vives: 1895), I--II, q. 90, art. 4.

[3]Canon 80: Consult also Brys, *De Dispensatione in Iure Canonico* (Brugis: Beyaert, 1925), 16.

[4]" . . . it is quite fitting that the Church establish special rules, make allowances for the various characters and customs of men, reward the meritorious, and make concessions contrary to law or outside the same: hence the reason for privileges." Cicognani, *Canon Law* (authorized English version by Rev. J. O'Hara and Rev. F. Brennan, Philadelphia: Dolphin Press, 1935), 779.

but she has merely exercised an integral part of that power.[5]

During the early centuries of the Church, privileges were wont to be granted only directly by the Pope,[6] and hence, at this time, direct concession was the only recognized source of privileges. Later, however, with the gradual development of canonical jurisprudence, custom and prescription, which were acknowledged as legitimate sources of rights not contained in general law, became recognized sources of privileges as well.[7] Then, in the Middle Ages, another source of privileges was introduced into the administrative policy of the Church. It attained a great deal of influence for it became one of the richest sources of privileges. It is this source, technically known as Communication of Privileges, which serves as the subject matter of this dissertation.

The dissertation itself, which will be limited to a study of the theory of communication of privileges, is divided into three parts. The first part is devoted to an analysis of the nature of the institute and to a study of its species and its modes of operation. Because of the profound influence of the documents authorizing communication on the institute of communication itself, on its development, and on its interpretation, a chapter in the first part is devoted to a study of these documents.

The second part of the dissertation treats of the historical development and operation of the institute. Since the benefits of the institute of communication were en-

[5]"Breviter intelligi potest quod, quicumque potest constitutionem facere et quatenus et in quibus potest, et privilegium . . . dare potest." Hostiensis, *Summa Aurea* (Venetiis: 1570), lib. V. tit. 33, *de privilegiis et excessibus privilegiatorium,* § *Quis possit privilegium concedere.*

[6]Van Hove, *Commentarium Lovaniense in Codicem Iuris Canonici* (5 vols., Mechliniae-Dessain: 1939), vol. I, *De Privilegiis--De Dispensationibus,* p. 6. This latter work, which is cited frequently in this dissertation, will be referred to as *De Privilegiis.*

[7]Cf. Van Hove, *De Privilegiis,* pp. 69-97.

joyed almost exclusively by religious institutes, it is unavoidably necessary to stress this aspect of the institute in the historical section. Without studying the institute of communication in conjunction with its application to the religious organizations within the Church, it would be impossible to evaluate the institute properly, for its frequent, if not continued use, in favor of religious institutes guided the formulation of most of the legal and doctrinal rules which govern its operation.

The third part of this dissertation contains a commentary on Canons 64 and 65. Since the dissertation is restricted to a study of the theory of communication in general, an explicit treatment of communication of privileges in favor of specific subjects as provided by the Code[8] does not fall within the scope of this dissertation.[9]

Before proceeding with an analysis of the juridic institute of communication, the writer takes this opportunity to communicate his heartfelt gratitude to his religious superiors, the late Rt. Rev. Abbot Justus Wirth, O.S.B. and his successor, the Rt. Rev. Abbot Lawrence Vohs, O.S.B., for having favored him with the privilege of advanced studies in Canon Law at the Catholic University of America. He is indebted to the members of the Faculty of the School of Canon Law for their helpful guidance and gracious assistance. Finally, he is deeply grateful to his confreres, relatives, and friends who aided him in any way in the preparation of this work.

[8]Cf. Canons 613, § 2, 713, § 1, 722, § 2. *Codex Iuris Canonici* (Pii X Pontificis Maximi iussu digestus Benedicti Papae XV auctoritate promulgatus, Romae: Typis Polyglottis Vaticanis, 1918).

[9]For an explicit treatment of communication of privileges in favor of religious and especially for a detailed analysis of the implications of Canon 613, § 1, the reader is referred to the following works: Vasto, *De Communicatione Privilegiorum praesertim inter Religiones* (Aquilae in Vestinis: Italia, 1936, hereafter cited as *De Communicatione Privilegorium*. Tatjer, "De Communicatione Privilegiorum inter Religiones," *Apollinaris* (Romae, 1928--), V (1932), pp. 468-486; Larraona, "Questio Canonica," *Commentarium pro Religiosis* (Romae, 1920--), III (1922), pp. 205-213.

PART ONE

THEORY OF COMMUNICATION OF PRIVILEGES

CHAPTER I

THE INSTITUTE OF COMMUNICATION

ARTICLE I. NATURE, ETYMOLOGY, AND DEFINITION OF COMMUNICATION

While the canons of the Code of Canon Law embody most of the rights enjoyed by the members of the Church, the Code itself acknowledges that it alone is not the exclusive source of rights for those members. It acknowledges this fact by stating that "privileges can be acquired not only by means of direct concession of competent authority and by means of communication, but also by means of legitimate custom and prescription."[1] Thus, the Code provides that privileges, which constitute special normative rights contrary to or beyond the provisions of law,[2] can be acquired in four distinct ways, one of which is communication.

The word "communication" is derived from the Latin word *communicatio*, which, in turn, has its foundation in the word *communis*, meaning "common to several, or to all."[3] According to popular usage, both in early as well as late Latin, the word communication had two fundamental meanings. According to one meaning, which considers the word from the viewpoint of the active agent, it signifies the action of making common or imparting.[4] Thus a person is said to communicate something to others. According to the other meaning, which considers the word from the viewpoint of the passive agent, it signifies the

[1]Canon 63, § 1. Author's translation.

[2]Concerning the nature and definition of a privilege, consult *infra*, pages 35-37.

[3]*A New Latin Dictionary*, founded on the translation of Freund's Latin-German Lexicon, edited by E. A. Andrews, revised, enlarged, and in great part rewritten by Charlton T. Lewis and Charles Short, (American Book Company, 1927) s. v. "communicatio," "communis."

[4]*Loc. cit.*

action of participating.[5] Thus, for example, persons professing one faith are said to communicate in that faith.

These two accepted meanings of the word, according to popular usage both in early and late Latin, were retained with some necessary modifications when the term was introduced into juridic terminology. In popular usage, the word "communication", signifying the action of an active agent, implies that the agent participates in the use of the communicated item with the recipient.[6] When the word communication is used in this sense in juridic terminology, the agent who imparts a privilege by communication does not share in the participation of that privilege with the recipient. Moreover, communication, used in the sense of common participation in popular usage, can be applied to the enjoyment of any object which is common to many. Hence, if the word is used loosely in reference to privileges, persons who enjoy a privilege which is common to a group, regardless of the source of acquisition, enjoy a communication of privileges.[7] This, however, is not precise juridic terminology, according to which persons are said to enjoy a communication of privileges only as a consequence of the special action of the agent or grantor. The result of this action produces a communication of privileges among the recipients.

Even before the appearance of the word communication itself, which subsequently became the accepted title of the

[5]*Thesaurus Linguae Latinae, editus auctoritate et consilio Academiarum Quinque Germanicarum, Berolensis, Gottingensis, Lipsiensis, Monacensis, Vindobonensis* (6 vols., 1906-1912), s.v. "communicatio." Consult also, Du Cange, *Glossarium Mediae et Infimae Latinitatis conditum a Carolo du Fresne Domino du Cange auctum a monachis ordinis S. Benedicti* (editio nova a Leopold Favre, 10 vols., Paris, 1937), s. v. "communicatio."

[6]" . . . victoria legionibus communicabo."—*A New Latin Dictionary, loc. cit.*

[7]E. g. " . . . that all subjects of Great Britain should enjoy a communication of privileges." *A New English Dictionary on Historical Principles*, edited by James A. H. Murray (9 vols., Oxford Clarendon Press: 1893), s. v. "communication."

source of privileges which is studied in this dissertation, other derivatives of the word *communis* were used in reference to this source.[8] The principal effect of the institute of communication—a resulting community of privileges among many subjects—warranted the use of these derivatives of the word *communis* both before and after communication became the accepted juridic title. Communication, however, and its verb form communicate are more precise because they describe the operation of the institute both from the viewpoint of the grantor and the grantee.

In accord with the provisions of Canon 63, § 1 communication can be defined loosely as a source of privileges. The inadequacy of such a definition, however, is immediately evident in view of the fact that it fails to note any characteristic mark which would distinguish communication from direct concession, custom, and prescription, which institutes also can be defined as sources of privileges. That there is a distinction in nature between these institutes is obvious from their difference in name. This difference is constituted by the manner in which the nature of the privilege is specified and by the norms which govern the acquisition and existence of the privileges acquired through these sources.

In an effort to classify and to note the precise nature of the institute of communication, canonists, both pre-Code and modern, define or describe this source in various

[8]Thus, for example, Pope Julius II instituted communication of privileges by stating: " . . . privilegia omnia . . . inter ipsos communia esse."—Const. *Militantis Ecclesiae,* 15 iul. 1507—*Bullarum Diplomatum et Privilegiorum Sanctorum Romanorum Pontificum Tauriensis Editio, auspicante Cardinali Francisco* Gaudé (25 vols., Augustae Taurinorum, 1857-1872), V, 455. Henceforth, this work will be cited as *BRT*. " . . . omnia privilegia inter Mendicantes de Apostolica auctoritatis plentiudine communicavimus."—Leo X, Const. *Dudum per nos,* 10 dec., 1519—*BRT*, V, 732; " . . . privilegiorum communionem . . . "—Iulius II, *Etsi ad benemerendum,* 17 iunii, 1598—BRT, V, 471.

ways,[9] and although these definitions and descriptions differ in some respects, all contain the same common de-

[9] "Communicatio privilegiorum consistit in participatione et concessione quadam privilegii quia superior privilegium quod uni simpliciter concesserat, etiam ad alterum extendit." Reiffenstuel, *Ius Canonicum Universum* (5 vols. in 7, Parisiis, 1864-1870), lib. V. tit. 33, n. 53; Ferraris, *Bibliotheca Canonica, Iuridica, Moralis, Theologica, necnon Ascetica, Polemica, Rubristica, Historica* (8 vols., Parisiis, 1860-1863), s. v. "privilegium." Hereafter cited *Prompta Bibliotheca.*

"Communicatio privilegiorum in eo consistere quod ius uni concessum per aliquod privilegium, alteri etiam conceditur per quandam extensionem, vel certe per quandam multiplicationem talis privilegii, ut nomine communicationis significare videtur." Suarez, *Opera Omnia* (26 vols., Parisiis: 1856-1866), vol. VI, *Tractatus de Legibus,* lib. 8, c. 16, n. 1. This latter work, which is always implied whenever reference is made to Suarez, will be cited as *De Legibus.*

"Communicatio privilegiorum est extensio privilegii uni concessi ad alterum ex concessione superioris ecclesiastici." Coronata, *Institutiones Iuris Canonici ad Usum Utriusque Cleri ac Scholarum* (5 vols., Taurini: Marietti, 1928-1935, Vol. I, 2 ed. 1939), I, 101. Hereafter this work will be cited *Institutiones.*

"Privilegiorum communicatio est privilegium quoddam generale vel speciale quo certae personae, societates, loca, participant plus vel minus plene, privilegiis aut gratiis directe aliis personis concessis . . . " Vermeersch, A., *De Religiosis Personis et Institutis Tractatus Canonico-Moralis* (2 vols., Brugis, 1907-1909. Vol. I, 2 ed., 1907; Vol. 2, 4 ed., 1909. Hereafter this work will be cited as *De Religiosis Institutis et Personis.*

"Privilegiorum communicatio est beneficium principis, vi cuius privilegium uni concessum ad alium extenditur. Extenditur quidem formaliter, i. e., non est materialiter iterata alteri personae concessio privilegii iam priori concessi; sed alteri formaliter ad instar prioris concessionis tribuitur." Vermeersch—Creusen, *Epitome Iuris Canonici* (3 vols. Mechliniae: Dessain: Vol. I, 6 ed., 1937; Vol. II, 5 ed., 1934; Vol. III, 5 ed., 1936), I, n. 181.

"Communicatio privilegiorum est privilegium quo participantur privilegia aliis concessa, secundum verborum concessionis vim." Vasto, *De Communicatione Privilegiorum,* p. 42, n. 73.

The same definition is given by Mocchegiani, P., *Iurisprudentia Ecclesiastica ad usum et commoditatem utriusque cleri* (3 vols., Ad Claras Aquas: 1904-1905), II, n. 683. This work will be cited *Iurisprudentia Ecclesiastica.*

nominator, namely: communication is a source by means of which a person is permitted to acquire those privileges which are first acquired by another. Since all definitions and descriptions of communication, including those not noted here, contain this common element, there can be no doubt that this is the distinctive feature of communication. Of itself, however, it is not radical enough to distinguish communication from other sources through which a person can acquire those privileges which are first acquired by another. Communication does not merely permit a person to acquire another's privileges, but, more fundamentally, it implies that the actual acquisition of a privilege through this source depends upon the privileges of another. When a person is favored with the benefits of communication, the competent authority does not specify the nature of the privilege which is to be acquired by the beneficiary of communication,[10] but he simply permits the person favored with his benevolence to acquire the privileges of another, implying that the nature of his privilege is to be specified by the nature of the privilege first acquired by another. Thus, the privileges of one beneficiary become the proximate or mediate cause of the privileges which are to be acquired by the one who is favored with the benefits of communication. The competent authority is always the ultimate cause of the origin, specification, and existence of privileges. This principle holds true even when communication is permitted, but communication itself is of no practical value to a beneficiary if the proximate cause is non-existent,[11] or for some other reason not liable to communication.[12] In the acquisition of a privilege by means of communication there is always some dependence of the privilege to be acquired upon a privilege previously ac-

[10]" . . . non est materialiter iterata alteri personae concessio privilegii iam priori concessi . . . " Vermeersch—Creusen. *loc. cit.*

[11]Cf. *infra.* pages 14,130-134.

[12]Cf. *infra.* pages 130-167.

quired by another,[13] because the origin, essence, and, at times, even the very existence of a privilege to be acquired through communication depends upon the essence and existence of the privileges acquired by a person whose privileges are made available to another.[14] The dependence of one privilege upon another is so essential to the notion of communication as a source of privileges that without it the superior's benevolence could not be actualized.[15] It is this dependence of the privilege to be acquired upon the previously acquired privileges of another which constitutes the formal distinctive element of communication and thereby sets it apart from other sources of privilege. Communication, then, is a source through which a person is permitted to acquire another's privileges, which act as the proximate or mediate cause for the privileges to be acquired.

Thus, communication is different from direct concession, which implies that a privilege derives its essence and existence immediately from the grantor. Communication differs from custom by virtue of the fact that a privilege acquired through custom derives its nature and existence through the acts of the person himself in accord with the provisions of law.[16] Finally, communication is distinct from prescription. However, the distinction between these two sources of privilege cannot be based on the distinctive

[13]"Communicatio . . . semper involvit aliquam relationem ad priorem quamdam concessionem."—Van Hove, *De Privilegiis*, n. 136. The word concession is to be understood in an accomodated sense, thus including privileges acquired through custom and prescription.

[14]"Utriusque formae (communicationis) hoc commune est ut concessa 'ad instar' privilegia a privilegiis directe concessis interpretationem sumant." Vermeersch—Creusen, *Epitome Iuris Canonici*, I, n. 181. The extent of the dependence of one privilege upon another is determined by the specific form of communication which is made operative in a particular case.

[15]" . . . deficiente termino a quo (i. e., privilegio iam altero concesso), idipsum fundamentum communicationis corrueret, ac proin ipsum beneficium seu favor principis." Vasto, B., *De Communicatione Privilegiorum*, p. 43.

[16]Cf. Canons 25-30.

characteristic of communication because another's privilege is the mediate cause of a privilege acquired through either source. In order to draw a distinction between these two sources, another element must be taken into consideration. While another's privilege is the mediate cause of a privilege acquired through prescription, the mediate cause itself becomes the property of the one who prescribes, and the one who first possessed the privilege is deprived of it. In communication, the privilege which serves as the proximate cause remains in the possession of the person whose privileges are made the object of communication.

Besides noting that communication permits the acquisition of another's privileges, canonists also note that the benefits of this source are not available to any beneficiaries unless the acquisition of privileges through this source is permitted by a competent superior. That the competent superior's intervention is necessary in order to effect communication of privileges is evident from the fact that members of society cannot acquire any special rights unless their acquisition is permitted, implicitly or explicitly, by competent authority. A privilege is conceded explicitly to a beneficiary through direct concession or communication, either by provision of law or by a special act of competent authority. Privileges are also granted expressly when the law itself sanctions certain modes of acquisition, such as, custom or prescription. Privileges are granted implicitly when a beneficiary is virtually included in a concession expressly made to another. Thus, persons closely affiliated with a grantee are virtually included in a concession even though they are not expressly mentioned when the object of the privilege is entirely favorable, when it does not prejudice the rights of others, and when the object of the privilege is not contrary to law. Beneficiaries are also virtually included within a concession expressly made to others when concessions of the above mentioned kind would be completely nullified unless affiliates of the grantee to whom the concession is made were implicitly included in the concession.[17] Persons who are thus virtually included in concessions expressly made to others are sometimes said to acquire those privileges through communication.[18] In such instances, however, the word communication is used in a non-technical or popular sense and it is not to be confused with the juridic institute of communication. Through the operation of non-technical communication, some persons automatically become beneficiaries of privileges which are not explicitly given to them. Through the institute of communication, persons become the beneficiaries of privileges previously acquired by another because they are explicitly made the beneficiaries of those privileges by an express provision of law or by an act of competent authority. Unless such persons were explicitly made the beneficiaries of privileges previously acquired by another, those privileges could not be acquired without the express provision of law or competent authority. The juridic institute of communication, then, cannot serve as a source of privileges unless it is made available by law,[19] by a special act of the legislator outside of law,[20] or by an

[17]Cf. Suarez, *De Legibus*, lib. 8, c. 10, nn. 1-7.

[18]Suarez, *De Legibus*, lib. 8, c. 10, n. 7.

[19]Communication of privileges was permitted by law to the mendicant orders when Pope Leo X issued the Constitution *Dudum per nos*. 10 dec., 1519—*BRT*, V, 732.

The Code permits communication of privileges in Canons 613, § 2, 713, § 1, 722, §2.

"Communicatio ista potest . . . statui a lege generali quae modo universali et in antecessum omnia vel varia privilegia alicuius personae et institutis communia reddat." Vermeersch—Creusen, *Epitome, Iuris Canonici*, I, n. 181.

[20]This may be done by means of rescript or oral grant. "Concedi potest per indultum speciale, quod interpretandum est iuxta regulas generales, attentis tamen clausulis specialibus additis." Van Hove, *De Privilegiis*, p. 148, n. 151.

act of the competent superior.[21]

Although canonists are in perfect agreement when they indicate the distinctive feature of the institute of communication, they are not in perfect agreement when they classify the institute. Thus, curiously enough, the institute of communication is classified as a law,[22] a privilege,[23] and as a benefit emanating from competent authority.[24] Manifestly, these different classifications of the institute are confusing. By virtue of the fact that direct concession, custom, or prescription are never classified in this way, even by the above mentioned authors, it seems rather strange that communication, which, like the other sources, is an instrumental cause of a privilege should be classified as a law or a privilege or a benefit emanating from authority. Communication, like the other sources of privilege, is acknowledged by law as a legitimate source of privileges.[25] Furthermore, it can be made available to particular beneficiaries by means of law, as it was made available to the mendicant orders by Pope Leo X,[26] and as it is made

[21]A distinction is made between a legislator and a competent superior because only the former can permit the acquisition of privileges contrary to law. On the other hand, a superior, with or without the power of jurisdiction, can permit the acquisition of privileges which do not affect any law as long as the superior has competence over the subject to whom the privilege is granted as well as the object of the privilege which is granted. Cf. Salmanticenses, *Cursus Theologiae Moralis* (6 vols. in 3, Venetiis, 1728), IV, tract. 18, c. 1, punct. 1, nn. 4-5; Van Hove, *De Privilegiis*, n. 43.

[22]Pignatelli, Iac., *Consultationes Canonicae* (11 vols. in 4, Coloniae Allobrogum: 1700), X, consult. 1, n. 26.

[23]Mocchegiani, *Iurisprudentia Ecclesiastica*, II, n. 683; Vasto, *De Communicatione Privilegiorum*, p. 42, n. 73;; Vermeersch, *De Religiosis Personis et Institutis*, I, n. 351.

[24]Vermeersch-Creusen, *Epitome Iuris Canonici*, I, n. 181. It might be noted here that the definition given by Vermeersch in *De Religiosis Personis et Institutis* is radically different. Cf. *supra* page 4.

[25]Cf. Leo X, Const. *Dudum per nos*, 10 dec., 1519—*BRT*, V. 732; Canon 63.

[26]*Loc. cit.*

available to particular beneficiaries by the Code of Canon Law.[27] However, because the institute is sanctioned by law or because it is sometimes permitted by means of law does not mean that it itself can be classified as a law, any more than direct concession, custom, or prescription can be classified as such. Similarly, it is inaccurate to classify communication as a privilege or a benefit emanating from competent authority. Communication might be called such if these terms were used in their popular rather than their technical significance. If communication can be classified in this way, then every other source of privileges can be placed in the same categories. However, to avoid confusion and insure juridic precision, it is preferable to refrain from classifying communication in this way. Obviously, canonists are mindful of the distinction between cause and effect when they refrain from classifying law, direct concession, custom, and prescription as a privilege or a benefit emanating from a competent authority when these institutes serve as a source of privileges. That same distinction must be kept in mind when communication is classified. Hence, to avoid an indiscriminate use of technical juridic terms, it would be more precise to classify communication as a source of privileges from the viewpoint of the grantee. From the viewpoint of the grantor it can be classed as a method of granting privileges, which the competent superior can concede through whatever means he wishes to do so.[28]

Considered from the viewpoint of the grantee, communication can be defined more fully as a lawfully constituted source for acquiring those privileges which are first acquired by another. From the viewpoint of the grantor, it can be defined as lawfully constituted method of imparting the previously acquired privileges of one beneficiary to another. More in accord with the intrinsic meaning of the word, communication can be defined as a juridic insti-

[27]Cf. Canons 713, § 1, 722, § 2.

[28]Suarez, *De Legibus*, lib. 8, c. 15, n. 1.

tute by means of which beneficiaries are permitted to enjoy privileges in common, or a juridic institute through which privileges are made common to many. Yet, despite the fact that these definitions preserve the intrinsic meaning of the word, they do not describe the precise nature of the institute for they do not indicate that the privileges which are made common to many are first acquired by a beneficiary who is technically styled the primary grantee. Though the intrinsic meaning of the word does not suffice for a precise definition of the institute of communication, it cannot be overlooked entirely because the institute of communication always implies that the primary grantee and the beneficiary of communication enjoy the communicated privileges in common. However, by stressing the formal element of communication, the institute is better defined as a source by means of which competent authority permits a person to acquire another's privileges which serve as the mediate cause for the beneficiary of communication.

By the will of the grantor or because of the status of the beneficiaries who are permitted to acquire the privileges of another, the institute accomplishes its purpose—to make privileges common to many—in two ways. In some instances, communication effects a multiplication of the privilege which is imparted to others, as a result of which the beneficiary of communication acquires an independent privilege in much the same way as he would if it were conceded directly. When the final object of the institute of communication is achieved in this fashion, there is only a necessary formal and not a material similarity between the privilege which is enjoyed in common by the primary grantee and the beneficiary of communication. In other instances, the final object of the institute is accomplished by retaining the numerical identity of a privilege, which is merely extended to others besides the primary grantee. By virtue of this difference in the manner in which the final object of the institute of communication is realized, the institute has traditionally been divided into two species, which are incorporated into the Code of Canon Law.[29] These two specific forms of communication, which will be analyzed more thoroughly in the succeeding articles, are: (a) Communication *in forma aeque principali,* and (b) Communication *in forma accessoria.* During the course of this dissertation, the former will be styled equal communication,[30] whereas the latter will be referred to as accessory communication.

In view of the fact that there is a distinct difference between these two species of communication, many of the above-mentioned definitions or descriptions of communication, which purport to be generic, can be called into question by virtue of the fact that the noun "extension" or the verb "extend" are used to signify the manner in which the final object of communication is realized.[31] In strict juridic terminology, the extension of a privilege signifies the increase of the object of the privilege or its application to a greater number of subjects. However, in either case, the privilege which is extended remains numerically one. When the grantor extends a privilege to others besides the original grantee, he does not favor the subjects of the extension with a numerically distinct and independent privilege. If the word "extension" or any of its derivatives

[29]Canons 64, 65.

[30]It must be admitted that the word 'equal' is not a satisfactory translation of *aeque principaliter.* Since there is no exact counterpart for the term in English, it is extremely difficult, if not impossible, to translate it satisfactorily. However, in order to avoid the constant use of unwieldy Latin terminology in the text, as well as unwieldy English combination of words, perfect accuracy will be sacrificed for facility of expression. Notwithstanding this expedient adaptation, the full import of the Latin terminology is by no means discarded. Whenever the word equal is used in conjunction with communication, it is used with the connotation inherent in the term *aeque-principaliter,* which signifies that the privilege which is communicated is equally independent as the one which serves as its model. Hence, the beneficiary who acquires a privilege through this form of communication can enjoy it independently of the primary grantee.

[13]Consult the definitions given by Coronata, Vermeersch-Creusen; the descriptions offered by Reiffenstuel and Ferraris.—*Supra,* page 4.

are used loosely, then communication, generically, might be defined or described as the extension of a privilege. If it is used with its strict juridic connotation, and this is the use presumed in law, then it is not proper to refer to communication in general as the extension of a privilege. In effect, accessory communication is nothing other than the extension of a privilege to others besides the primary grantee. Equal communication, however, can never be referred to as such.

The characteristic marks of the juridic institute of communication can be described clearly and briefly by indicating what constitutes its formal, material, and final object. Thus, the acquisition of another's privilege which serves as the proximate cause for its creation, is the formal object of the institute. Its final object, as already noted, consists in effecting a community of privileges. Its material object is a privilege, whose nature in relation with the institute of communication is analyzed in a later chapter. Considered from the viewpoint of its material object, the institute of communication, both equal and accessory, is divided into complete or incomplete communication.[32] Accordingly, communication is considered complete when all privileges are made the material object of communication; incomplete, when the effectiveness of the institute is restricted to certain kinds of privileges. In practice, such a division is superfluous because it seldom happens that communication permits a beneficiary to acquire all of the primary grantee's privileges.

Article 2. Species of Communication

A. *The Notion of Equal Communication*

Equal communication, which is also styled absolute or perfect,[33] is effected when a competent superior imparts

[32]Pejska, *Ius Canonicum Religiosorum* (3 ed., Friburgi: Brisgoviae, Herder: 1927), p. 29.

[33]Reiffenstuel, *Ius Canonicum Universum*, lib. V. tit. 33, n. 54.

the privileges of one beneficiary to another in such a way that the subject favored with communication acquires a separate and independent privilege. Since it has already been stated that the acquisition of a privilege by means of communication always entails the dependence of one privilege upon another,[34] it would seem paradoxical to assert that equal communication implies the acquisition of an independent privilege. However, paradoxical as the assertion might seem, it is not so in reality, because it does not imply that one privilege is dependent upon another and independent of it at the same time. A privilege acquired through equal communication depends upon another only for its origin and essence.[35] Its subsequent existence, however, is in no way subject to the privilege from which it derives its origin and essence. Assuredly, such a dependence, at least of origin, is absolutely essential, because communication would be ineffective without it,[36] but when a privilege is acquired through equal communication it automatically ceases to depend upon the privilege from which it receives its very existence and through which its nature is determined.

In accord with the final object of the institute,[37] equal communication enables many subjects to partake of the same privileges, but in achieving this aim it produces as many numerically distinct privileges as there are beneficiaries of communication.[38] Manifestly, then, equal com-

[34]Cf. *supra*, pages 8 and 9.

[35]" . . . quoniam non pendent ab aliis (a privilegiis primariis) quoad conservationem, sed quoad productionem." Navarrus, *Opera Omnia* (6 vols. Venetiis: apud Ionannem Guerilium, 1618), vol. III, *Commentarium de Iubilaeo*, c. 541, n. 26. Hereafter cited *Commentarium de Iubilaeo*.

[36]Cf. *supra*, page 6.

[37]" . . . hoc enim est proprium communicationi ut idem privilegium commune sit pluribus."—Vasto, *De Communication Privilegiorum*, p. 42: "Communicare est commune reddere."—Van Hove, *De Privilegiis*, n. 136.

[38]Suarez, *De Legibus*, lib. 8, c. 16, n. 2: Philips, *Kirchenrecht* (7 vols., Regensburg: 1845-1872), V. 122: Cicognani, *Canon Law*, p. 704.

munication effects a multiplication of the primary grantee's privileges.[39] By virtue of equal communication a beneficiary acquires full and independent ownership of the privilege thus communicated in the same way as he would if it were granted directly.[40] Now, in view of the fact that the person who is favored with the benefits of equal communication acquires an independent privilege, it logically follows that the privilege thus acquired can be used independently of the subject whose privileges are communicated to another. As a matter of fact, it has always been the common opinion that the party to whom a privilege accrues through equal communication can use the privilege against the subject to whom it was given originally and through whom it is acquired by another.[41] Some authors defend this opinion without qualification, implying that it can be used indiscriminately against the primary gran-

[39]" . . . dici potest multiplicatio numerica eiusdem privilegii."—Suarez, *De Legibus*, c. 16, n. 15. In citing Suarez on this point, Vasto implies that Suarez contradicts himself when the former writes: "Communicatio privilegii non est eius multiplicatio, sed extensio, et quasi applicatio. (*De Legibus*, lib. 8, c. 16, n. 2)—"Vasto, *De Communicatione Privilegiorum*, p. 45, n. 75. The implication which Vasto makes is incorrect because the statement itself is not Suarez's teaching on this point. Suarez clearly states that this is what some canonists teach.

[40]"Privilegium uni corpori vel personae concessum communicatur alteri proprie et aequaliter, ita ut ex propria persona illo uti possit, non minus quam ipse posset, si primo et per se fuisset communicatum ei privilegium." —Didacus ab Aragonia, *Dilucidatio Privilegorium Ordinum Regularium* (Bononiae: 1765), tract, 1, c. 8, n. 1; " . . . quia religio communicans [per communicationem in forma aeque principali] in privilegiis ita ea propria sibi facit, ac si primo et per se essent communicata . . . "—Salmanticenses, *Cursus Theologiae Moralis*, II, tract. 18, c. 1, punct. 7, § 2, n. 102.

[41]Cf. Tatjer. "De Communicatione Privilegiorum inter Religiones." *Apollinaris*, V (1932), p. 465.

tee.[42] The more reasonable view on this point, however, is the one proposed by those canonists who teach that a privilege acquired through equal communication can be used by the mediate grantee against the primary grantee only in court in order to defend himself against any damage which would result from the primary grantee's use of the same privilege.[43] The beneficiary of communication has the right to defend himself against the primary grantee's use of the same privilege because the one who asserts his privilege to avert damage has a stronger right than the one who seeks to make a gain.[44]

Although the actual acquisition of a privilege through equal communication is indirect or mediate, the privilege thus acquired has the same stability as a privilege which is granted directly. In view of the fact that documents through which communication is permitted are replete with expressions indicating that a privilege acquired through equal communication is to merit the same consideration in law as a privilege which is granted directly,[45] there can be no doubt that the mode of acquisition is the

[42]Rodericus, H. *Quaestiones Regulares et Canonicae Enucleatae* (Lugduni, 1534), p. 836, n. 53. Hereafter cited *Quaestiones Regulares et Canonicae Enucleatae.* Tamburini, *De Iure Abbatum et Aliorum Praelatorum, tam Regularium quam Saecularium Episcopis Inferiorum* (3 vols. in 1, Coloniae Aggripinae, 1691), D. XVII, quest. 4. Hereafter cited *De Iure Abbatum.*

[43]Cf. Salmanticenses, *Cursus Theologiae Moralis,* IV, tract. 18, l. 1, punct. 7, § II, n. 102; Ferraris, *Prompta Bibliotheca,* s. v. "privilegium", n. 29; Tatjer, *op. cit.,* p. 465; Vasto, *op. cit.,* p. 68, n. 94.

[44]Michiels, *Normae Generales Iuris Canonici* (2 vols, Lublin-Poloniae: Universitas Catholica: 1929), II, 379. Hereafter cited *Normae Generales.*

[45]" . . . ita ut illis (privilegiis) praedicta congregatio . . . uti, frui, et gaudere possit, et valeant, perinde ac si specialiter expresse concessa fuissent . . ."—Pius VI, Const. *Inter multiplices,* 14 dec., 1892—*Bullarii Romani Continuatio Summorum Pontificum* (19 vols., Prato: 1756-1883), VI, 2569. Hereafter cited *BRC.*

" . . . gaudere libere et licite possint et valeant, perinde ac si illa ei specifice et particulariter concessa fuissent . . . "—Urbanus VIII, *Const. Salvatoris nostri,* 12 ian., 1632, *BRT,* XVI, 67.

only mark of difference between the status of a privilege acquired through equal communication and one acquired through direct concession. Yet, though the difference seems slight, it is of utmost importance. By virtue of its priority in time[46] a privilege acquired through direct concession would always take precedence over the same privilege acquired through communication when a conflict of privileges would arise between equally privileged parties. Moreover, according to present law,[47] the possible communicability of a privilege depends upon the mode of acquisition. The Code prescribes that privileges must be conceded directly before they can be acquired through communication, thus excluding communicated privileges from further communication.

In view of the fact that privileges acquired through equal communication are endowed with the same stability and independence as privileges which are granted directly,[48] it logically follows that privileges acquired through the former source are in no way subject to the modifications which affect the model after it has served its purpose of determining the nature of a privilege acquired through equal communication. Now, if a privilege acquired by means of equal communication is immune from any modifications which affect the model privilege because it becomes independent of the model privilege, then, logically, the latter privilege is also immune from the modifications which affect the former.[49] Consequently, if either privilege is lost, revoked, increased, or diminished, the other is in no way affected by any of these modifications. If any of these modifications proceed from the grantor—e.g., revocation, increase, decrease,—the privileges are affected

[46]A privilege cannot be acquired through communication of either species unless it is first acquired by another.

[47]Canon 64.

[48]Cf. *supra,* page 16.

[49]Suarez, *De Legibus,* lib. 8, c. 15, n. 5.

only when the respective privileged parties are expressly notified. If the modifications depend upon the acts of the privileged party—e.g., loss, renunciation, non-use, abuse,—the privileges of either party are lost only when either is directly responsible for the acts which lead to the loss of the privilege.

From the time that the institute of communication began to receive explicit treatment in canonical works, canonists have unanimously adhered to the teaching that privileges acquired through equal communication cannot be affected by the loss, revocation, increase, or diminution of the primary grantee's privileges which serve as the model for the privileges that are acquired through communication.[50] Canonists could not but adhere to this teaching, which is a logical outcome of the connotation inherent in the term *aeque - principaliter*,[51] whence equal communication received its official juridic title. Thus there never was and logically could not have been any variation in the teaching of pre-Code canonists about this feature of equal communication, which, fundamentally, is the whole theory underlying equal communication. In spite of the fact that the Sacred Congregation of Indulgences issued one isolated pronouncement, which completely contradicts this traditional doctrine,[52] the Code itself gives legal sanc-

[50] Cf. for example, Castro Palao *Opus Morale*, (6 vols. in 3, Lugduni: 1682), I, tract. 3, disp. 4, punct. 2, § 9, n. 3; Suarez, *De Legibus*, lib. 8, c. 16, n. 12; Reiffenstuel, *Ius Canonicum Universum* (7 vols., Parisiis: 1864-1870), lib. V, 33, n. 69; Rodericus, H. *Questiones Regulares et Canonicae Enucleatae*, p. 830, n. 38; Bouix, *Tractatus de Iure Regularium* (3 ed., 2 vols. Parisiis: 1883), II, pars. 5, p. 77.

[51] Cf. *supra*. page 20.

[52] Although the response cited on page 170 might accurately reflect the mind of the legislator relative to equal communication in general, canonists correctly note that the response cannot actually serve as a general interpretation of doctrine of equal communication of privileges because it is a particular response (given to the Third Order of St. Francis), and especially because it pertains only to indulgences acquired through equal communication. Cf Piatus Montensis, *Praelectiones Iuris Regularis* (3 ed., 2 vols., Tornaci: Casterman, 1906), II, q. 143, n. 1.

tion to the constant, unvarying teachings of canonists by stating that the consequences of equal communication are contrary to those resulting from accessory communication.[53]

B. *Subjects of Equal Communication*

Communication, like any other source of privileges, is available only to those who are favored with its benefits by law or by a competent superior, for unless the competent authority permits or sanctions the acquisition of a privilege it cannot be acquired validly. Together with this necessary condition, without which a privilege cannot be acquired, a beneficiary of communication must possess certain qualifications before he can acquire any privileges whatsoever, and certain specific qualifications before he can be favored with the benefits of equal communication. Though all persons, physical or moral, who are subject to a superior are capable of acquiring privileges from him,[54] a beneficiary must necessarily be the subject of law before he can acquire a privilege providing him with normative right contrary to the provisions of the law.[55] Moreover, privileges contrary to law can be conceded only by the one who enacts the law. In accord with these prerequisites any physical or moral persons can acquire privileges directly from the competent superior or indirectly through relation to things or places in which privileges might be vested. Just as any of these beneficiaries might acquire privileges through direct concession, so it is possible for these same beneficiaries to acquire them through communication. Although the institute of communication has been actually used only in favor of moral persons such as religious institutes, universities, confraternities, etc.,

[53]Canon 65.

[54]Cf. Suarez, *De Legibus*, lib. 8, c. 9, n. 3.

[55]Van Hove, *De Privilegiis*, p. 45, n. 43.

there is no solid reason to prove why this source of privileges cannot be used in favor of individual physical persons. However, the use of the institute in favor of the latter is only a matter of speculation, whereas its use in favor of moral persons is a matter of historic fact.

Because a beneficiary of equal communication becomes the owner of an independent privilege which is exactly the same as a privilege which is first acquired by another and later imparted to him, it is only reasonable to presuppose that equal communication postulates some special requisites besides those ordinarily required of a beneficiary of privileges. Thus, it seems reasonable to presuppose that beneficiaries of equal communication must be (1) juridically similar to the one whose privileges are communicated; (2) juridically independent of the person whose privileges are communicated. Though such special requisites have never been demanded by positive law, the actual operation of the institute offers sufficient proof to show that they were presupposed. The absence of these requisites would seem to contradict the nature of the institute because it is unlikely that the grantor would permit a person of dissimilar juridic condition or one juridically dependent upon the primary grantee to enjoy exactly the same privileges independently of the primary grantee and to profit by all the advantages inherent in equal communication.

The first condition, i. e., juridic similarity, is fulfilled by those beneficiaries who belong to the same class, enjoy the same rank, dignity, or position. Undoubtedly, it was in consideration of these qualifications that equal communication was permitted between religious institutes, universities, lay societies, etc. Theoretically, it would seem desirable to demand that there be perfect similarity between the beneficiaries of equal communication. Such perfect similarity was even demanded by Pope Julius II when he prescribed that muneral privileges granted to the Dominican order be communicated only to the corresponding dignitaries of the Franciscan order.[56] However, in view of the fact that equal communication of privileges was permitted between Mendicants and Regulars,[57] between Congregations and Regulars,[58] it would be difficult to determine just how far the prerequisite of perfect similarity could be pressed, because there certainly is no perfect similarity between these religious institutes.[59]

The second requirement demands that a beneficiary of equal communication be juridically independent of the primary grantee. In view of the fact that a beneficiary favored with equal communication acquires an independent privilege which is immune from the modifications which affect the primary grantee's privilege, it is reasonable to demand this requirement in order to offset the legal absurdity which would otherwise be created. Thus, if a beneficiary, subject to a primary grantee in jurisdictional matters would acquire the latter's privileges through equal communication, it would imply that the beneficiary could use privileges in contradiction to the rights which the primary grantee enjoys by virtue of jurisdiction over the beneficiary of equal communication. So too, it would be unreasonable for a society, which depends upon a primary grantee for its establishment to acquire the privilèges of that primary grantee through equal communication.

Finally, as a necessary condition for equal communication, it is necessary that the above.mentioned qualifications exist simultaneously. Thus, a person might possess juridic similarity with another, but if he is subject to the jurisdic-

[56]Cf. Bulla, *Alias ad supplicationem,* 1 iun. 1509—*Bullarium Ordinis Praedicatorum,* editum a Th. Ripoli (8 vols., Romae: 1729-1740), IV, 258.

[57]Cf. Pius V, Const. *Ex supernae,* 16 aug. 1567—*BRT,* VII, 584.

[58]Cf. Clemens XIV, *Supremi Apostolatus,* 16 nov. 1769—*BRC,* V, 73.

[59]Cf. Canon 488, 2°.

tion of the other, the acquisition of the latter's privileges through equal communication would be out of question. If, on the other hand, a beneficiary is juridically independent, but of dissimilar condition or inferior rank, it is not at all probable that equal communication would be permitted.

C. *The Notion of Accessory Communication*

The second species of communication, technically known as communication *'in forma accessoria'*,[60] is a source by means of which a beneficiary acquires a privilege which is completely dependent upon another. Besides being dependent upon the primary grantee's privilege for its origin and essence, which dependence is essential to either species of communication, a privilege acquired in accessory form depends upon the primary grantee's privilege for its continued existence[61] and its quality throughout its existence. This complete dependence of the privilege acquired in accessory form is customarily, though not adequately, defined by the axiomatic rule of law, which states that "it is fitting for the accessory to follow the nature of the principal."[62] The wording of the rule itself implies that the rule is not inflexible, and just as any other rule of law admits of exceptions, [63] this rule also admits them.[64] A

[60]It has already been noted that this species will be called accessory communication during the course of this dissertation. Cf. *supra*, page 12. Some canonists refer to this form as imperfect or relative communication. Cf. Piatus Montensis, *Praelectiones Iuris Regularis*, II, q. 141, n. 4, p. 111; Michiels, *Normae Generales*, II, 362.

[61]" . . . ab ipso enim pendet non tantum in fieri, seu quoad acquisitionem privilegii, sed et in esse, seu in conservari."—Vasto, *De Communicatione Privilegiorum*, p. 49, n. 79.

[62]"Accessorium naturam sequi congruit principalis."—Regula 42, R. J. in VI°.

[63]Cf. Reh, *The Rules of Law and Canon Law* (Romae: apud Pont. Universitatis Gregorianae: 1939), pp. 58-63.

[64]Cf. Reiffenstuel, *Ius Canonicum Universum*, vol. VI, *Tractatus de Regulis Iuris*, pp. 73, 74.

privilege acquired in accessory form is completely dependent upon the primary grantee's privileges not merely because it is acquired in accessory form, but especially because the privilege which is made the object of communication remains numerically one and the same privilege.[65] It is simply applied or extended by the competent superior to others besides the one to whom it was originally given. The latter grantee retains complete ownership and control of the privilege,[66] while the beneficiary of accessory communication is merely assimilated to the primary grantee in order that he may enjoy the same privilege as the primary grantee. Thus, a beneficiary of accessory communication can enjoy the same privilege—materially and formally—provided he himself remains capable, only as long as the primary grantee possesses the privilege. Since the beneficiary of accessory communication does not acquire an independent privilege, it is intrinsically impossible for the privilege acquired through accessory communication to be independent of the modifications which affect the primary grantee's privilege. Hence, if it is increased, diminished, or revoked for the primary grantee, it is necessarily[67] increased, diminished, or revoked for the beneficiary of accessory communication. If it is lost by the primary grantee, it is automatically lost by the beneficiary of accessory communication.[68]

In view of the fact that accessory communication, in an efficient sense, does not produce an independent privilege, it might well be classified as the extension of a privilege to others besides the primary grantee,[69] which obviously

[65]" . . . est idem privilegium, non tantum specie, sed etiam numero quod uni primo et alteri, ratione primi communicatur."—Suarez, *De Legibus*, lib. 8, c. 16, n. 2.

[66]Cf. infra, page 177-185.

[67]Schmalzgrueber, *Ius Ecclesiasticum Universum* (5 vols. in 12, Romae: 1843-1845), lib. V, tit. 33, n. 77.

[68]Cf. Canon 65; cf. also, *infra*, page 185-188.

[69]Didacus ab Aragonia, *Dilucidatio Privilegiorum Ordinum Regularium*, tract. 1, c. 8, n. 1; Suarez, *De Legibus*, lib. 8, c. 16, n. 12.

can be effected by competent authority, although it is unlawful for subjects themselves to claim a privilege through extension.[70] However, despite the fact that it has always been considered unlawful to presume that a privilege expressly given to one beneficiary cannot be claimed by another, another principle conflicting with the former is also admitted by canonists.[71] According to this principle it is maintained that privileges expressly given to one beneficiary can be claimed by others who are closely affiliated with the beneficiary by virtue of the relationship of an accessory to principal, as for example the relation of lay servants to religious orders, of novices to religious, etc.[72] While canonists admit that privileges can be acquired by beneficiaries who are not expressly included in a grant but are nevertheless closely affiliated with the beneficiary, they also stress that the acquisition of privileges in this fashion is not the result of an extension, but of a lawful comprehensive interpretation.[73] Moreover, only those privileges can be acquired in virtue of such a relationship which are not contrary to law or prejudicial to the rights of third parties, and only when the nature and purpose of the privilege demands the inclusion of accessory beneficiaries in order to prevent the privilege from being frustrated. However, the application of this principle demands careful consideration and prudent judgment, lest privileges

[70]Cf. Van Hove, *De Privilegiis*, p. 163-176, where in commenting on Canon 67 he presents the traditional principles concerning the extension of privileges.

[71]Rodericus, E., *Quaestiones Regulares et Canonicae Enucleatae*, I, Quaest. 13, n. 22; Castro Palao, *Opus Morale*, I, tract. 3, d., 4, p. 12, n. 1; Schmalzgrueber, *Ius Ecclesiasticum Universum*, lib. V, titi, 33, nn. 130-145; Suarez, *De Legibus*, lib. 8, c. 16, n. 14.

[72]"Non esse inconveniens ut sub principali veniat accessorium, quando finis et ratio privilegii illorum concomitantiam requirit."—*Suarez, De Legibus*, lib. 8, c. 10, n. 7.

[73]" . . . non est eius extensio, sed tantum interpretatio comprehensiva."—Schmalzgrueber, *op cit.*, lib. V, tit. 33, n. 131.

be claimed unreasonably and indiscriminately.[74]

Considering the nature of accessory communication and its frequent application to beneficiaries closely affiliated with religious, it can be inferred that this source of privileges is nothing other than an official and external recognition of the above-mentioned juridic principle. By expressly favoring affiliates of religious institutes, as frequently as the pontiffs did, with the privileges of religious, they certainly removed the doubts and uncertainties that were bound to arise when the application of the principle was left to the parties themselves. Moreover, by permitting communication of privileges to those who could claim them by reason of a virtual inclusion in the name of the principal beneficiary, the pontiffs not only expressly sanctioned an accepted juridic principle, but in doing so they further extended its scope by permitting the acquisition of privileges contrary to law, as well as privileges prejudicial to the rights of the third parties.[75]

D. *Subjects of Accessory Communication*

The actual operation of the institute of communication in history reveals that accessory communication served as a source of privileges almost exclusively for beneficiaries affiliated with religious orders. Thus, privileges were communicated in this fashion to nuns of the corresponding order of men,[76] to novices, servants, oblates, and benefactors of religious orders,[77] to third orders of seculars affiliated

[74]Cf. Suarez, *De Legibus,* lib. 8, c. 10, n. 8.

[75]While there was never any restriction against acquiring privileges contrary to law through communication, privileges prejudicial to the rights of third parties could not be acquired indiscriminately through this source. Concerning the acquisition of these privileges through communication, see *infra,* pages, 76-79.

[76]Cf. Sixtus IV, Const. *Sacri Praedicatorum,* 26 iul, 1479—*BRT,* V, 280; cf. also Piatus Montensis, *Praelectiones Iuris Regularis;* II, q. 141, n. 4, p. 111.

[77]Cf. Paulus III. Const. *Ratione congruit,* 3 nov. 1534.—BRT. VI. 173; Clemens VIII, Const. *Cum ex corpore,* 13 aug. 1525—BRT, VI, 92.

with religious,[78] and to confraternities aggregated to religious institutes.[79] Insofar as it can be determined, the only other beneficiaries of accessory communication, outside of affiliates of religious orders were lay societies (confraternities) erected by and aggregated to other lay societies (arch-confraternities),[80] in whose favor accessory communication still prevails by virtue of the Code.[81] At all events, accessory communication was and still is permitted only to persons closely affiliated with the primary grantee, not because of their own merits or similar juridic condition, but because of their connection with the primary grantee, to whom the beneficiaries of accessory communication seem to be assimilated in order that they may enjoy the privileges of the primary grantee.

Hence, judging from the actual operation of the institute of communication, it can be inferred that a beneficiary of accessory communication, if he is of dissimilar juridic condition, must be associated with the primary grantee in order to be favored with his privileges. This association or connection, which canonists accurately note as the only reason for which a beneficiary is permitted to acquire the privilege of the primary grantee,[82] can be realized in two ways,

78Cf. Leo X, *Dudum per nos,* 10 dec. 1519—*BRT*, V, 732.

79Cf. Parma, *Collectio Indulgentiarum Theologice, Canonice, ac Historice Digesta* (Ad Claras Aquas, 1897), n. 1371. Hereafter this work will be cited as *Collectio Indulgentiarum*. These beneficiaries can enjoy the privileges of religious only in accord with the provisions of the Constitution *Quaecumque* issued by Pope Clement VIII, 7 dec. 1604—*Codicis Iuris Canonici Fontes, cura Emi. Petri Card. Gasparri editi* (9 vols., Romae (later Civitate Vaticana): Typis Polyglottis Vaticanis, 1923-1939. Vols. VII-IX *ed. cura et studio Emi Iustiniani Seredi*), n. 192. Hereafter cited *Fontes*.

80Parma, *op. cit.*, n. 1371.

81Cf. Canon 722, § 2; cf. also, Vromant, G., *De Fidelium Associationibus* (Louvain: 1932), p. 106, note 2.

82Cf. Pichler, *Epitome Iuris Canonici iuxta Decretalium Libros Gregorianae Collectionis Explanati* (2 vols., Venetiis: 1741), lib. V, tit. 33, p. 665; Schmalzgrueber, *Ius Ecclesiasticum Universum*, lib. V, tit. 33, n. 77.

namely: by juridic dependence or simply by close affiliation. Juridic dependence upon the primary grantee would exist in the case of an association which is erected by and aggregated to the primary grantee. Although the Code itself prescribes that arch-confraternities acquire no right over the aggregated confraternity by virtue of the communication of privileges which is permitted,[83] still the aggregated confraternity is juridically dependent upon the arch-confraternity initially because it depends upon the latter for its establishment. Novices, for example, would be juridically dependent upon the religious with whom they are affiliated. By virtue of the fact that novices are not religious in the strict sense of the word, they could not acquire the privileges of religious unless a special concession were made in their favor. In the old law, this was permitted either through a reasonable application of the juridic principle explained above, or through communication.[84] In the present law, the privileges of the religious are conceded to them by law.[85] As a condition for communication, close affiliation with the primary grantee would be realized by lay servants of religious institutes.

Despite the fact that the history of the institute of communication offers sufficient evidence to prove that accessory communication generally operated in favor of beneficiaries who were in some way connected with the primary grantee, there is no solid reason why this form of communication should be restricted only to these beneficiaries who answer to these qualifications. Thus, the competent superior is in no way compelled to institute equal communication when he permits communication of privileges to autonomous subjects who possess juridic similarity. On the contrary, he is perfectly free to determine the mode of communication which should operate in favor of these beneficiaries. Although the very nature of things would preclude such

[83]Canon 722, § 2.

[84]Rodericus, E., *Questiones Regulares et Canonicae,* III, q. 52, art. 12.

[85]Canon 567.

freedom of choice when communication of privileges is permitted to those beneficiaries who are dependent upon or closely affiliated with the primary grantee, no such compelling reason exists when communication is permitted to subjects juridically independent of each other. Hence, it is not at all unreasonable for the competent superior to permit accessory communication to juridically independent or/and similar beneficiaries. If accessory communication were permitted under these conditions, the beneficiaries favored with such a communication would not acquire an independent privilege, as they do when equal communication is effected. In such instances, however, the relationship between accessory and principal would concern the privilege exclusively and not the beneficiaries,[86] and since the privilege would be acquired in accessory form it would naturally be completely subject to the nature and fate of the primary grantee's privilege.

ARTICLE 3. VARIANT DIVISIONS OF COMMUNICATION.

Although the two-fold division of communication into equal and accessory has been traditionally received by canonists of all time,[87] and later incorporated into the Code of Canon Law, there are some authors who favor different divisions of communication. Thus, Castro Palao[88] maintains that communication is effected in three ways. Basing his division on the efficient cause of communication, he maintains that the institute is made operative as follows: (1) when the competent superior aggregates other subjects

[86]Cf. *infra*, page 174.

[87]Cf. for example, Rodericus, H., *Quaestiones Regulares et Canonicae Enucleatae*, p. 830, n. 38; Bouix, *Tractatus de Iure Regularium*, p. 77; Piatus Montensis, *Praelectiones Iuris Regularis*, II, q. 141; Reiffenstuel, *Ius Canonicum Universum*, lib. V, tit. 33, n. 54; Cicognani, *Canon Law*, 783; Vermeersch-Creusen, *Epitome Iuris Canonici*, I, n. 181; Woywod, *A Practical Commentary on the Code of Canon Law* (5 ed., 2 vols., New York: 1939), I, n. 46.

[88]*Opus Morale* I, tract. 3, disp. 4, p. 2, § 9, nn. 1-5.

to the one who enjoys certain privileges in order that the aggregated subjects may enjoy the privileges of the former; (2) when the competent superior extends the privileges of one subject to another, who is to enjoy them in complete dependence upon the original grantee and his privilege; (3) when the same competent superior grants a subject the same privilege which is enjoyed by another in such a way that the latter's privilege is to serve as the model for the one to be acquired through communication. After its specification, the privilege acquired through the third method of communication becomes completely independent of the privilege upon which it is modeled. Palao expressly states that the second method signifies accessory communication, whereas privileges acquired through the third method are the products of equal communication. In view of the fact that this division is based on the efficient cause of communication, it merits some consideration. However, the distinction between the first and the second method —aggregation and extension— is only an accidental one in so far as the status of the privilege is concerned. In either case, the privilege remains one and the same, and the subjects of communication are completely dependent upon the primary grantee's privilege for the specification and the existence of theirs. Though Palao's division seems to depart from the traditional, it is fundamentally the same as the one which has always been accepted because it implicitly affirms that privileges acquired through communication are acquired either in accessory or equally principal form.

According to Pichler,[89] the unqualified use of the word communication or its equivalent in documents of communication constitutes a separate species of communication, distinct from accessory and equal communication. In offering this division, which is based on the wording of the documents, Pichler does not indicate whether a privilege

[89] *Epitome Iuris Canonici iuxta Decretalium Libros Gregorianae Collectionis Explanati,* lib. V, tit. 33.

acquired through such a communication becomes independent of the original privilege or whether it is acquired in accessory form.[90] Because communication is permitted without the use of any significant modifying terminology it does not necessarily imply that this constitutes a different species of communication. Either form can be permitted with or without the use of qualifying terminology. The division offered by Pichler, then, must necessarily be reduced to the traditional two-fold division in order to determine the exact nature of communication as well as the status of the privilege acquired through this source.

The third variant division of communication is the one offered by those authors who maintain that communication is effected through (1) aggregation or extension, (2) through concession *ad instar,* which is the genus of accessory and equal communication.[91]

Although these authors do not state that a privilege acquired through aggregation or extension, which incidentally, are properly identified, are acquired in accessory form, it cannot but be inferred that they are acquired in this way. By stating that communication is effected through concession *ad instar,* these canonists correctly imply that a privilege which is granted in this way must derive its nature from another's. However, they contradict the more common opinion of canonists[92] by stating that a privilege might be acquired in accessory or equally principal form

[90]See *infra,* pages, 69-73, concerning the identification of the institute when communication is permitted without any qualification.

[91]Schmalzgueber, *Ius Ecclesiasticum Universum,* lib. V. tit. 33, n. 88; Sägmüller, *Lehrbuch des Katolischen Kirchenrecht* (Freiburg im Breisgau: 1900), p. 98, n. 31.

[92]Cf. Barbosa, *Variae Tractiones Iuris* (5 vols. in 1, Lugduni, 1631), IV, *De Clausulis Usufrequentioribus,* claus. 5, p. 6. Hereafter cited *De Clausulis Frequentioribus.* Suarez, *De Legibus,* lib. 8, c. 16, nn. 2-7; Salmanticenses, *Cursus Theologiae Moralis,* IV, tract. 18, c. 1, punct. 7, § 1, n. 95; "Privilegium ad instar iisdem normis subest atque communicatio in forma aeque principali et est mere huius alia denominatio."—Van Hove, *De Privilegiis,* p. 139, n. 140.

through concession *ad instar*. It is true that the intrinsic significance of the phrase *ad instar*[93] does not reveal the manner in which a privilege is acquired. However, it has always been the more common opinion of canonists,[94] traceable to Roman Law jurists,[95] that a privilege granted through concession *ad instar* becomes independent of the privilege from which it derives its nature. In light of this more common opinion, therefore, it is incorrect to classify concession *ad instar* as the genus of equal and accessory communication.

Article 4. Modes of Communication

Just as in popular usage, the word communication can properly connote either a unilateral or a reciprocal transfer of an item, so the same connotation can be attached to the juridic term. In popular terminology, the distinction between these two meanings hinges on the preposition which accompanies the word "communication." Hence, the communication of something to someone implies a unilateral concession of something, whereas, a communication of some thing between or among persons implies the reciprocal transfer of items. The distinction between unilateral and reciprocal communication of privileges is founded on the same basis, and, naturally, the exact mode of communication can be identified only by studying the wording of the grant. Thus, when the superior communicates the privileges of one person to another, either by using the phrase "communicate to" or some other expression conveying the same idea, unilateral communication is effected.[96] On the other hand, if the superior uses any expression which connotes a mutual transfer of privileges, reciprocal communication is pro-

[93]Cf. Du Cange, *Glossarium Mediae et Infimae Latinitatis* (2 ed. 10 vols., Paris: 1937), IV, p. 382, s. v. "instar."

[94]*Ut supra,* note 92.

[95]Cf. *infra,* page 83.

[96]E. g., " . . . omnes et singulas gratias . . . ei communicavimus."—Pius VI, Const. *Iniuncti nobis,* 27 martii, 1787—*BRC*, VI, pars. 2, 1795

duced.[97] Unilateral communication implies that only the privileges of the person who serves as the intermediary for the communication are liable to acquisition through this source. The privileges of the beneficiary of communication cannot be acquired by the primary grantee. Hence, if the competent superior communicates the privileges of A to B and C, A cannot acquire the privileges of B and C by virtue of such a communication, nor can the latter acquire each other's privileges. Reciprocal communication alone permits such an exchange of privileges. When such a communication of privileges is permitted, as was the case among religious orders before the promulgation of the Code,[98] the privileges acquired by one of the parties can be acquired by any of the other parties of communication as long as the acquisition of particular privileges is not implicitly or explicitly proscribed.

[97]E. g., " . . . omnia privilegia inter Mendicantes . . . communicavimus . . . "—Leo X. Const. *Dudum per nos,* 10 dec. 1519—*BRT,* V, 732.

[98]Cf. *infra,* pages 111-114.

CHAPTER II

THE MATERIAL OBJECT OF COMMUNICATION

ARTICLE I. THE NOTION OF A PRIVILEGE IN RELATION TO THE INSTITUTE OF COMMUNICATION

Although the full title of the institute of communication —Communication of Privileges— restricts the material object of communication to privileges alone, there is ample evidence in the documents of communication to prove that it serves as a source for the acquisition of other favorable concessions, such as, favors, indulgences, dispensations, faculties, exemptions, immunities, indults, and rescripts.[1] There can be no question about the possible acquisition of these favors by means of communication as long as they are expressly mentioned in the documents by means of which communication is permitted. Furthermore, if any of these specific items is not expressly mentioned, but is properly considered a specific kind of privilege,[2] then its acquisition by means of this source is assured as long as positive rules or the nature of things does not prevent this. If, however, competent authority permits communication of privileges

[1]Pius VI, Const. *Militantis Ecclesiae Regiminis,* 2 iun, 1784—*BRC,* VI, pars. 1, 94; cf. also *Analecta Iuris Pontificii* (Romae: 1852-1868; Paris: 1869-1890), XIII, col. 1019, n. 863.

[2]Exemptions, and immunities, for example, can be classified as such. "The word exemption in ecclesiastical law means a privilege in virtue of which an individual or a community is withdrawn from the authority of his or its immediate superior and is put directly under the authority of a higher superior or his representative." Creusen, *Religious Men and Women in the Code* (3 ed. by Adam Ellis, translation by Edward Garesche, Milwaukee: Bruce Publishing Co., 1939), § 308.

Immunity, which is a specific kind of privilege, implies the exemption of ecclestiastical persons from the jurisdiction of secular tribunals and from certain obligations which the law imposes on citizens. Cf. Conte a Coronata, M., *Ius Publicum Ecclesiasticum* (2 ed. Taurini: Marietti, 1934), p. 194.

"Faculties are special privileges granted to a private person by the Roman Pontiff." Cicognani, *Canon Law,* p. 90.

alone, without any express mention of the above enumerated concessions,, and excluding specific types of privileges, the possibility of acquiring other favorable concessions by means of communication of privileges is called into question. If the indiscriminate use of the word privilege by authors of all time[8] were to serve as a standard for determining the extent of the word privilege and the extent of communication of privileges, then it would have to be admitted that all of the above mentioned items could be acquired by means of a document granting only a general communication of privileges. However, to accept the indiscriminate use of the word privilege as the standard whereby the object of communication is to be determined would lead to the admission that a privilege is merely a favorable concession, regardless of its specific nature and consequences. If a privilege were understood merely as a favorable concession, it would be useless to imply that there is a distinction between a privilege and other favorable concessions such as favors, rescripts, indults, dispensations and indulgences, and it would be superfluous to question the communicability of these concessions by means of communication of privileges. It cannot be denied that a privilege is a favorable concession, if one understands concession

[8] "Privilegium aliquando appellatur gratia, aliquando indultum, aliquando favor, aut rescriptum, aut indulgentia, aut etiam bulla."—Bonacina, *Opus de Morali Theologia* (2 vols. Venetiis: 1687), II, disp. 1, q. 3.; "Privilegium . . . quandoque . . . vocatur . . . rescriptum, diploma, indultum, principale, favor, gratia, etc."—Reiffenstuel, A., *Ius Canonicum Universum*, lib. V, tit. 33, § 1, n. 6; "Privilegium est favor, indulgentia, vel aliud quidpiam, alias ex iure non concessum."—Salmanticenses, *Cursus Theologiae Moralis*, II, tract. 18, c. 1, *de privilegiis*, punct. 1, n. 1. Among present canonists, Augustine maintains that communication of privileges includes dispensations, commutations, spiritual favors, and indulgences.—(Bachofen), Charles Augustine, *A Commentary on the New Code of Canon Law* (8 vols., St. Louis: Herder, 1921-1929, vol. II, *Religious*, 5 ed. 1938), p. 334; hereafter cited as *Religious;* "In communicatione privilegium idem audit ac gratia, indulgentia, praerogativa, favor, immunitas, exemptio, facultas indultum, etc." Vasto, *De Communicatione Privilegiorum*, p. 43.

in an accomodated sense so as to include such legally approved sources of privileges as custom, prescription, and communication. However, it would seem to be more accurate to consider a privilege as the specific object of a favorable concession, or a specific object originating in the benevolence of competent authority, which, in the last analysis, is the source of all favorable concessions, which cannot otherwise be acquired.

Despite the variety of definitions ascribed to a privilege by authors of all time,[4] there is no doubt that, objectively

[4]Both before the introduction of the institute of communication, and even until the present day, the etymology of the word "privilege" formed and forms the basis of the variety of definitions ascribed to it. During the earlier period of canonical jurisprudence, a privilege was defined as a private law, in contrast to a law which is enacted for the common good. "Privilegia sunt leges privatorum, quasi privatae leges. Nam privilegium inde dictum est, quod in privato feratur." (C. 3, D. III; cf. also dictum post c. 16, C. XXV, Q 1.) While the identity between a law and a privilege was still retained, Pope Innocent III indicated that a privilege is a private law which grants something favorable or special: " . . . cum privilegium sit lex privata . . . nec esset privata, nisi aliquid specialiter indulgeret."—C. 25, *Abbate,* X, *de verborum significatione,* V, 40. More advanced juridic analysis has proved that a privilege cannot be identified with a law, and although many canonists still define a privilege as a 'private law', it is unanimously admitted that a privilege can be called a law only by analogy insofar as it obliges others to respect the rights constituted by a privilege. Cf. Reiffenstuel, *Ius Canonicum Universum,* lib. 1, tit. 3, *de rescriptis,* n. 50; Zallinger, *Institutiones Iuris Ecclesiastici* (5 vols. Romae: 1823), lib. V, tit. 33, nn. 262-263; Phillips, *Kirchenrecht* (7 vols., Regensburg, 1845-1872), V. 103-105; Sägmüller, *Lehrbuch des katolischen Kirchenrechts,* n. 33, p. 195; Roelker, *Principles of Privilege According to the Code of Canon Law,* The Catholic University of America Canon Law Studies, n. 35 (Washington: The Catholic University of America, 1926), pp. 4-8; hereafter cited *Principles of Privilege.*

A privilege cannot be identified with a law for the following reasons: it does not need official promulgation—notification is sufficient; it is not necessarily an obligatory norm of action; it always connotes a favor. It is evident, however, that the reasons for which the identity between a law and a privilege is discredited, as well as the opinion that a privilege can be called a law only by analogy, are applicable only to those privileges acquired by a source other than law.

considered, a privilege is a special right. Many of the definitions of a privilege consider it as the efficient cause of a special right.[5] Undoubtedly, the definition of a privilege from this viewpoint can be traced to the original connotation in Roman Law, where it was considered an odious private law attached to individual persons,[6] and although it did not connote an odious or burdensome law in ecclesiastical law, still it continued to be defined as the efficient cause of a special right. It would seem to be preferable to consider a privilege as the object or the effect of an efficient cause. From this viewpoint a privilege would not be considered as the cause of a special right, but the special right itself which is created by competent authority. It is only from this viewpoint that a privilege can be distinguished from other favorable concessions, and it is only in this way that other favorable concessions might be excluded from communication of privileges. Considered from this viewpoint, a privilege can be defined as a special, objective right created by competent authority or acknowledged as such by it.[7] The creation of such a special right constitutes a

[5]A privilege is a private law conceding a special favor. Ph. de Angelis, *Praelectiones Iuris Canonici* (6 vols. Romae: 1877-1891) V. 33, t. 4, p. 324; Lehmkuhl, *Theologia moralis* (Friburgi Brisgoviae, 1897), I, n. 215. Those who are not in favor of calling a privilege a private law substitute other words such as 'constitution": cf. Herincx, *Summa Theologica Scholastica* (Antwerpiae, 1680), tr. 3, disp. 4, q. 3, n. 53. Others define a privilege as *"ius singulare"* which grants a special right. cf. Vermeersch-Creusen *Epitome Iuris Canonici*, I, n. 128.

[6]Cf. Cicognani, *Canon Law*, p. 778.

[7]The authority which has the competence to create such a special right is the legislator, who may do so by any means whatsoever. Besides the legislator, who alone is competent to grant a privilege contrary to the law, any superior who has jurisdiction or merely dominative power over a subject, depending upon the nature of the privilege which is granted, has the power of creating such a special right. Privileges which have their origin in custom or prescription must be acknowledged by competent authority before they can receive lawful existence. If provisions of law for obtaining such privileges are fulfilled, the privileges are automatically approved.

lawful norm of action contrary to or beyond the provisions of law for the person in whose favor such a special right is created.

Except for the note of specialty attached to such a right, which constitutes a lawful norm of action contrary to or beyond the provisions of law, there is no other characteristic that can be applied to privileges in general. Most of the qualities which are usually described as characteristic of a privilege,—such as, the liberty of using or not using the special right, the liberty of accepting or rejecting the special right without promulgation— are not characteristic of those privileges which are created by law. But specialty or exclusiveness of the right applies to these as well as to any other privileges, and as such it is the only generic quality which is a common characteristic of all privileges. The consideration of the other characteristic of a privilege must be reserved for that portion of this work in which privileges are divided according to their various species. However, before consideration is given to the division of privileges, the nature of other favorable concessions in ecclesiastical law will be noted.

Article 2. Dispensations

In view of the fact that a dispensation was frequently identified with a privilege contrary to the law, it is necessary to determine whether the nature of the entities warranted the identification, and whether a dispensation could thereby be included within the scope of communication of privileges.

Because both privileges contrary to the law and dispensations were considered exceptions to the law, these two items were commonly identified with each other during the time of the decretists.[8] Later authorities[9] admitted the identity

[8]Cf. Brys, *De Dispensatione in Iure Canonico* p. 102-103.

[9]Sanchez, *De Sancto Matrimonii Sacramento Disputationum Libri Decem, in Tres Tomos Distributi* (Venetiis, 1712), lib. VIII, disp. 1, n. 1; Billuart, *Cursus Theologiae iuxta Mentem Divi Thomae* (Parisiis, 1878), IV, De Legibus, diss. 5., art. 3.

without any qualifications, while others, as Suarez,[10] maintained that only those dispensations, whose effects were permanent, could be identified with a privilege contrary to the law. Thus, Suarez incorrectly maintained that perpetuity was an essential characteristic of a privilege.[11] Yet while Suarez himself teaches that some dispensations can be called privileges, he asserts that it is the common opinion of his time that these two entities are distinguished from each other.[12] Although there were some authorities who still identified a privilege contrary to the law with a dispensation, Schmalzgrueber[13] and Reiffenstuel[14] developed a clear distinction between these entities. This clear cut distinction has been accepted without question since their time.[15]

According to the opinion of these authorities, a privilege is to be distinguished from a dispensation for these reasons: a dispensation always involves an exception contrary to the law, while a privilege can constitute a right beyond as well as contrary to the law. Furthermore, a dispensation differs from a privilege contrary to the law by virtue of the fact that a dispensation merely removes or suspends the efficacy of a law in a particular case.[16] A privilege, like a dispensation, removes an obligation imposed by law, but,

[10]*De Legibus,* lib. 8, c. 2, n. 10.

[11]"Nota essentialis privilegii nequit esse eius perpetuitas vel stabilitas, qua privilegium contra ius diversificaretur a dispensatione; haec stabilitas potius est consectarium creationis iuris specialis objectivi, quam eius nota essentialis, cum perpetuitas in privilegio deficere possit." Van Hove, *De Privilegiis,* n. 22.

[12]*De Legibus,* lib. 8, c. 2, n. 10. Suarez indicates that Mandosius and Rebuffus were two of the authorities who sponsored this opinion.

[13]*Ius Ecclesiasticum Universum,* lib. V, tit. 33, n. 5.

[14]*Ius Canonicum Universum,* lib. I, tit. 3, de rescriptis, n. 30.

[15]Cf. Michiels, *Normae Generales,* II, 327; Reilly, *The General Norms of Dispensation,* The Catholic University of America, Canon Law Studies, n. 119 (Washington: The Catholic University of America Press, 1939), p. 3, p. 40.

[16]"Dispensatio, seu legis in casu speciali relaxatio . . . "—Canon 80.

unlike a dipensation, it substitutes a special normative right in place of the obligation of the law, which it removes or suspends.

Although the negative operation of a dispensation and the positive operation of a privilege seem to form a solid basis for a distinction between the two entities, it may be questioned whether this can serve as the basis for a distinction between dispensations and all privileges contrary to the law. Undoubtedly, dispensations from impediments, irregularities, and vindictive penalties can be accurately considered mere facts which remove certain obstacles that prevent persons from enjoying juridic benefits which cannot accrue to them because of those obstacles. It would be absurd even to imply that dispensations such as these might be acquired by means of communication of privileges. This is impossible not only because they are fundamentally different from privileges, but also because they are given to particular persons for particular reasons, which would not be realized if communication of them as privileges were invoked. However, it seems reasonable to presume that some dispensations-e.g., dispensations from the law of fast and abstinence, dispensations from the observance of feast days prescribed by law, dispensations from the obligation of reciting the office in choir— might be acquired by means of communication of privileges because privileges contrary to the law were identified with dispensations or even because there is so close a resemblance between some dispensations and privileges. Those dispensations which exempt from the obligations imposed by certain laws not only remove the efficacy of the law in certain cases, but also acknowledge the lawfulness of an action contrary to the obligation which is removed. The same lawful norm of action might result from a privilege granted contrary to such laws. Whether the course of action becomes lawful by implication, which happens in the case of dispensations, or whether the norm of action becomes lawful by the establishment of a positive right through a privilege, the effects are identical. In both instances there is hardly an alternative norm of action. If, for example, a competent superior dispenses a subject from the law of fasting or from the obligation of reciting office in choir, it is not very likely that a different course of action would be prescribed if the same exemptions from law would be granted by means of a privilege. Hence, any attempt to draw a distinction between such dispensations and privileges would result in an argument about words. For this reason, Van Hove maintains that the difference between such dispensations and privileges is based on the mode of concession and not on the object of the concession.[17]

The difference in the mode of concession would not entail a difference between the effects produced by either one. However, despite the similarity of effects, the difference in the mode of concession would help to determine whether such dispensations could be included under communication of privileges. Dispensations of any kind cannot be included under a communication of privileges because they are given for a specific cause, and even though such a dipensation could be identified with a privilege, its acquisition through communication could hardly be admitted because it has always been the common opinion that privileges granted for special reasons cannot be acquired through this source.[18]

ARTICLE 3. FAVORS *(Gratiae)*

According to the terminology of the Roman Curia, any favorable grants, including privileges and dispensations,[19]

[17] *Op. cit.*, n. 32.

[18] Cf. Schmalzgrueber, *Ius Ecclesiasticum Universum*, lib. V, tit. 33, n. 83: Reiffenstuel, *Ius Canonicum Universum*, lib. V, tit. 33, n. 62.

[19] Piatus Montensis, *Praelectiones Iuris Regularis*, II, q. 134; Suarez, *De Legibus*, lib. 6, c. 2, n. 11.

were called favors (gratiae).[20] Accordingly, a favor may be classed as the genus of various favorable concessions, and as such can be distinguished from a privilege as a genus is distinguished from a species.[21] The fundamental difference between a favor and a privilege rests in the fact that the beneficial concession itself, whatever it might be, is considered a favor, whereas a privilege, which itself is a favor, is a special normative right which renders a person immune from the obligation of law.[22] In view of this obvious difference between the two items, it would be incorrect to deduce that communication of specific favors, such as privileges, could effect the communication of all favors. The communication of a specific or lesser item could by no means include the communication of the genus or the greater item.

Article 4. Indulgences

Although indulgences were at times called privileges,[23] and although it was asserted that communication of privileges included communication of indulgences,[24] the intrinsic difference easily discovered between these two items does not warrant the identification, or the claim that indulgences

[20]"On appelle ainsi ä Rome les dispenses, les mandats, les provisions des bénèfices, la rèhabilitation en matiere des crimes, et tous les autres rescrits qu'ill est loisible au Pape de refuser ou d'accorder.' André *Cours Alphabetique et Methodique de Droit Canon* (2 vols. in 1, Paris: 1844), s. v. "grace."

[21]Schmalzgrueber, *Ius Ecclesiasticum Universum*, lib. V, tit. 33, n. 6; Coronata, *Institutiones*, I, n. 85.

[22]Suarez, *De Legibus*, lib. 6, c. 2, n. 11.

[23]Salmanticenses, *Cursus Theologiaė Moralis*, IV, tract. 18, c. 1, *de privilegiis*, punct. 1, n. 1.

[24]Didacus ab Aragonia, *Dilucidatio Privilegiorum Ordinum Regularium*, I, VIII, 18; Parma, *Collectio Indulgentiarum*, n. 1374, where he maintains that only those indulgences which were granted for a general cause could be communicated by means of communication of privileges, admitting that it was almost impossible to distinguish such indulgences: "Difficulter satisfieri interrogationi cum omnimoda certitudine."; Cf. Tatjer, "De Communicatione Privilegiorum inter Regulares," *Apollinaris* V, (1932), 466-467; Augustine, *Religious*, 334.

can be acquired by means of communication of privileges. An indulgence[25] is indeed a favorable concession—a kind of absolution—but it cannot be considered a privilege because it establishes no positive normative right whereby a person may posit lawful acts contrary to or beyond the law, or may omit certain acts prescribed by the law. According to Suarez, it was the common teaching of his day not to identify privileges with indulgences.[26] In spite of the fact that Suarez denies the identity between privileges and indulgences, Parma[27] asserts that Suarez and Rodericus sponsored the opinion that indulgences could be acquired by means of communication of privileges in general. This assertion, however, is absolutely incorrect as to Suarez because Suarez clearly draws a distinction between the two concessions.[28] Rodericus, on the other hand, admits that indulgences can be acquired by means of communication, but that this is possible only when documents of communication expressly permit the communication of indults, by means of which indulgences were frequently granted.[29]

If indulgences could be properly identified with privileges, it is doubtful whether the Pontiffs would have expressly mentioned indulgences in the documents granting communication as they so frequently did. Moreover, the Code

[25]Indulgentia est remissio "coram Deo poenae temporalis debitae pro peccatis, ad culpam quod attinet iam deletis, quam ecclesiastica auctoritas ex thesauro Ecclesiae concedit pro vivis per modum absolutionis, pro defunctis per modum suffragii".—Canon 911.

[26]"Indulgentia vero habet speciem quoddam privilegii, communi tamen usu non ita vocatur, nec solet comprehendi sub nomine privilegiorum in generalibus rescriptis Pontificum nisi mentio illius proprio nomine fiat. . . . indulgentia . . . non est facultas aliquid agendi, vel non agendi, quam privilegium specialiter significat . . . "—Suarez, *De Legibus*, lib. 6, c. 9, n. 10. "Indulgentiae sensu proprio non sunt privilegia." —Piatus Montensis, *Praelectiones Iuris Regularis*, II, 9, 103.

[27]*Op. cit.*, no. 1374.

[28]*Loc. cit.*

[29]Rodericus, E. *Quaestiones Regulares et Canonicae Enucleatae*, I, q. 55, n. 106.

itself follows this practice by expressly mentioning indulgences in reference to communication.[30] It can hardly be doubted that there is a difference between indulgences and privileges, and for this reason it is to be maintained that indulgences cannot be acquired by means of communication of privileges.[31] If, however, communication of indulgences was specifically permitted, their communicability was to be judged according to the same rules that applied to the communication of privileges.

Although a clear distinction was drawn between indulgences and privileges in the old law,[32] the problem about the acquisition of indulgences through communication of privileges was not settled with absolute certitude in the old law.[33] Nor is there any uniform opinion on this problem

30"Per aggregationem communicantur omnes indulgentiae, privilegia et aliae gratiae spirituales communicabiles . . . "—Canon 722, § 1.

31Since rescripts usually served as the instrument whereby communication was permitted, the words of the rescript had to be interpreted according to their proper meaning, which precluded the possibility of extending the meaning of the rescript to items not expressed therein. Cf. Reiffenstuel, *Ius Canonicum Universum*, lib. 1, tit. 3, n. 19; O'Neill, *Papal Rescripts of Favor*, The Catholic University of America, Canon Law Studies, n. 57 (Washington: The Catholic University of America), p. 100; Cf. also Canon 49.

32Cf. Suarez, *De Legibus*, lib. 6, c. 9, n. 10.

33Commenting on the opinion favored by Emmanuel Rodericus, (*Quaestiones Regulares et Canonicae Enucleatae, sive Resolutiones Quaestionum Regularium* [3 vols. in 1, Antwerpiae, 1628], q. 55, art. 20.), who maintained that the indulgences attached to the feast days of the Franciscans were communicated to the feast days of the Dominicans, Mocchegiani makes these remarks: "At opinio huiusmodi, inspecta saltem moderna praxi, non videtur sustineri. . . . Quoad hanc sententiam hodierna praxis aliter docet et communis fidelium sensus contrarium ostendit . . . . Ob theologorum dissensiones circa hanc materiam, ob eorum hesitationes in asserendo vel negando, in extendendo vel coarctando memorato privilegio (i.e. communicationis) . . . . ob tantas incertitudines non amplius fidunt . . ." *Iurisprudentia Ecclesiastica*, I, nn. 1374, 1383.

" . . . relinquimus onus hoc, quod non tam facile est, illis quorum interest."—Melata, *Manuale de Indulgentiis* (Romae: 1892), as quoted by Tatjer, who himself writes: " . . . solutio non clare constat, nam auctores concordes non inveniuntur."—"De Communicatione Privilegiorum inter Regulares, *Apollinaris*, V, (1932), 466.

today. Vasto[34] maintains unequivocally that indulgences are included within communication of privileges. Following the opinion sponsored by Tatjer,[35] Van Hove admits that indulgences were probably included within communication of privileges as long as there was no commonly accepted and clear cut distinction between indulgences and privileges.[36] In one place, Augustine maintains that the incommunicability of indulgences was the more probable opinion even in the old law;[37] in another place, he favors the opinion that indulgences are included within the scope of communication of privileges.[38]

Article 5. Rescripts and Bulls

Since resripts and bulls[39] were sometimes called privileges,[40] it might be presumed that communication of privi-

[34]*De Communicatione Privilegiorum*, p. 43.

[35]*Op. cit.*, 458.

[36]*De Privilegiis*, n. 150, note 1.

[37](Bachofen), Augustine, *Compendium Iuris Regularium* (Neo-Eboracensis: Benziger: 1903), p. 311.

[38]Thus he maintains that the communication of privileges as enjoyed by nuns in virtue of Canon 613, § 2 includes the communication of indulgences. *Religious* (5 ed., 1938), p. 334.

[39]In pre-Code law a rescript was defined as "a written reply given by the Pope to someone's consultation, report, or petition."—Maroto, *Institutiones Iuris Canonici ad Norman Novi Codicis* (3 ed., 2 vols., Romae: 1921), n. 278. Contrary to present legislation, pre-Code law did not apply the word rescript to documents issued by Ordinaries. Cf. Canon 36, § 1. Hence, in reference to communication of rescripts before the Code, this restricted meaning of the word "rescript" is to be applied.

Considering the subject matter of the rescripts, the latter are divided into (a) rescripts of justice, (b) rescripts of favor, (c) mixed rescripts. Matters pertaining to the administration of justice are contained in rescripts of justice. Dispensations, privileges, indulgences, honors, and other favorable concessions are granted by means of rescripts of favor. Finally, matters pertaining to the administration of justice, as well as the concession of favors are disposed of by means of rescripts. Cf. Reiffenstuel, *Ius Canonicum Universum* lib. I, tit. 3, nn. 28-30; Cocchi, *Commentarium in Codicem Iuris Canonici ad Usum Scholarum* (8 vols. Taurinorum Augustae: Marietti, 1931-1940), I (5 ed., 1938), 158.

[40]*Supra*, page 34, n. 3.

leges effects the communication of these. Such a presumption, however, is unlawful in spite of the fact that they were sometimes called privileges,[41] because rescripts are intrinsically different from privileges, which fact is acknowleged by authors of all times.[42] The basic difference between rescripts and privileges rests on the fact that the former are documents by means of which privileges are conveyed. As a result of this difference, which is comparable to the intrinsic difference between an instrumental cause and its effect, the acquisition of rescripts by means of communication of privileges is undoubtedly ruled out. If the distinction between a rescript and a privilege were not acknowleged, then other favors distinct from privileges, could be claimed under communication of privileges by virtue of the fact that many such favors are granted by means of rescripts. In order to prevent such an unrestricted interpretation of communication of privileges,[43] the difference between rescripts and privileges is of the greatest importance.

On many occasions the Pontiffs expressly mentioned rescripts in documents granting communication. In such instances, the communication of rescripts cannot be questioned, but even then, the express mention of rescripts cannot be interpreted to mean that all rescripts, regardless of their contents, are subject to communication. On the contrary, the contents of the rescript must be examined in order to determine the nature of the favor contained therein, and the acquisition of these favors through express mention in grants of communication is to be determined according to the rules pertaining to communication of privileges.

[41]*Loc. cit.*

[42]Cf. e. g., Cocchi, *op. cit.*, I, n. 114; Conte a Coronata, *Institutiones*, I, 85.

[43]" . . . privilegium est stricti iuris, et ideo extendi non debet ultra verba formalia et expressa."—Suarez, *De Legibus*, lib. 8, c. 10, n. 2.

ARTICLE 6. INDULTS

Another favorable concession, whose acquisition through communication of privileges might be claimed, is an indult. Admitting the fact that indults are frequently identified with privileges,[44] a seventeenth century canonist points out that an indult is a special kind of favor which removes an impeding obstacle and permits a person to enjoy a right provided by law. For this reason, it is to be distinguished from a privilege, which merely grants a right not provided by law.[45] By virtue of this definition, however, an indult cannot be distinguished from a dispensation. Using the examples offered by this authority, it would be more accurate to classify an indult as a specific kind of rescript of favor. In fact, he himself acknowledges the fact that a contemporary canonist sponsored this opinion. There seems to be no doubt that this was the original and more accurate meaning of the word indult, which received its title from the use of some form of the word *indulgere* in the dispositive part of the rescript.[46] Despite the fact that this was the original connotation of the word "indult," it is certain that it was later considered a favorable concession

[44]"Saepissime unum pro alio accipitur."—Amydenius, Th. *Tractatus de Officio et Iurisdictione Datariae et de Stylo Datariae* (2 vols., Venetiis: 1654), I. c. 15, n. 1, p. 80: c. also *supra*, page 34.

[45]"Indultum est gratia quaedam, quae fit illi, qui de iure uteretur, nisi esset impeditus decreto contrario, videlicet simplex remotio obstaculi. Privilegium vero est gratia, quae conceditur illi cui de iure non competit."—Amydenius, *loc. cit.*

[46]Cf. the example given by Amydenius: "Indulgemus, ut possessiones et alia mobilia et immobilia, quae ad personas fratrum, si in saeculo mansissent ratione successionis, vel quocumque alio iusto titulo contigissent, petere, percipere, ac retinere, libere valeatis." *loc. cit.* By means of this indult, the Pontiff permitted professed monks to enjoy their right of inheritance which they lost by profession. Hence, the Pontiff removed the obstacle which impeded this right, and now permitted them to exercise that right in favor of the monastery to which they were professed, in accordance with the demands of the vow of poverty, namely, that whatever is acquired by the monk, is acquired for the monastery.

which could not be clearly distinguished from a privilege.[47] According to the modern opinion an indult is still considered a favorable concession whose characteristic mark is the note of impermanence, on the basis of which it is distinguished from a privilege.[48] Although the temporary nature of an indult is undoubtedly its characteristic mark according to modern opinion, it cannot be determined whether it was characterized in this way in the old law. Hence, as long as an indult constituted a special normative right which was not of a temporary nature,[49] it could not be excluded from communication as long its acquisition through this source was guided by the accepted rules.

As a result of the observations made in the foregoing pages concerning the nature of various favorable concessions and their acquisition through communication, the following conclusions are made. First of all, only those favorable concessions which can be classified as specific kinds of privileges —favorable concessions, which constitute special normative rights— can be acquired by means of communication of privileges, provided that the rules of communica-

[47]André, *Cours Alphabétique et Méthodigue de Droit Canon, s.v.* "indult."

[48]"Indultum est quaelibet largitio favorabilis aliquem determinatum actum ponendi, et eatenus a privilegio differt, quod ad tempus tantum tribuitur, dum, e contra privilegium est largitio permanens, v.g., facultas dispensandi a lege abstinentiae ad quinqennium est indultum."—Beste, *Introductio in Codicem* (Collegeville, Minnesota: St. John's Abbey Press, 1938), p. 55.

"Indults are quasi-privileges, differing from privileges strictly so-called in this respect, that indults are not necessarily perpetual. They are faculties and favors which the legislator benevolently grants for a time, either outside the law or contrary to the same."—Cicognani, *Canon Law,* 477.

[49]According to pre-Code opinion, sanctioned by the Code, privileges cannot be acquired by means of communication if they are granted for a determined length of time. Cf. Didacus ab Aragonia, *Dilucidatio Privilegiorum Ordinum Regularium,* tr. 1, q. 8, n. 5; Antonius a Spiritu Sancto, *Directorium Regularium* (Lugduni: 1661), tr. 1, disp. 1, sect. 3, n. 43; Cf. Canon 64.

tion, which will be treated later,[50] do not prevent their acquisition through this source. Secondly, the indiscriminate use of the word privilege cannot be followed as a standard according to which the extent of communication of privileges is to be determined. The intrinsic nature of the various favorable concessions and not the inaccurate use of the word "privilege" is to determine their classification and possible acquisition through this source. Thirdly, other favorable concessions, which differ from privileges as such, cannot be acquired by means of communication of privileges unless those favorable concessions are expressly mentioned in the documents. If they are expressly mentioned in the documents of communication, their acquisition is to be judged according to the nature and circumstances of the grant, applying the rules that pertain to communication of privileges. However, if beneficial concessions such as favors, indulgences, rescripts, etc., can be acquired by means of communication, it would be more in accord with precise juridic terminology to say that these favorable concessions are acquired by means of communication alone, and not by communication of privileges.

Undoubtedly the pre-Code canonists, who assert that favorable concessions other than privileges as such can be acquired through communication, base their contention on many documents in which such favorable concessions are expressly enumerated. If their teaching is not based on this foundation, then it is based on the popular, rather than the juridic use of the word "privilege." In so far as it can be determined, none except Suarez speculate about the possible acquisition of other favors, intrinsically different from privileges, when communication of privileges is permitted.[51] Thus, he maintains that favors, dispensations, indults, indulgences, etc., can be acquired through communication when privileges alone are mentioned, because privi-

[50]Cf. *infra,* pages 128-167.

[51]Cf. Suarez, *De Legibus,* lib. 8, c. 19, n. 10.

leges demand a broad interpretation.[52] However, in other sections of his treatise on privileges, Suarez himself draws a sharp distinction between, for example, privileges and dispensations,[53] privileges and indulgences,[54] and also states that privileges (considered as the efficient cause of a special right) should not be extended beyond the tenor of their words.[55] To reach absolute certainty on this question in so far as the pre-Code doctrine is concerned seems to be a physical as well as a moral impossibility, but there is no doubt that the intrinsic difference between favorable concessions and privileges is acknowledged by advanced juridic opinion, which is recognized by the Code of Canon Law. For this reason it is incorrect to maintain, as some modern authorities do, that communication of privileges alone includes the communication of other favorable concessions with which privileges were frequently identified in the old law.[56]

Article 7. Division of Privileges in relation to the Institute of Communication

In view of the fact that the extent of communication of privileges depends upon the nature of specific privileges, it is necessary to present, at least in summary fashion, a division of privileges which will facilitate the classification of privileges, when they are referred to by their technical title.

(A) Considering the nature of the source through which privileges can be acquired, the Code of Canon Law divides them into four groups.[57] From this viewpoint, privileges

[52]*Loc. cit.*

[53]*De Legibus,* lib. 8, c. 2, n. 10.

[54]*De Legibus,* lib. 8, c. 9, n. 10.

[55]*De Legibus,* lib. 8, c. 10, n. 2.

[56]Vasto and Augustine are two present day authors who maintain that communication of privileges includes communication of other favorable concessions. Cf. Augustine, *Religious,* p. 334; Vasto, *De Communicatione Privilegiorum,* p. 43.

[57]Canon 63.

are divided as follows by the Code: those which are acquired a) by direct concession of competent authority; b) by custom c) by prescription; d) by communication. It would probably be more precise to classify privileges into five distinct groups from the viewpoint of the source of acquisition. Such a five-fold division is warranted by the fact that the first source, which is listed in Canon 63 is not exclusive. The phrase " direct concession by competent authority " is used generically by the Code, and thus includes any competent authority such as the law itself, the legislator, or any competent superior. As long as a privilege is specifically defined and granted to a determined person, such a privilege is acquired by means of direct concession, whether it be granted by law or by a special act outside of law.[58]

Even though privileges acquired by law, as well as those acquired by means of a special act outside of law, are products of direct concession, it is better to separate the privileges produced by these two sources into distinct classes because their mode of acquisition as well as their interpretation is governed by different norms. Moreover, there has never been any doubt or disagreement among canonists about the proper classification of privileges which are acquired by direct concession outside of law, whereas there is no such uniformity among canonists about the classification of those special rights which are acquired by law.[59] Since the former have always been considered true privileges, their communicability, considered objectively, cannot be called into question. However, the communicability of the latter privileges is not so certain because of the difference of opinion among authors. For these reasons, then, privileges can be grouped in the following classes by virtue of the source through which they are acquired: a) direct concession of competent authority by means of a special act out-

[58]Michiels, *Normae Generales*, II, 358.

[59]Cf. Van Hove, *De Privilegiis*, nn. 61-64 for references to those authors who uphold these conflicting opinions.

side of law; b) direct concession by law; c) custom; d) prescription; e) communication.

(a) Privileges acquired by direct concession outside of law.

Among those privileges which are acquired by direct concession outside of law are included all special normative rights which are specifically defined for a particular person (physical or moral), who is the immediate beneficiary of the superior's benevolence. Hence, regardless of the method employed by the competent superior,[60] privileges are acquired by means of this source when the superior defines the exact nature of a privilege and grants it immediately to a beneficiary.

(b) Privileges acquired by law.

Within this group are included those special normative rights which are established by universal or particular law. Privileges in this group are composed mainly of those special rights, which are technically called *'iura singularia'*.[61] Their possible inclusion within the scope of communication of privileges depends upon whether they are

[60]A rescript or oral concession can be used by the competent superior in making such a concession. If a privilege is granted in answer to a petition, such a privilege is granted *ad instantiam;* if, on the other hand, it is granted out of pure liberality on the part of the superior, it is conceded *motu proprio.* The manner in which the privilege is conceded, i. e., by rescript or oral concession, determines the force as well as the probative value of the respective privilege. Cf. Canon 79; Suarez, *De Legibus,* lib. 8, c. 2, n. 2; Roelker, *Principles of Privilege,* pp. 17-19; Cicognani, *Canon Law,* pp. 826-827.

[61]For the want of a better English title, these will be called 'exceptional rights'. Exceptional rights are positive laws, universal or particular, enacted in consideration of the special juridic condition of certain persons within a society. Exceptional rights are primarily laws, and as such can be established only by the legislator within the limits of his competence, observing the general conditions required for the enactment of a law.—Cf. Van Hove, *De Privilegiis,* n. 68. Since these rights are established by law, they must be promulgated officially before they can become a lawful norm of action.

properly called privileges or not. Exceptional rights were considered privileges in the old law,[62] just as they are called privileges by the Code,[63] but in spite of this official use of the word privilege, there has never been any uniform opinion among canonists at any time about the exact classification of these exceptional rights.[64]

In so far as these laws provide favorable rights which are restricted to persons enjoying special dignities, or to persons belonging to a special class within a society ruled by common law, they are marked with the note of specialty, which is a distinctive mark of privilege in general,[65] and by virtue of this characteristic, exceptional rights can be called privileges in the true sense of the word. The source of acquisition —law or concession outside of law— might form the basis for a distinction between privileges widely so-called and privileges strictly so-called,[66] but it does not destroy

[62]CC. 2 and 27, X, *de privilegiis et excessibus privilegiatorum,* V. 33.

[63]Canons 123, 239, 625.

[64]D'Annibale denies the juridic similarity between exceptional legal rights and privileges properly so-called, but admits that they were generally considered identical.—*Summula Theologiae Moralis* (3 ed., 3 vols., Romae: A. Saraceni, 1908), I, n. 277, note 1. "Privilegia clausa in corpore iuris fere omnia sunt beneficia legis tum generalia . . . tum specialia . . . quae iura singularia sunt potius quam privilegia."—Zallinger, *Institutiones Iuris Ecclesiastici,* lib. V, tit. 33, nn. 262. Exceptional rights were also called common privileges.—Cf. Bernardus Papiensis, *Summa Decretalium,* ed. E. Th. Laspeyeres (Ratisbonae: 1860), lib. V, tit. 28, p. 255. " . . . iura singularia, si sint favorabiles, vocantur privilegia, sed sensu improprio."—Van Hove, *De Privilegiis,* n. 65, p. 66; " . . . *privilegium late sumptum* (*iura singularia*) is not thereby an improper privilege . . . A real concession is made and the word privilege is properly employed."—Roelker, *Principles of Privilege,* p. 8.

[65]Cf. *supra,* page 38.

[66]Cicognani, *Canon Law,* 780; Conte a Coronata, *Institutiones,* I, p. 97; Cappello, *Summa Iuris Canonici* (3 vols. Romae; Apud Aedes Universitatis Gregorianae: vols. I-II, 2 ed., 1932-1934; vol. III, 1933). I, n. 168, note 13. These canonists distinguish between privileges widely so-called and strictly so-called on the basis of the mode of acquisition. Thus, a privilege acquired by law is a privilege widely so-called; one acquired through direct concession is a privilege strictly so-called.

the nature of a privilege, which is a special objective normative right, regardless of the source through which it is acquired. Hence, it cannot be maintained that privileges acquired by law are privileges only by analogy, or privileges improperly so-called.

Relative to the institute of communication of privileges, the question of the proper or improper use of the word privilege in reference to exceptional rights is not too important. In most cases, communication of privileges is superfluous as a source for these special rights because all members of the same group or dignity (e. g., religious, religious superiors) already enjoy exceptional rights by provision of law. Nevertheless, if it were possible to acquire such special rights through communication,[67] undoubtedly the official use of the word privilege in reference to exceptional rights, both in the old as well as present law, would supersede the conflicting opinions of canonists, and consequently these rights would fall within the scope of communication of privileges.

(c) Custom.

Although lawful custom[68] had long been an acknowledged source of special rights,[69] there has been no uniform opinion

[67]The possibility may arise in the case of those exceptional rights which are established by particular law. Hence, if exceptional rights are established for religious in one diocese, the religious of another diocese can claim these special rights if communication of privileges is permitted between these distinct groups. At least in one instance communication of exceptional rights was permitted expressly. " . . . item . . . iuraque singularia, quibus familiae singulae privatim utebantur, fruebantur, ac prorsus omnia quae differentiam aut distinctionem quoque modo sapiant, nulla sunto . . ." Leonis XIII *Pontificis Maximi Acta* (22 vols., Romae, ex typographia Vaticana: 1881-1903), 4 Oct., 1897, XVII, 296.

[68]"Ius per similium alicuius actuum frequentium acquisitum."—Bouix, *De Principiis Iuris Canonici* (Parisiis: 1882), p. 351. "A sola communitate legis recipiendae capace introduci potest, non a singularibus personis, quae praescriptione tantum iura acquirere possunt."—Van Hove, *De Privilegiis*, n. 71.

[69]C. 13, *Novit*, X, *de iudiciis*, II, 1 (a. 1204); c. 6, D. 64. (Pope Gelasius, a. 492-496); c. 8, C. IX, Q. 3, (Pope Nicholas, a. 864).

among canonists at any time as to the proper classification of these rights. However, although some authorities denied and still deny that rights acquired by custom are true privileges,[70] it has always been the prevailing opinion that custom can produce special normative rights contrary to or beyond the law, and that these special normative rights can be called true privileges.[71] The prevalent opinion of canonists merely acknowledges the true nature of consuetudinary rights, which cannot be called anything else but true privileges. It is true that the norms which govern the acquisition of special rights through custom are different from the norms which govern the acquisition of privileges, but this difference is only accidental. It does not constitute an essential difference between special normative rights themselves, and hence it is incorrect to maintain that consuetudinary rights are not true privileges. Because they are true privileges, their acquisition through communication of privileges is conceivable, and, in fact, it was expressly admitted by canonists, without a dissenting voice, that communication could serve as a source for the acquisition of

[70]Pichler, *Epitome Iuris Canonici iuxta Decretalium Libros Gregorianae Collectionis Explanati*, lib. V, tit. 33, n. 10; Toso, *Ad Codicem Iuris Canonici Commentaria Minora* (5 vols., Romae: 1927), I, p. 156. Ojetti's view represents the opinion of those who claim that custom does not produce a true privilege, by writing: "Melius dici consuetudinem obtineri vim privilegii, quam consuetudine vel praescriptione privilegium acquiri."—*Commentarium in Codicem Iuris Canonici* (4 vols., Romae: 1927-1931), I, 282.

[71]Bonacina, *Opus de Morali Theologia* (2 vols., Venetiis: 1687, II, disp. 1, q. 3, punct. 1, n. 2-3; Pirhring, *Ius Canonicum Nova Methodo Explicatum* (5 vols. in 4, Dillingae: 1674-1678), lib. V, tit. 33, n. 11; Wernz, *Ius Decretalium* (6 vols., Romae et Prati: 1898-1905), I, n. 160, 2; Schmalzgrueber, *Ius Ecclesiasticum Universum*, lib. V, tit. 33, nn. 94-95; Cappello, *Summa Iuris Canonici*, I, n. 168, note 13.

privileges acquired through custom.[72] Although most modern authors admit that special rights produced by custom are true privileges, which fact is acknowledged by the Code itself in Canon 63, they question the effectiveness of communication of privileges as a source for these rights on the basis of the restriction contained in Canon 64, wherein it is prescribed that only those privileges which are granted directly can be acquired through communication.[73]

(d) Prescription.

The old law[74] as well as the Code[75] acknowledge prescrip-

[72]"Item . . . censentur communicata privilegia per praescriptam consuetudinem acquisita, quae habet vim privilegii, licet de his nulla apud alias religiones fit specialis concessio a Sede Apostolica emanata."—Rodericus, H., *Questiones Regulares et Canonicae Enucleatae,* p. 839, n. 57; "Communicatio generalis privilegiorum includit privilegia non solum a Pontificibus concessa, sed etiam ex consuetudine acquisita."—L. Maria Sinistrari de Ameno, *De Delictis et Poenis* (3 vols. Romae: 1754), I, tit. 7, § 10, p. 446; Cf. also Pius VI, Const. *Iniuncti nobis,* 27 Mart, 1787—*BRC,* VI, pars. 2, 1795. In this constitution privileges acquired through custom are expressly listed as the object of communication.

[73]An analysis of this question is reserved for the commentary on Canon 64. Here it may be noted that Berutti, Roelker, Vasto, Michiels, and Toso deny the effectiveness of communication in this case. Berutti, Ch., *Institutiones Iuris Canonici* (6 vols., Taurini—Romae: Marietti, 1936-1938), I, p. 155; Roelker, *Principles of Privilege,* p. 49; Vasto, *De Communicatione Privilegiorum,* p. 60; Toso, *Ad Codicem Iuris Canonici Commentaria Minora,* I, p. 154; Michiels, *Normae Generales,* II, 362. Other canonists, such as Coronata and Wernz-Vidal, accept this opinion with the qualification that those privileges only which are acquired through immemorial or centenary custom may be acquired through communication of privileges. Cf. Coronata, *Institutiones,* I, n. 92; Wernz-Vidal, *Ius Canonicum* (7 vols. in 8, Romae: Universitas Gregoriana, 1923-1938), I, n. 293.

[74]C. 2, *Dilectus,* X, *de capellis monachorum et aliorum religiosorum,* III, 37, (Innocentius III, a. 1201); C. 50, *Cumana ecclesia,* X, *de electione et electi potestate,* I, 6, (Gregorius IX, a. 1229).

[75]Canon 63.

tion[76] as a source of special normative rights. However, just as in the case of special rights acquired through custom, there has been much difference of opinion among authors of all time about the proper nomenclature of the special rights acquired through prescription. Many pre-Code canonists admitted that prescription served as the source of true privileges;[77] others denied this with the added qualification that prescription could produce a special right similar to a privilege, without offering any suggestion as to how such a special right might be classified.[78] Modern authorities[79] who deny that special rights acquired through prescription can be called true privileges, base their contention on the argument that prescription produces a subjective rather than an objective normative right, which is the distinctive characteristic of a privilege. This argument, however, is not conclusive because the existence of such a right as a lawful norm of action depends ultimately upon the benevolence of competent authority. It is perfectly true that the special right is already in existence, and that the action whereby it will eventually be transferred to another person originates with the subject who is capable of acquiring the special right in this way. However, the action by means of which such a special right can be acquired

[76]"Adiectio dominii vel alieni iuris peremptio, per continuationem possessionis temporis a lege definito." "Praescriptio vel usucapio est exceptio ex tempore legibus definito substantiam capiens, quae actioni personali vel in rem opponitur." Cf. Reiffenstuel, *Ius Canonicum Universum*, lib. II, tit. 26, n. 12; Veermersch-Creusen, *Epitome Iuris Canonici*, II, n. 828.

[77]Castro Palao, *Opus Morale*, I, tract. 3, disp. 4, punct. 2, § 5, n. 2; Schmalzgrueber, *Ius Ecclesiasticum Universum*, lib. V, tit. 33, nn. 94, 95; Reiffenstuel, *Ius Canonicum Universum*, lib. V, tit. 33, n. 39; Ferraris, Prompta Bibliotheca, VI, s. v. "privilegium," art. 1, n. 20; Wernz-Vidal, *op. cit.* I, n. 294.

[78]Pichler, *Epitome Iuris Canonici iuxta Decretalium Libros Gregorianae Collectionis Explanati*, lib. V, tit. 33, n. 10; Zallinger, *Institutiones Iuris Ecclesiastici*, lib. V, tit. 33, n. 267.

[79]Darmanin, "Consuetudine e portio paroecialis," *Perfice Munus* (Turin: 1926—), XII (1937), pp. 152-154; Van Hove, *De Privilegiis*, pp. 33-35.

is sanctioned by law, and it can become a lawful norm of action for another only when the conditions prescribed by the law are fulfilled.[80] If the provisions of law are observed, the special right becomes a lawful norm of action not because a subject has established the right, but because the benevolence of law sanctions the acquisition of a special right in such fashion. Such a special right might be called subjective, but only in so far as the action of prescription originates in the subject. When the time element is completed in accord with the provisions of law, the special right becomes an objective norm of action, whose existence depends upon the benevolence of law. By virtue of this, special rights acquired by prescription are true privileges, and as such might be acquired by means of communication of privileges as long as no implicit or explicit restrictions preclude their acquisition through this source. One such restriction which immediately presents itself is the one which unequivocally prohibits the acquisition of purely personal privileges through communication.[81] Since prescription is usually, though not exclusively, a source of privileges for individuals[82] the acquisition of such privileges through communication is out of the question. However, if privileges are acquired through prescription by a community, there is no reason why they cannot be acquired by another community through communication. There is no available evidence to prove that such privileges were considered incommunicable. Nor is there any positive evidence to prove the opposite. However, since the acquisition of privileges acquired through custom was expressly permitted, an argument from analogy favoring the communicability of privileges acquired through prescription would be valid. Those authorities who maintain that privileges acquired through custom cannot be included within the scope of com-

[80]Cf. Canons 1508-1512.

[81]Cf. *infra,* pages, 153, 161.

[82]Privileges can be acquired through prescription by communities as well as individuals. Cf. Suarez, *De Legibus,* lib. 8, c. 1, n. 11.

munication apply the same restriction to privileges acquired by prescription, maintaining that the acquisition of such privileges is outlawed by Canon 64, which prescribes that only those privileges which are acquired by direct concession are liable to communication.

(B) Considered in its relation to law, a privilege can be: (1) contrary to the law; (2) beyond the law; (3) according to the law.

(1) A privilege contrary to the law constitutes a norm of action whereby a person can lawfully perform an act prohibited by law, or omit an act which is prescribed by law. Hence, the privilege of anticipating divine office from noon of the preceding day would come under the first class, whereas exemption from the jurisdiction of a superior would be an example of the latter. By virtue of these different effects produced, privileges contrary to the law are classified as positive privileges or negative privileges.

(2) The concession of a special right not provided by law and not prohibited by it is called a privilege beyond the law. Thus, for example, the title of a minor basilica is a privilege beyond the law because it does not involve a derogation of law, nor can it be obtained without the permission of the competent superior.[83] The most common privileges beyond the law are faculties,[84] whose classification as privileges beyond the law has seldom been questioned.[85]

(3) The existence of a few examples of so-called con-

[83]Van Hove, *De Privilegiis,* n. 36.

[84]"Facultates habituales quae conceduntur vel in perpetuum vel ad praefinitum tempus aut certum numerum casuum, accensentur privilegiis praeter ius."—Canon 66, § 1.

[85]Hinschius and Schulte are two of the authors who have denied that faculties can be classed as privileges. Cf. Hinschius, *Das Kirchenrecht der Katholiken und Protestanten in Deutschland* (6 vols., Berlin, 1869-1897). Vols. I-IV, *System des katholischen Kirchenrechts* (Berlin, 1869-1888), III, p. 808; Schulte, *Das katholische Kirchenrecht* (Giessen, 1860), I, p. 143.

cessions according to the law,[86] as well as official confirmation of privileges, seems to have suggested this classification. However, none of these examples can be called a privilege because none conceded a new and special right. The examples found in the old law were only declarations or specific applications of the common law.[87]

(C) By reason of the subject to whom privileges are granted, they cán be grouped into two large divisions — personal and real—, which in turn are subdivided according to the nature of the person or reality to which the privileges are given.

Personal privileges are those which are given directly to persons themselves, but since the nature of a juridic person varies, personal privileges must be divided accordingly. Hence, personal privileges are (a) commonly personal, (b) individually personal, (c) corporate. Commonly personal are those which are conceded to a body of persons (e. g. religious order) so that individual members may enjoy special rights by virtue of their membership in the group to which the privileges are granted. Individually personal are those which are directly granted to private individuals, not because of their connection with a moral person, or because they enjoy a certain dignity, but in consideration of their own personal merits. Such privileges are purely personal and must not be confused with those which are enjoyed by private individuals in virtue of their membership in class or because they enjoy a certain dignity. Corporate privileges are those which are given to a moral person (e. g., religious community) as such. Such privileges can be used only when the moral person acts as a unit. Hence these privilges are different from those which are given

[86]C. 1, X, *de rescriptis*, I, 3 (Alexander III, a. 1174-1181); c. 26, X, *de iureiurando*, II, 24 (a. 1206).

[87]"Concessio quae fit tantum secundum ius commune . . . privilegium dici non debet.—Bernardi Papiensis, *Summa Decretalium*, p. 254; "Privileges according to the law are not proper privileges because no precise concession is made." Roelker, *Principles of Privilege*, p. 31.

directly to a moral person for the benefit of individuals.

Real privileges are those which are granted to places or things, not to favor those places or things themselves,[88] but to benefit the persons who have some connection with those places or things. Real privileges are divided into: a) local—those which are granted to a place (e. g., a diocese) ;(b) muneral—those which are granted to a dignity (episcopate) or office (rectorship) ;(c) properly real—those which are vested in tangible things, such as a church or statue.

In connection with the institute of communication, the distinction between personal and real privileges is of major importance. This is especially true in the case of purely personal and muneral privileges.[89] In actual practice, however, it is oftentimes difficult to distinguish between these privileges. When such a doubt arises and the words of the grant do not offer a solution to the problem, the following rules are to be followed: A privilege is considered real if it is not contrary to the common law, or prejudicial to the rights of a third person.[90] If, on the contrary, it is prejudicial to the rights of a third party and is contrary to the common law, it is considered personal.[91] The motive of the granting of the privilege will oftentimes help to determine its proper classification. Hence, if a privilege is given to a person because of his merits it is certainly personal. If, on the contrary, it is given to a person because he enjoys

[88] " . . . res et loca sunt iurium incapaces."—Van Hove, *De Privilegiis*, n. 12.

[89] Cf. *infra*, pages, 153-154.

[90] Salmanticenses, *Cursus Theologiae Moralis*, tract. 18, c. 1, *de privilegiis*, punct. 3, n. 18.

[91] Sanchez, *De Sancto Matrimonii Sacramento Disputationum Libri Decem, in Tres Tomos Distributi*, lib. III, disp. 1, n. 4.

a special dignity, there is no doubt that such a privilege is real. Finally, a privilege enjoyed by an individual is personal if it is given for a determined length of time; real, if it is vested in the office.[92] However, in order that a privilege may be classified as a real privilege by virtue of its permanence, it must be absolutely and not relatively permanent. Hence, although a privilege is permanent for a particular subject, it is still a personal privilege if it ceases with the death of a person. However, if a privilege is given to a person with the provision that it can be transferred to his successors, such a privilege enjoys absolute permanence, provided it is not expressly revoked, and is therefore a real privilege.

(D) By reason of their objective nature privileges can be favorable or odious.[93] At first glance, it would seem that such a division implies that not all privileges are favorable concessions. This, however, is not the case. All privileges are favorable rights in so far as the grantee himself is concerned. Some privileges, however, are injurious to the rights of another and for this reason are called odious.[94] Privileges which in no way prejudice the rights of another are favorable.[95]

[92]Cicognani, *Canon Law*, p. 782.

[93]The distinction between favorable and odious privileges was important in pre-Code law, according to which favorable privileges were to be interpreted liberally, and odious privileges strictly. Cf. Antonius a Spiritu Sancto, *Directorium Regularium*, tract. 1, disp. 1, n. 10; Suarez, De Legibus, lib. 8, c. 6, n. 4; Salmanticenses, *Cursus Theologiae Moralis*, II, tract. 18, c. 1, *de privilegiis*, punct. 3, n. 26. In present law, this distinction is not too important because the Code does not demand a different interpretation for odious and favorable privileges except in Canon 76.

[94]E. g., the privilege of not paying tithes; exemption from jurisdiction of a superior.

[95]E. g., the privilege of hearing Mass during the time of an interdict.

CHAPTER III

PAPAL DOCUMENTS IN RELATION TO THE INSTITUTE OF COMMUNICATION

Any study of the institute of communication would be incomplete without some explicit treatment of the papal documents by means of which communication of privileges is made available as a source of privileges for members of the Church.[1] Pontifical documents merit this attention because the institute of communication proper to ecclesiastical law owes its origin and development to them. It was in these documents that some of the general norms[2] that were to regulate the operation of the institute were first enunciated, and it was through the medium of pontifical documents alone that communication of privileges was

[1]Although communication of privileges is at times permitted through other sources besides papal documents, strictly so-called, this study is restricted to the latter because they form the bulk of the documents through which communication of privileges is permitted.

[2]Here, the word general is not used in the sense of comprehensive or all-embracing as applying to the institute of communication under all circumstances. The only general norms which can be traced to pontifical documents are those which pertain to special classes of persons. Thus, for example, Pope Sixtus IV (Const. *Regimini universalis ecclesiae*, 31, aug. 1474—*BRT*, V, 217) prescribed the norms which must be followed in determining the manner in which privileges attached to the office of religious superiors are to be communicated. Cf. *infra*, pages 150-153. Clement VIII (Const. *Quaecumque a Sede Apostolica*, 7 dec. 1604—*BRT*, IX, 138) enacted regulations concerning communication in favor of confraternities. Hence, because these regulations were enacted by means of Constitutions, strictly so-called, they were endowed with the force of law and were to be observed whenever communication of privileges was permitted to persons belonging to these classes. The only comprehensive regulations applicable to communication were the traditional doctrinal rules pertaining to the consequences of the two specific forms of communication. Outside of these comprehensive norms pertaining to communication at all times, and the more limited general norms which applied to communication in favor of particular persons within a special class, no other all-embracing or general positive regulations were enacted before the promulgation of the Code.

permitted before the promulgation of the Code.[3] However, though these reasons would demand a detailed analysis of the juridic force, nature, and interpretation of the various kinds of documents by means of which communication was regulated and through which it was permitted,[4] the limits of this dissertation preclude such a detailed analysis.

Next in importance to the legal force of some of the Constitutions pertaining to the institute of communication, is the terminology of the dispositive part of the documents through which communication is permitted. This feature of the documents is especially important in relation to this study because it furnishes the clues for identifying (1) communication itself, (2) its specific nature, (3) its precise limits in regard to the material object.

(1) In spite of the fact that there is no uniform or exact terminology through which communication can be identified, it is by no means difficult to determine when this source is permitted to serve as the source for acquiring privileges. Hence, whenever the wording of the document indicates

[3]The assertion that pontifical documents were the only medium through which communication of privileges was permitted does not imply that other methods were not employed by the pontiffs. Hence, in theory, communication could be permitted by means of an oral grant ('vivae vocis oraculo'). However, though this was possible theoretically, there is no evidence to show that communication was ever effected by means of an oral grant.

[4]Before the promulgation of the Code, communication of privileges was permitted by means of such papal documents as constitutions, rescripts of favor, bulls, briefs, indults, and simple or mixed rescripts. Cf. Cicognani, *Canon Law*, pp. 81-96 for a description and analysis of these documents. Cf. also, Van Hove, *Commentarium Lovaniense in C. I. C.*, vol. I, tom. IV, *De Rescriptis* (Mechliniae-Dessain: 1936); O'Neill, *Papal Rescripts of Favor*.. Whenever a pontifical document is entitled as a constitution in this dissertation, it is not to be inferred that the title is used in its strict juridic meaning, i. e., a pontifical act by means of which a law is enacted. In accord with the opinion proposed by Cicognani, who states that "all pontifical acts may be called constitutions", (Cf. Cicognani, *Canon Law*, p. 80), the title is used in a wide sense. If it is necessary to use the title in its strict connotation, this will be indicated in the text of the dissertation, rather than in the reference made in the footnote.

that the specification of a privilege granted to a person is dependent upon the nature of a privilege acquired by another, there is no doubt whatsoever that communication is effected in such cases. It matters little what words are used by the grantor when he imparts the privilege already acquired or to be acquired by one to another. As long as this dependence of one privilege upon another is implied by the terms of the document, it can safely be presumed that the privilege is to be acquired by means of communication.[5] Moreover, in order that a person might claim the benefits of communication, it is not absolutely necessary that the documents contain no mention of specific privileges. Specific privileges can be mentioned, as they frequently were, without destroying the force of the document in granting communication. In those instances when specific privileges are mentioned, the fact of communication can still be observed in the requirement that the precise nature of a specific privilege is to be derived from the nature of the

[5]The following excerpts from papal documents serve to demonstrate how communication can be identified despite the lack of uniformity in terminology. " . . . eidem congregationi Lateranensi etiam concedimus ut omnibus privilegiis . . . congregationi S. Iustinae concessis ipsa quoque congregatio Lateranensis pariformiter potiri et gaudere possit et valeat . . . "— Sixtus IV, Const. *Dum ad universos*, 23 aug. 1476—*BRT*, V, 234: " . . . omnibus et singulis privilegiis . . . in suo firmitate persistenibus in omnibus et per omnia, perinde ac si . . . huiusmodi privilegia a principio congregationi Cassinensi . . . specialiter et expresse concessa fuissent."— Iulius II, Const. *Super cathedram pastoralis*, 22 nov. 1503—*BRT*, V, 40. All other documents that are referred to in this dissertation exhibit the same distinguishing mark—i.e., dependence of the privileges to be acquired by one person upon the privileges enjoyed by another—and thus all documents of communication are fundamentally the same in this respect.

specific privilege enjoyed by the one whose privileges are communicated.[6]

(2) Secondly, the terminology of the documents is important because the wording of these offers the only absolute standard for identifying the specific nature of communication. Considering the contrariety in the consequences resulting from the distinct species, there can be no question about the importance of identifying the specific nature of communication.

The use of the term *aeque- principaliter* in the documents of communication offers unmistakable evidence that equal communication is effected,[7] for it is this terminology which gave rise to the technical juridic title of equal communication, namely, *communicatio in forma aeque principali.* The communication of a privilege *aeque principaliter* signifies that the person favored with such a communication is not only made equal to another in regard to the use of a privilege, but more important is the fact that he is made a principal beneficiary,[8] as a result of which he is able to possess the privilege in his own right and use it independently of the person whose privilege serves as a model for the specification of his.[9]

Although equal communication can be best identified by virtue of the phrase *aeque principaliter,* it is not to be inferred that documents of communication must necessarily

[6]e.g. "Ita ut omnibus et singulis exemptionibus . . . quibus alii conventus ordinis et provinciae praedictorum utuntur, fruuntur, et gaudent, uti, frui, et gaudere libere et licite possit . . . "—Pius VI, Const. *Ex iniuncto nobis,* 28 nov. 1783—*BRC,* VI, pars. 2, 1308. The express mention of exemptions in this document and in others that follow the same pattern implies that the person favored with the privilege of exemption must ascertain the extent of his exemption from the nature of the exemption enjoyed by the other person.

[7]" . . . vos quoque aeque principaliter, sicut ipsi, uti, potiri, et gaudere, libere et licite valeatis . . ."—Clemens VII, *Religionis zelus,* 3 iun. 1528—*BRT,* VI, 113.

[8]Pignatelli, *Consultationes Canonicae,* X, consult. 1, n. 30.

[9]Antonius a Spiritu Sancto, *Directorium Regularium,* tract. 1, disp. 1, sec. III, n. 14.

contain this expression in order to effect equal communication. Other expressions besides *aeque principaliter* are used just as frequently in documents of communication, and point to equal communication just as unmistakably as the phrase *aeque principaliter.* Among such expressions are any phrases by means of which the grantor implies that the privileges acquired by the person favored with communication are to merit the same consideration as a privilege which is mentioned specifically and granted directly to the primary grantee.[10] Finally, it is lawful to presume that equal communication is effected when a privilege is granted *ad instar*. It has already been noted[11] that the concession of a privilege *ad instar* can be interpreted as productive of equal communication. However, it was also noted at that time that the phrase *ad instar* is interpreted in this manner not by virtue of its intrinsic or natural meaning, but by virtue of its juridic meaning which is derived from the prevailing opinion of jurists. There is no doubt that the more common opinion of jurists can establish a standard juridic meaning for legal terminology. Hence, by virtue of the fact that a juridic meaning can be established in this way, it is not only lawful to maintain that equal communication is effected when a privilege is granted *ad instar,* but this connotation must necessarily be attached to the phrase because the juridic meaning of words and phrases always prevails in law.

Besides the above mentioned expressions which are clearly indicative of equal communication, documents of

[10]The following excerpts from pontifical documents are representative examples of expressions which effect equal communication without the use of the term *aeque principaliter.* " . . . ut omnibus et singulis privilegiis . . . gaudere libere et licite possint et valeant, perinde ac si illa ei specifice et particulariter concessa fuissent . . . "—Urbanus VIII, Const. *Salvatoris nostri,* 12 ian. 1632—*BRT,* XVI, 67; " . . . ita ut illis (privilegiis) praedicta congregatio . . . in posterum uti, frui, et gaudere possit . . . perinde ac si specialiter, expresse, . . . concessa fuissent . . . "—Pius VI, Const. *Inter multiplices,* 14 dec., 1792—*BRC,* VI, 2569.

[11]Cf. *supra,* page 31.

communication contain two other expressions whose precise connotation presents some difficulty when an attempt is made to determine the specific nature of communication which is effected by these expressions. These two expressions are: *pariformiter* and *sine* (or *absque*) *ulla differentia.* On a number of occasions the privileges of one person were granted to another in such a way that the person favored with the communication was permitted to enjoy the privileges equally with *(pariformiter)* and without any distinction *(sine ulla differentia)* from the person whose privileges were communicated.[12] It is difficult to ascertain what form of communication is produced when these expressions alone are used in documents of communication because the intrinsic meaning of the expressions favors accessory communication, while the actual operation of the institute of communication argues against it. There would be a solution for this dilemma if, as in the case of the phrase *ad instar,* the meaning of these expressions could be gauged from the opinions of authors. Unfortunately, however, there is no such simple solution because it seems that no pre-Code canonist has attempted to explain the connotation attached to these expressions. Some modern canonists seem to imply that equal communication is produced when these expressions are used,[13] but the paucity

[12]E. g. " . . . in omnibus et per omnia pariformiter et absque ulla differentia perpetuo uti et gaudere libere et licite possint." —Sixtus IV, Const. *Dum ad universos regulares,* 23 aug. 1476—*BRT,* V, 234.

[13]Michiels refers to equal communication as *"communicatio pariformis",* thus implying that *"pariformiter"* is synonymous with *"aeque-principaliter".* *Normae Generales* (2 vols., Poloniae: 1929), II, 363. In discussing the significance of the terminology in documents of communication, Vasto seems to favor exclusion of equal communication only when the status of the persons favored with communication argues against this form or when the terminology of the documents is obviously opposed to it. Moreover, it is certain that he favors an identity between the term *"aeque-principaliter"* and the phrase *"sine ulla differentia"* by virtue of the fact that he borrows this expression to describe the effects of equal communication. Cf. *De Communicatione Privilegiorum,* p. 50.

and indirectness of these opinions makes them practically worthless.

Considered in the light of their intrinsic meaning, the two above-mentioned expressions produce the following effects when they are used by the grantor in documents of communication. On the strength of these terms, used separately or conjunctively, persons favored with communication are given an equal right to enjoy the same privileges as the primary grantee and all distinction is abolished between these persons insofar as the enjoyment of those privileges is concerned. By producing these effects, the terms themselves do not indicate whether the privilege which is acquired by virtue of such a grant is a product of accessory or equal communication. The distinction between the two latter species of communication pertains more to the consequences affecting the acquired privileges rather than their use, which factor is uppermost in the mind of the grantor when he communicates the privileges of one person to another *pariformiter* and *sine ulla differentia.*[14] Hence, in view of the fact that equal communication implies that the nature of a privilege acquired in this way is not subject to the vicissitudes of the primary privilege, and vice versa, it is more logical to infer that a privilege communicated *pariformiter* or *sine ulla differentia* is the product of accessory communication rather than that of equal communication. It is only by virtue of accessory communication that the person favored with such a grant would enjoy the privilege equally and without any distinction. If *pariformiter* and *sine ulla differentia* implied equal communication, the equality and lack of distinction which the grantor intended to effect would cease to exist just as soon as the nature of one privilege (either the one possessed by the primary grantee or the one acquired by the subject of communica-

[14]E. g., " . . . vobis praedictis eremitis, ut omnibus et singulis privilegiis . . . uti et gaudere pariformiter et absque ulla differentia libere et licite valeatis." Sixtus IV, Const. *"Sedes apostolica"*, 27 maii, 1474—*BRT*, VI, 213.

tion) were changed in any way or if it were lost. Therefore, it would be more logical to infer that the terms *pariformiter* and *sine ulla differentia,* considered objectively, effect accessory communication. However, in spite of the fact that this is the correct objective interpretation of these expressions, it will be seen presently that, under certain circumstances, it is lawful to infer that these terms produce equal communication when the status of the subjects favored with such a communication of privileges is taken into consideration.

Although precise terminology is the surest standard for determining the specific nature of communication, there are times when such clear terminology is wanting, and in the absence of such terminology reasonable doubts are bound to arise. Thus, the competent superior might permit communication of privileges without qualifying the nature of communication in any way[15] or by qualifying its nature with terminology whose precise connotation is not clearly evident. In such instances, the status of the subjects favored with communication offers the only clue for the solution of the doubt. Hence, if it is evident that the subjects to whom privileges are communicated are juridically dependent upon or closely affiliated with the person whose privileges are communicated, there can be no question that accessory communication is effected. It is not so easy, however, to determine the nature of communication when obvious terminology is not used in documents by means of which autonomous subjects of parallel rank are favored with communication of privileges. Autonomy of jurisdiction and equality of rank do not necessarily imply that equal communication is effected. *Per se* such a condition is not opposed to accessory communication, nor is the superior constrained to grant equal communication to persons who possess these qualifications. However, though the grantor is free to grant

[15] E. g., "Privilegia . . . omnibus monasteriis eiusdem congregationis . . . ac omnibus dicti ordinis monialibus et monialium locis sint communia . . ." Leo X, Const. *Etsi a summo,* 4 iul, 1513—*BRT,* V, 545.

either form of communication to such persons, the question still remains: What form of communication takes place between juridically independent subjects of parallel rank when the terminology used in the documents of communication is not clear on this point? The answer to this question can be found in the actual operation of the institute of communication. In the great majority of documents permitting communication of privileges between juridically independent subjects of parallel rank (e. g., distinct religious orders, universities, confraternities, etc.) unmistakable terms are used in order to produce equal communication in favor of such subjects. If it does chance to occur that communication is permitted to subjects who enjoy the same status and at the same time are independent of each other, it is certainly lawful to judge the nature of communication in these comparatively few instances in the light of actual operation of the institute. Hence, it can safely be presumed that, in the absence of precise terminology, equal communication is intended between autonomous subjects of parallel rank. The wealth of positive evidence which exists to prove the operation of equal communication under such circumstances would weaken any argument in favor of accessory communication.

Although documents of communication abound with technical expressions clearly indicative of equal communication, there is a dearth of such significant expressions insofar as accessory communication is concerned. In fact, neither the word "accessory" nor any of its derivatives can be found in any documents of communication. The word "accessory," which is used frequently in legal terminology in opposition to principal, seems to have been borrowed by canonists in order to show that a privilege acquired through this form of communication is completely dependent upon the privilege which serves as the model. In view of the fact that pontifical documents reveal a total absence of the term accessory or any phraseology similar to it, it is reasonable to ask how this form of communication can be identified. This can be done only by ascertaining the status of the persons who are favored with communication of privileges. Therefore, accessory communication must be presumed when, without specifying the nature of communication, the grantor communicates the privileges of one person to another who is juridically dependent upon or closely affiliated with the person whose privileges are communicated. The same conclusion must be reached when such subjects are expressly included within the terms of a grant by means of which autonomous subjects are favored with equal communication. Thus, if equal communication is permitted to two religious orders and secondary persons are included within the scope of such a communication, the implication is that the distinct religious orders become independent beneficiaries of the communicated privileges whereas the persons dependent upon them or affiliated with them enjoy only accessory communication. In actual practice, accessory communication was enjoyed by nuns subject to orders of men, by secular third orders aggregated to and subject to religious orders, by novices, postulants, and oblates affiliated with religious orders, by lay societies canonically erected by religious orders, etc. Hence, whenever it is evident that persons are favored with privileges of a primary grantee merely because of their dependence upon or affiliation with the primary grantee, accessory communication must necessarily take place because this is the only form of communication feasible under such circumstances. Under these circumstances the status of the persons absolutely excludes the possibility of equal communication.

However, in spite of the fact that juridic dependence or close affiliation offer an absolutely flawless objective criterion for identifying accessory communication when the terminology itself offers no enlightenment, it seems as though there are instances when accessory communication should be presumed even when such an objective criterion does not exist. Hence, it would seem to be reasonable to infer that, in the absence of clear terminology, accessory communication is effected in favor of a person, who, despite his autonomy, is inferior in rank to the person whose privileges are communicated. Such a condition would seem to favor accessory communication in order to prevent the person of inferior rank from becoming more privileged than the person whose privileges are communicated. Judging from actual operation of the institute of communication, there is no doubt that equal communication was permitted only to autonomous persons of parallel rank. However, considered also from the viewpoint of its actual operation, it is equally certain that parallelism of rank did not imply absolute juridic equality or similarity. This is evident from the fact that equal communication was expressly permitted between mendicant and non-mendicant orders, between regulars and congregations, between religious orders of men and religious orders of women. Obviously, the only parallelism that existed between these various autonomous persons was a parallelism based on membership in the same general class. However, despite the fact that these distinct religious institutes belong to one and the same class, (i. e., religious) there are differences between them which admit of a distinction in degree or rank. Certainly, religious institutes in which solemn vows are taken enjoy a greater degree of pre-eminence than those in which simple vows are taken; clerical religious institutes enjoy a superiority over lay institutes; pontifical institutes rank higher than diocesan institutes, etc. Hence, notwithstanding the fact that it would seem more reasonable to restrict communication to that which is accessory when doubtful or uncertain terminology is used in making this source of privileges available to persons of inferior rank, the historical operation of the institute can be invoked in order to claim equal communication. If such reasoning from analogy is permissible —and there is no reason why it should not be— inferiority in rank would not be opposed to equal communication as long as the person who is favored with a communication of privileges belongs to the same class as the one whose privileges are communicated.

The foregoing discussion concerning the identification of the specific nature of communication can be summarized as follows: Equal communication alone can be identified through the terminology of the documents. However, in following this objective method, equal communication can be detected with absolute certainty only when the expressions *aeque-principaliter, perinde ac si* etc., and *ad instar* are used by the grantor to effect communication of privileges. In order to determine the specific nature of communication when the terminology of the documents does not clearly indicate this, the status of the subjects to whom communication is permitted offers the only clue for ascertaining the species of communication. Hence, in view of the fact that equal communication was expressly permitted only to autonomous persons enjoying juridic similarity, it can reasonably be presumed that this form of communication is effected in favor of any persons possessing these qualifications even when the nature of communication is not expressly specified. Finally, no other form but accessory communication can operate in favor of those persons who are in any way dependent upon or affiliated with the person whose privileges are communicated.

Another feature closely connected with the specific nature of communication is the distinction between the two modes —unilateral and reciprocal— according to which communication might operate. Although this aspect of communication is treated in detail in another place,[16] it is important to note at this point that, in practice, only equal communication is subject to this distinction in modes of operation. More important, however, is the fact that the terminology of the documents, as ambiguous as it might be in other respects, never leaves any room for doubt insofar as the mode of operation is concerned, and consequently it

[16]Cf. *supra*. pages 31, 32.

is incorrect to invoke an argument from analogy on this point.

(3) Lastly, the terminology of the documents of communication is important because it alone reveals the exact scope of this source of privileges in regard to the material object. In this respect, the wording of the documents is the only means of ascertaining whether communication serves as a source only for the privileges which are in existence at the time when communication is permitted, or whether this source is valid also for those privileges which will be granted in the future. From the wording of a great number of documents it would be difficult to determine whether communication is restricted to those privileges already acquired by the primary grantee prior to the issuance of the document of communication or whether it also extends to those privileges which will be acquired by him in the future. Thus, on many occasions, the pontiffs favored persons with this source of privileges by permitting them "to use, and enjoy" the privileges of another.[17] Though it would seem that such wording would not preclude the acquisition of privileges which would be acquired by the primary grantee in the future, it was the consensus of pre-Code canonists that such privileges could not be acquired by means of communication unless they were expressly included within the terms of the document.[18] Hence, according to the com-

[17]E. g., " . . . ita ut omnibus et singulis privilegiis . . . quibus alii conventus . . . utuntur, fruuntur, et gaudent, uti, frui, et gaudere libere, ac licite possit . . . " Pius VI, Const. *Ex iniuncto nobis,* 28 nov. 1783—*BRC,* VI, par 2, p. 1308.

[18]Cf. Rodericus, H. *Questiones Regulares et Canonicae,* 838, n. 55: Cf. also Suarez, *De Legibus,* lib. 8, c. 16, n. 16. Among modern canonists only Van Hove and Vasto offer any opinion on this point. The former upholds the opinion commonly accepted before the Code by teaching it expressly: "Requiritur ergo mentio specialis ut communicatio sese extendat ad concedenda."—*De Privilegiis, n.* 147. The latter upholds the same opinion implicitly:" . . .supposita . . . concessa communicatione etiam pro in futurum concedendis privilegiis."— *De Communicatione Privilegiorum,* p. 55.

mon opinion of canonists communication can never be invoked as a source of privileges which would be granted to the primary grantee after the permission to acquire privileges through communication has been given, unless future privileges are expressly mentioned. In order to attach such effects to communication, it is not enough that the terminology itself does not oppose such an interpretation, but the document must contain an explicit statement permitting the acquisition of those privileges which would be acquired in the future by the primary grantee. Such an explicit permission would be contained in the document if the grantor states that the person favored with communication can acquire "not only those privileges which have been conceded, but also those which will be conceded."[19] In the light of this common opinion which teaches that communication, objectively considered, is restricted to those privileges which have already been acquired by the person whose privileges are communicated, it is important to consult the terminology of particular documents in order to insure a correct interpretation of communication on this point.

On the basis of the difference in the terminology of the dispositive part of the documents of communication, pre-Code canonists were wont to make a two-fold distinction: (1) those documents by means of which communication of privileges was permitted in general terms;[20] (2) those

19" . . . omnia et singula privilegia . . . concessa, vel in posterum concedenda . . . "Pius VI, Const. *Inter multiplices,* 14 dec. 1792—*BRC,* VI, 2569.

20" . . . terminis generalibus simpliciter tantum conceptis . . . "—Pichler, *Epitome Iuris Canonici iuxta Decretalium Libros Gregorianae Collectionis Explanati,* lib. V, tit. 33, *de privilegiis,* II, p. 665. The following document offers an example of such a communication conceived in general terms: "Privilegia . . . universae huic congregationi . . . ac omnibus dicti ordinis monialibus et monialium locis sint communia . . . " Leo X, Const. *Etsi a summo,* 4 iul. 1513—*BRT,* V, 545.

documents in which specific privileges as well as other favorable concessions were listed.[21] The distinction, which obviously has a solid foundation in reality, has an important bearing on the efficacy of communication, for the communicability of a certain class of privileges depends upon the above-mentioned difference in the terminology of the documents of communication. Although most documents of communication, objectively considered, would seem to permit the acquisition of all privileges, Pignatelli[22] maintains that privileges which are prejudicial to the rights of a third party[23] cannot be acquired by virtue of a document of communication which contains general terminology. In support of this opinion, the eminent canonist offers two Rota decisions[24] which denied the validity of certain privileges because they were claimed on the strength of documents which permitted only a general communication of privileges. Concluding his discussion about the differences in the terminology of the documents and the peculiar effects of the respective types, Pignatelli states that any privileges which are prejudicial to the rights of a third party cannot be acquired by means of communication unless the document expressly mentions such specific privileges, as, for example, exemptions, immunities, etc. Although Pignatelli himself offers no reasonable explanation for his opinion, it

[21]Canonists generally referred to such terminology as "communicatio in terminis praegnantibus concepta". Cf. Piatus Montensis, *Praelectiones Iuris Regularis*, II, q. 143, ad II, n. 3. Such a communication is effected by terms like the following: " . . .omnes et singulas gratias, concessiones, indulgentias, peccatorum remissiones, praerogativas, favores, immunitates, exemptiones, facultates, privilegia, indulta, tam spiritualia, quam corporalia, qualiacumque illa essent . . . de Apostolicae auctoritatis plenitudine communicavimus."—Leo X, Const. *Dudum per nos*, 10 dec., 1519—*BRT*, V, 732.

[22]*Consultationes Canonicae*, X, const. 199, n. 25.

[23]E.g., Exemption from the authority of the bishop; privilege of not paying tithes. In short, any privilege which would deprive another of a right given to him by law.

[24]S.R. Rota, *in Vallisoletana quartae funeralis coram Iusto*, 19 apr. 1606; *in Valentina decimarum coram Lancellota*, 28 nov. 1603—*Loc. cit.*

can be explained very conveniently in the light of the opinion proposed by Pichler,[25] who teaches that communication of privileges permitted by means of unqualified terminology serves as the source for ordinary privileges alone, whereas documents containing a list of specific privileges permit the acquisition of extraordinary privileges as well. In view of the fact that privileges prejudicial to the rights of a third party were frequently enumerated in documents of communication,[26] it can be maintained with Pichler that such were extraordinary privileges and could not be acquired by means of a general communication of privileges because a "general concession does not include those privileges which are worthy of special mention."[27] There can be little doubt that privileges prejudicial to the rights of a third party can be properly classified as extraordinary privileges and as such are to be excluded from a general communication of privileges. However, it should be remembered that these are not the only privileges that are to be classified as extraordinary privileges. Over and above these extraordinary privileges, there are those which merit the same classification by virtue of the fact that they are rarely granted by the Holy See. In view of the fact that the classification of such privileges depends upon the changing practice of the Holy See, it is quite difficult to offer an accurate illustrative list of such extraordinary privileges.[28] Privi-

[25]*Op. cit.*, V, 33, *de privilegiis*, II, p. 665.

[26]Cf. *supra*, page 76, note 21.

[27]Pichler, *loc. cit.;* "In generali concessione non veniunt ea quae quis non esset verisimiliter concessurus."—Reg. 81, R. J. in VI°.

[28]Judging from a Rota decision passed in 1637, it is certain that the privilege of granting benefices reserved to the Holy See and the privilege of electing a temporary abbot of a Benedictine monastery were privileges which were rarely granted by the Holy See. S.R. Rota coram Molines, 26 dec. 1637—Corazza, *Sacrae Rotae Romanae Decisiones coram Rev. J. Molines* (6 vols. in 5, Romae: 1728), II, p. 849. Some authors classified exemption from observing an interdict as such a privilege. Cf. Petra, *Commentarium ad Constitutiones Apostolicas* (5 vols. in 2, Venetiis, 1729), V, 296, n. 10; Pignatelli, *Consultationes Canonicae*, X, consult. 1, n. 24.

leges, which are properly considered extraordinary by virtue of the fact that they are granted rarely, are excluded not only from communication of privileges permitted by means of unqualified terminology, but also from communication permitted with the broadest and most comprehensive terminology. Thus, if a privilege pertaining to the election of abbots were considered extraordinary, and of infrequent concession, it could not be acquired by means of communication even though the document mentioned privileges pertaining to elections. In order to acquire privileges such as these it is necessary that their nature be defined in exact and specific terms.[29]

In regard to the exclusion of privileges prejudicial to the rights of a third party, care must be taken to avoid the unwarranted opinions of those canonists who maintain unequivocally that all privileges prejudicial to the rights of a third party can never be acquired by means of communication, regardless of the differences in the terminology by means of which communication is permitted.[30] It is sound jurisprudence, indeed, to consider privileges prejudicial to a third party incommunicable if and when a general communication of privileges is permitted, but to maintain that such privileges are incommunicable even when they are expressly mentioned would imply that the grantor has no intention of conceding such a privilege despite the fact that he expressly mentions it. It is obviously incorrect to maintain that prejudicial privileges cannot be acquired through communication of privileges when they are expressly mentioned as communicable by the grantor. Such an interpretation would contradict the grantor's express benevolence, which

[29]Cf. Corazza, *loc cit.;* Piatus Montensis, *Praelectiones Iuris Regularis,* II, q. 143 ad II, n. 3.

[30]" . . . nam privilegia . . . quae involvunt praeiudicium tertii . . . non conferuntur per solam communicationem sed indigent speciali mentione."— Monacelli, *Formularium Legale Practicum* (Venetiis: 1706), tit. 6, n. 26; Cf: also *Analecta Iuris Pontificii,* IX (1867), col. 385. The author of this article favors the same opinion as the one upheld by Monacelli.

certainly should not be frustrated by an incorrect interpretation of clear and explicit terminology.[31] If under ordinary circumstances, concessions should be interpreted in favor of the grantee,[32] it would be absolutely erroneous to maintain that a person does not receive a privilege when it is expressly mentioned.

Along with being a decisive factor in determining the communicability of privileges prejudicial to the rights of a third party, the difference in the terminology of the documents determines the acquisition of other favorable concessions, which are intrinsically different from a privilege.[33] Calling to mind the above mentioned distinction it is noted that some documents of communication simply permit a communication of privileges, whereas others contain a list of specific privileges as well as other favorable concessions. In so far as it can be determined, there is no author who indicates the necessity of making this distinction in regard to the possible acquisition of favorable concessions, which are distinct from privileges. In treating of communication of privileges, most authors seem to imply that other favorable concessions, intrinsically different from privileges, are implicitly included within the scope of communication, and, as a matter of fact, some authors[34] teach this explicitly. If certain kinds of specific privileges cannot be claimed by virtue of a simple communication of privileges, it is reasonable to maintain that those favorable concessions, which, of their nature, are entirely different from a privilege cannot be acquired on the strength of such a communication of privileges. It is to be admitted that there were periods

[31] " . . . maxime cavendum est ne verba privilegii inania reddantur."—Suarez, *De Legibus*, lib. 8, c. 15, n. 12.

[32] " . . . ea semper adhibenda interpretatio, ut privilegio aucti aliquam ex indulgentia concedentis videantur gratiam consecuti."—Can. 68. Cf. Roelker, *Principles of Privilege*, pp. 72-82, esp. p. 76.

[33] The intrinsic difference between a privilege and other favorable concessions is treated on pages 48-73, *supra*.

[34] (Bachofen), Charles Augustine, *Religious*, p. 334. Vasto, *De Communicatione Privilegiorum*, p. 43.

during the history of canonical jurisprudence when there was no clearly defined distinction between a privilege and other favorable concessions, but eventually such a distinction was made and the different favorable concessions were placed in separate categories. Hence, it is in harmony with advanced juridic thought to distinguish between privileges and other favorable concessions and to insist upon the incommunicability of other favorable concessions when a simple communication of privileges is permitted.

It is a well known fact that, in the present economy, the institute of communication enjoys a relatively insignificant efficacy compared to that which characterized its operation before the promulgation of the Code. However, despite the fact that its efficacy has diminished to a great extent, it is not to be assumed that the distinctive terminology of the documents and the rules which must be observed in interpreting it properly have no significance whatsoever today. On the contrary, the norms which guided the interpretation of the institute, whose operation in former days was effected by means of special documents, are still applicable, substantially at least, for the proper interpretation of the institute today, whether its benefits are permitted by law or by means of a special document outside of law. If permitted by means of a special document outside of the common law of the Code, the rules of the Code concerning the interpretation and force of such documents,[35] together with the prescriptions of the Code on communication[36] must be observed. However, except for the provisions of the Code regarding the efficacy of communication in favor of particular persons[37] and the introduction of a new restriction concerning

[35]If permitted by means of a constitution, strictly so-called, Canons 8, 9, 10, and 17-23 would be of greatest importance; if by means of rescript, Canons 36-62 would apply.

[36]Canons 64, 65.

[37]Canons 613, 713, 722.

the efficacy of the source in general,[38] the correct interpretation of the institute of communication still depends upon the pre-Code norms, most of which had their origin, directly or indirectly, in the terminology of the documents of communication which were issued before the Code.

The significance of the terminology of the documents for the correct interpretation of the efficacy of communication is accurately described by Suarez,[39] who writes: "In order to understand the quantity and quality of communication, the words of the document must be investigated from the viewpoint of the subject of communication as well as the mode of communication, observing, at the same time, all general norms concerning the interpretation of the documents."[40]

[38]The Code prescribes that only those privileges which are directly conceded are liable to communication. Canon 64.

[39]*De Legibus*, lib. 8, c. 16, n. 1.

[40]Author's translation. Cf. also Salmanticenses, who write: "Unde verba indulti attente considerandae sunt, tum ex parte eius cuius privilegia communicantur . . . tum ex parte eius cui communicantur." *Cursus Theologiae Moralis*, tract. 18, c. 1, *de privilegiis*, punct. 7, n. 80.

PART TWO
HISTORICAL SYNOPSIS

CHAPTER IV

THE ORIGIN OF THE INSTITUTE OF COMMUNICATION

In order to trace the origin of the juridic institute of communication, it is necessary to go back to Roman Law, for it is an accepted fact, explicitly ackowleged by many canonists,[1] that a special form of concession used therein inspired the legal institute which is the subject of this study. One should consult Roman Law not only because of the external and possibly fortuitous resemblance between the special source found therein and the institute of communication, but especially because the interpretation and effects produced by equal communication depend, for the most part, on the interpretation of that particular law[2] by the early Roman Law jurists.

By virtue of this law, all orphanages, churches, and hospitals conducted by a certain Nicon and his successors were permitted to enjoy all the privileges already received or to be received by the Church of Constantinople.[3] Instead

[1]Castro Palao, *Opus Morale,* I, tr. 3, disp. 4, punct. 2, § 8, n. 1; Suarez, *De Legibus,* lib. 8, c. 15 nn. 1 and 7; Vasto, *De Communicatione Privilegiorum,* p. 61, n. 90; Van Hove, *De Privilegiis,* p. 136, n. 136.

[2]C. (1, 3) 34 (35). *Corpus Iuris Civilis* (3 vols., Berolini, apud Weidemmanos, 1928-1929), Vol. II, *Codex Iustinianus,* ed. stereotypa decima, P. Krueger. *Glossa Ordinaria* (Lugduni: 1549) cites this particular law as 33, and since this is the edition of the *Corpus Iuris* which was used by the early Roman law jurists, it is cited in the same way by them.

[3]"Domus etiam aliasque res superius nominatas ad curam memorati viri pertinentibus vel postmodum quolibet modo ad eius sollicitudinem vel qui post eum ad eiusdem orphanatrophi curam vocati fuerint perventuras *ad instar* maioris venerabilis ecclesiae vel nunc adipiscitur vel postea merebitur, perpetuo potiri pietatis intuitu decernimus."—*Loc. cit.*

of specifying the privileges that were to be acquired by the beneficiaries mentioned in this law, the legislator simply stated that they were to enjoy the same privileges as the Church of Constantinople.[4] Thus, it is evident that these who, by this statute, were permitted to enjoy the same privileges as those given to the Church of Constantinople depended upon the privileges of that church for the specification of theirs. The law is clear enough on this point because there is no other way in which the beneficiaries could determine the quality of their privileges except by consulting those which were first granted to the Church of Constantinople. However, the law itself does not reveal whether its beneficiaries were to acquire independent privileges, identical with the privileges of the primary grantee, or whether they were simply permitted to enjoy the privileges of the primary grantee along with it and subject to the same modifications which affected its privileges.

The answer to this doubt was first proposed by Roman Law jurists, notably Baldus de Ubaldis (1319-1400), whose opinion was later adopted by Castro Palao and Suarez and acknowledged by all canonists since their time. Of itself, the particular law, to which reference has been made, would hardly have attracted the attention of Roman Law jurists because, insofar as it can be determined, this is the only law in which concession *ad instar* appears. That it did attract the attention of the early commentators of Roman Law can be attributed to the fact that privileges had already been granted in this fashion to the Universities,[5] for which reason the problem must have been one of practical

4" . . . ad instar maioris venerabilis ecclesiae . . . "—*Loc. cit.*

5Cf. *infra,* page 93. This fact is acknowledged by Baldus de Ubaldis in the summary preceding his commentary on C. (1, 3) 33. "Studium Tholossanum habet omnia privilegia studii Parisiensis . . . Studium Aurelianum gaudet privilegiis studii Tholossani . . . :" *Commentaria in XI Codicis Libros* (3 vols., Venetiis: 1572).

as well as theoretical importance. Relative to the effects of concession *ad instar*, Baldus de Ubaldis settled one fundamental point, from which all other deductions logically flow. Thus, contrary to the impression conveyed by the law itself, which seems to imply that the privileges of the primary grantee are not multiplied and distributed as distinct entities among the new beneficiaries, this jurist maintained that the privileges acquired through concession *ad instar* were dependent upon the primary grantee's privilege only for their origin and essence,[6] as a consequence of which the cessation of the primary grantee's privilege does not spell the cessation of the privilege acquired through concession *ad instar*.[7] There can be no doubt that this interpretation of concession *ad instar* served as the foundation for the more elaborate opinions of later authors.[8] Thus, basing their opinions on the ideas first proposed by Baldus de Ubaldis, canonists developed the theory which can be summarized as follows: 1.) A privilege acquired through concession *ad instar* is a numerically distinct privilege, which is necessarily an exact duplicate of the primary grantee's. 2.) The model privilege and its reproduction are both self-subsistent entities, and although the latter is an imitation of the former it is not dependent upon the former except for its specifications because the primary grantee's privi-

[6]" . . . relatio habet se . . . per modum causae fiendi. . . . sufficit quod in principio sit vera relatio quia in instanti [i. e., at the time that the quality of the privilege is determined] consumit suum effectum, ita quod amplius non dependet a relatione sed debet formam impressam . . . "—*Loc. cit.*

[7]" . . . quod studio Aureliano sint concessa omnia privilegia studii Tholossani. Deinde studium Tholossanum cassatur et eius privilegia annihilantur. . . . quaerit utrum per hoc annihilata est privilegia studii Aureliani? Guilielmus determinat contra quia cum a principio sit studio Aureliano ius quaesitum ex casu proveniente in alio, non in se illud ius amittit . . . "—*Loc. cit.*

[8]Cf. Castro-Palao, *Opus Morale*, I, tract. 3, disp. 4, punct. 2, § 8; Suarez, *De Legibus*, lib. 8, c. 15; Antonius a Spiritu Sancto, *Directorium Regularium*, tract. 1 ,disp. 1, sect. 2, nn. 33-34.

lege serves to interpret the grantor's mind.[9] 3.) The increase of the primary grantee's privilege does not thereby cause the increase of the privilege which it models. This, however, applies only to concession *ad instar* which does not permit a beneficiary to acquire those privileges which will be granted to the primary grantee in the future. Objectively, concession *ad instar* serves as a source only for those privileges which had been granted to the primary grantee.[10] There are instances, however, when a beneficiary of concession *ad instar* is permitted to acquire those privileges which have already been acquired by the primary grantee and those which will be acquired.[11] Under such circumstances any increase of the primary grantee's privileges is available to the beneficiary of concession *ad instar* because such an increase is comparable to a new concession. 4.) The revocation or loss of the primary grantee's privilege, however, does not, under any circumstances, cause the destruction of the privilege which it models.

If a comparison is made between concession *ad instar* and communication, it will be seen immediately that there is a close resemblance between these two sources of privilege. First of all, both sources imply that the specification of the privilege to be acquired by the beneficiary depends upon a privilege acquired by another. Secondly, both equal communication and concession *ad instar* produce an independent privilege which is not effected by the increase, diminution, or loss of the primary grantee's privilege except when either source is made available for the

[9]" . . . utrumque privilegium stat per se ut reipsa distinctum, et licet sit ad instar prius concessi, ab eo tamen non dependet, sed istud tantum fuit adductum in exemplum et similitudinem ad determinandam voluntatem concedentis." Grueber, X., *De Privilegiis Religiosorum,* edidit Amort (Augustae Vindelicorum: 1747). This citation is taken from Vasto, *De Communicatione Privilegiorum*, p. 64.

[10]Cf. Suarez, *De Legibus,* lib. 8, c. 15, n. 2.

[11]Cf. C. (1, 3) 34 (35); Cf. also Iulius II, Const. *Copiosus,* 6 apr. 1552—*BRT,* VI, 455.

acquisition of the primary grantee's future privileges, in which case the beneficiary of either source profits by the increase of the primary grantee's privileges. Hence, in so far as the specification of a privilege is concerned, communication of either species is identical with concession *ad instar*. In so far as the status of an acquired privilege is concerned, perfect similarity exists only between concession *ad instar* and equal communication. Though some canonists favor the opinion that concession *ad instar* can effect the acquistion of a privilege in either accessory or equally principal form,[12] and although one canonist maintains there is an absolute identity between accessory communication and concession *ad instar*,[13] by far the greater majority of canonists acknowledge perfect identity only between equal communication and concession *ad instar*.[14] Despite the fact that there is an obvious difference between the effects of accessory communication and concession *ad instar*, at least one canonist identifies these two sources of privilege and, in doing so, maintains that it is erroneous to hold otherwise.[15] Though it seems impossible to maintain that there is an identity between concession *ad instar* and accessory communication, still it must be admitted that there is some foundation in fact for the opposite opinion.

[12]Cf. *supra*, page 30.

[13]Cf. *infra*, note 15.

[14]Suarez, *De Legibus*, lib. 8, c. 16, n. 1-17, especially nn. 4-5; Pignatelli, *Consultationes Canonicae*, X, consult. 1, n. 25; Navarrus, *Commentarium de Iubilaeo*, 540, n. 26; *Collectanea in usum Secretarium Sacrae Congregationis Episcoporum et Regularium*, (ed. A. Bizzarri, Romae, 1885, p. 478, note 1; Van Hove, *De Privilegiis*, p. 137, n. 136. The opinion of all these canonists is summed up concisely by Castro Palao, who writes: "Inter huiusmodi privilegium [per communicationem in forma æque principali acquisitum] et privilegium ad instar nullam invenio aliquam in se differentiam . . . Quapropter omnia illa quae dicta sunt de privilegiis ad instar intelligi debent de hoc privilegii communicatione."—*Opus Morale*, I, tract. 3, disp. 4, p. 2, § 9, n. 1.

[15]Thus Oietti writes: " . . . qui aliter haec verba sumunt in errorem duci videntur." *Commentarium in Codicem Iuris Canonici*, I, 280.

This foundation exists in those documents where the terms connoting equal communication and the phrase *ad instar* are seemingly used in opposition to each other.[16] Both Suarez[17] and Van Hove[18] explain this apparent antithetic use of the terms *"aeque principaliter et ad instar"* by maintaining that they are not used in opposition to each other but to stress the effects of equal communication. This may well explain the terminology found in those documents where the terms are used conjunctively, but it cannot explain a document wherein the terms are used in obvious opposition to each other. Thus, in imparting the privileges of the Clerics Regular to the Discalced Passionists and the Congregation of the Holy Cross, Clement XIV informs the beneficiaries of communication that the privileges are communicated "—perinde ac si principaliter ipsis, ac specialiter, *non autem ad eorum instar concessa.*"[19] Assuredly, it is difficult to explain this combination which flatly contradicts the common opinion of canonists who maintain that equal communication and concession *ad instar* are different only in name. Obviously, the beneficiaries favored with the benefits of communication by virtue of this document acquire an independent privilege for it is expressly stated that the privileges of the Clerics Regular are given to the beneficiaries of the document as if they were granted specifically to a primary grantee. The concluding phrase seems to nullify this concession, but there

[16]Communicating the privileges of the Mendicant Orders to the Order of Clerics Regular, Pope Gregory XIV states that the privileges are communicated "perinde ac si illis nominatim et in specie concessa fuissent, singula et omnia privilegia . . . non solum ad eorum instar sed pariformiter et aeque principaliter." Const. *Ad uberes fructus,* 15 Oct., 1622—*BRT*, XII, 749. Another example of the apparent antithetic use of these terms appears in a Constitution issued by Pope Pius II to effect communication of privileges between the Cassinese and Mt. Olivet Congregations of Benedictines.—Const. *Licet,* 5 Oct., 1462—*BRT*, V, 169.

[17]*De Legibus,* lib. 8, c. 16, n. 8.

[18]*De Privilegiis,* n. 136.

[19]Const. *Supremi Apostolatus,* 16 nov. 1769—*BRC*, V. 73.

is no way of ascertaining the exact explanation of this combination where terms connoting the same effects are mutually exclusive of each other. However, in spite of the fact that the terms *principaliter* and *ad instar* are expressly used in opposition to each other in this isolated instance, even the terminology of this document does not postulate an identity between concession *ad instar* and accessory communication. The lack of a reasonable explanation for the strange juxtaposition of the above mentioned terms must be acknowledged, but at the same time the identity between equal communication and concession *ad instar*, as acknowledged by the consensus of canonists, cannot but be preserved. With these preliminaries concerning the similarity between communication and concession *ad instar*, the history of the institute of communication in the Church's system of privileges will now be considered.

Although it is generally admitted that the institute of communication is nothing other than concession *ad instar* under a different name, and though it is also admitted that the origin of communication can be traced ultimately to the Justinian Code and proximately to a law which appears in the Decretals,[20] some authorities assert that communication served as a legitimately constituted source of privileges as early as the seventh century. Although no documentary evidence can be found to support this assertion, the Bollandists maintain that communication of privileges was enjoyed by the monastic orders during this time.[21]

[20]C. 2, *de privilegiis*, V, 7, in VI°. Cf. Suarez, *De Legibus*, lib. 8, c. 15, nn. 1 and 7; Van Hove, *De Privilegiis*, n. 136; Cicognani, *Canon Law*, 789.

[21]In a work which was written to refute the teachings of a certain R. D. Verhoeven concerning monastic privileges, the Bollandists write: "Hinc intelliget parum apte R. D. Professorem supra recitatis verbis significasse tunc temporis non extitisse communicationem privilegiorum quae nunc inter eiusdem instituti monasteria, aut inter similes ordines nunc existit." —*Examen Historicum et Canonicum Libri R. D. Verhoeven* (Bruxellis: 1847), 161.

A review of early papal documents in authorized collections[22] fails to reveal the existence of any document which might substantiate the claim made by the Bollandists. Moreover, no other authorities acknowledge the existence of the institute of communication as a lawful source of privileges for religious institutes before the reign of Pope Eugene IV (1431-1447).[23] The Bollandists base their assertion on the assumption that such an institute must have existed to maintain an equality in the matter of privileges especially between the founding monasteries and their new establishments. Perhaps it is reasonable to suppose that some kind of expedient source of privileges existed between the mother houses and their new establishments, but it cannot be proved that such a source was instituted by papal concession. On the contrary, the general law of the Church and the procedure usually followed in granting privileges during the early centuries point to a total absence of any lawful form of communication, whereby a newly founded monastery would automatically acquire the privileges enjoyed by its mother house.

The absence of any lawful form of communication may be proved from the customary practice of the pontiffs in granting monasteries the privilege of free election of an abbot,[24] which privilege was frequently granted to monasteries during that period in which communication of privileges, according to the Bollandists, was supposed to

[22]*BRT*, I-III: Jaffé, P. *Regesta Pontificum Romanorum ab condita ecclesia ad annum* 1198 (Leipsig, 1887, 2, ed., cura Wattebach, Loewenfeld, Kaltenbrunner, Ewald, 2 vols. in 1, Lipsiae: 1885-1888) Hereafter this work will be cited: Jaffé, *Regesta Pontificum*.

[23]De Luca, *Theatrum Veritatis et Iustitiae* (16 vols. in 9, Colloniae Agrippinae: 1706), I, discept. 38; Cf. also Van Hove, *De Privilegiis*, p. 11, n. 1.

[24]Cf. Parsons, *Canonical Elections*, The Catholic University of America. Canon Law Studies, n. 118 (Washington: The Catholic University of American Press, 1939), pp. 34-39. The author clearly shows that free election was enjoyed by virtue of special concessions from the 6th to the 11th centuries.

have been in operation.

From the general law of the church, which prescribed that monasteries were subject to the authority of bishops[25] it is inferred that the election of an abbot was not official until it was confirmed by the bishop of the diocese wherein the monastery was situated.[26] Although this conclusion seems far-fetched, it is supported by the legislation of the Council of Toledo, which affirms the bishop's right to institute an abbot.[27] The same conclusion is further substantiated by many papal documents which conclusively prove that subjection to the bishop in abbatial elections was the accepted rule in the early centuries of monasticism, and that the exemption from the bishop's intervention in this matter was considered a special privilege.[28] When the pontiffs began to exempt monasteries from episcopal intervention in abbatial elections by favoring them with the privilege of free election, they made the concessions to separate monasteries by means of separate documents,[29] none of which offer any evidence to prove that the privilege was to be communicated to its new establishments. Nor are there any documents during this period to prove that some monasteries were permitted to enjoy the privileges of other monasteries, whose privileges were to serve as the model for the specification of privileges to be acquired by the former. If the pontiffs departed from

[25]Council of Chalcedon (451), Canon 4—Hardouin, *Acta Conciliorum et Epistolae Decretales ac Constitutiones Summorum Pontificum* (12 vols., Parisiis: 1715), II, 602. Hereafter cited *Hardouin*.

[26]Chapman, J., *Saint Benedict and the Sixth Century.* (New York: Longmans, 1929), p. 60, n. 1.

[27]Council of Toledo (633), Canon 51—Hardouin, III, 585.

[28]Thus, for example, two monasteries founded by King Sidebert received this privilege from the same pontiff by means of separate documents. Cf. *BRT*, I, 314. Cf. also Benedictus II, Const. *Cum Romanae Sedis*, 7 Oct., 855—*BRT*, I, 301; Jaffé, *Regesta Pontificum*, n. 2663; Nicholas I. Breve, *Convenit apostolico*, 28 apr., 863—*BRT*, *I*, 314; *Jaffé*, *Regesta Pontificum*, 2717.

[29]*Ut supra*, note 28.

the customary practice of granting specific privileges to specific monasteries by means of separate documents, even to monasteries belonging to a federation, they listed all the monasteries of the federation in one and the same document and specified the privileges that were granted, thus making a cumulative direct concession.[30] If the institute of communication were a valid source of privileges during the early history of monasticism, it is reasonable to suppose that some document could be found to prove that privileges were granted to some monasteries in such a way that the privileges were to derive their nature from the privileges enjoyed by other monasteries.

Although the institute of communication, under the form of concession *ad instar* was not introduced into the church's system of privileges until the early part of the twelfth century,[31] a papal document appearing in the latter part of the eleventh century[32] gives evidence of a trend toward the introduction of a practical institute for expediting grants of privileges through which some uniformity in the matter of privileges might be achieved among religious organizations. Thus, Pope Urban II issued a Bull to the Abbot of Monte Cassino,[33] informing him that the monasteries and churches of the congregation were to enjoy the same privileges as the monastery of Monte Cassino. This

[30]A spurious document favoring the monastery of Volturno and its dependencies with specific privileges offers a good example of such a cumulative grant. Although the document is a spurious one, it offers an excellent example to show the high regard that is had for the specification of particular privileges as well as the explicit mention of specific beneficiaries. Cf. Paschal I, Const. *Divinis praeceptionibus* (no date given, 819)—*BRT*, I, 271; Jaffé, *Regesta Pontificum*, n. 2552.

[31]Gregorius IX, Const. *Olim operant*, 29 apr., 1233—*BRT*, III, 480; Potthast, *Regesta Pontificum Romanorum inde ab anno post Christum natum MCXCVIII ad annum MCCCIV* (Berolini: 1874), 9173. Hereafter cited Potthast, *Regesta Pontificum*.

[32]Urbanus II, Bulla, *Praeter generale*, 27 mart. 1097—*BRT*, II, 182; Jaffé, *Regesta Pontificum*, n. 5681.

[33]*Ut supra*, note 32.

statement alone closely resembles the terminology to be found in documents of communication in later years, but further resemblance between this document and documents of communication fails because the pontiff proceeds to specify the privileges and to list the beneficiaries who are to acquire the privileges of the monastery of Monte Cassino. Privileges were granted in the same way to the Congregation of Cluny[34] and the Congregation of Vallambrosa.[35] The express mention of specific beneficiaries within these congregations in papal documents through which privileges were granted in the ninth century offers proof that communication was not considered a lawful source of privileges. That privileges were claimed by others besides the beneficiary to whom they were granted expressly is an acknowledged fact.[36] Thus, the privileges enjoyed by the abbots of certain Benedictine monasteries[37] were claimed by the abbots of other monasteries,[38] as a result of which unlawful claim[39] the Council of Poitiers issued a decree prescribing that no abbot is permitted to wear gloves, sandals, or ring unless the privilege is expressly given to the abbot of a specific monastery.[40] Finally, in the

[34]Urbanus II, Const. *Cum omnium fidelium*, 9 ian. 1097— *BRT*, II, 176; Jaffé, *Regesta Pontificum*, n. 5676.

[35]Migne, P. J., *Patrologiae Cursus Completus, Series Latina* (221 vols., Parisiis: 1844-1864), CLI, 322. Hereafter cited MPL.

[36]Cf. Schreiber, G., *Kurie und Kloster im 12 Jahrhundert*, Kirchenrechtliche Abhandlungen von Dr. Ulrich Stutz, Heft. 65-68 (2 vols., Stuttgart: 1910), I, 157; II, 141-142; cf. also, Thomassinus, L., *Vetus et Nova Ecclesiae Disciplina circa Beneficia et Beneficiarios* (10 vols., Moguntiae: 1787), I, par. 1, c. 36, p. 279, n. 7. Hereafter cited as *Vetus et Nova Ecclesiae Disciplina*.

[37]The privileges here in question pertained to the wearing of the mitre and other episcopal garb.

[38]Cf. Schreiber, *loc. cit.*

[39]"Quod alicui gratiose conceditur trahi non debet aliis in exemplum."—Reg. 74, R. J. in VI°.

[40]Canon 6—Mansi, I., *Sacrorum Conciliorum Nova et Amplissima Collectio* (53 vols., Parisiis: 1901-1927), XX, 1123. Hereafter cited Mansi.

year 1206, Innocent III confirmed the existence of unlawful communication, when he granted exemption to the monastery of Evesham, prescribing that monasteries or churches subject to it cannot partake of this privilege unless it can be proved that they are expressly granted to those monasteries or churches.[41]

From all that has been said above, it is evident that the assertion made by the Bollandists about the existence and lawful operation of the institute of communication between monasteries is untenable. It is untenable because it cannot be supported by any documentary evidence and because the customary method of granting privileges argues against the fact of the introduction of the institute of communication before the thirteenth century.

With the establishment of many new Universities in the early part of the thirteenth century, the institute of communication, under the form of concession *ad instar*, was used for the first time as a method of granting privileges.[42] Ever since the Universities were first established they were made beneficiaries of numerous privileges by Popes, emperors, kings, princes, and municipalities. "The Popes, however, led all in generosity; and papal privileges were eagerly sought by both professors and students."[43] It is very likely that the accumulation of privileges in favor of the Universities influenced the pontiffs to revive the Roman Law concession *ad instar* by means of which concessions in favor of the new establishments could be granted more expeditiously. The more significant feature of this method of granting privileges, however, is the fact that a similarity between the Universities in the matter of privileges could be effected very expediently. Shortly

[41]" . . . in membris autem, videlicet in illis, quae non probantur exempta, diocesano Episcopo ipsum decernimus subiacere . . . "—C. 17, X, *de privilegiis et excessibus privilegiatorum*, V, 33; cf. also Potthast, *op. cit.*, n. 2660.

[42]Gregorius IX, Const. *Olim operant*, 29 apr., 1233—*BRT*, III, 480.

[43]Cicognani, *Canon Law*, p. 270.

after its introduction into the Church's system of privileges, Innocent IV (1244-1245) imparted the privileges of all the Universities to the students in Rome.[44] Subsequently, the privileges of the Universities were communicated in this fashion to other Universities on a number of occasions,[45] and not long afterwards it was invoked by the pontiffs as an expedient method of granting privileges to religious orders.

Except for the reference to unlawful communication in the twelfth century and the allegation made by the Bollandists concerning the operation of the institute of communication, only one other author[46] suggests that the institute of communication was introduced in favor of religious institutes before the reign of Eugene IV.[47] Thus, Rodericus is of the opinion that communication of privileges was permitted between the monasteries of the Cistercian Congregation and the Monastery of Chartreuse—the principal monastery of the congregation.[48]

Since this opinion, like the assertion made by the Bollandists, cannot be substantiated by any documentary evidence, it is better to assume with the majority of authors that the institute of communication was not introduced in favor of religious institutes before the reign of Pope Eugene IV (1431-1447), or probably not until the reign of Sixtus IV (1471-1484).[49] For practical purposes, the latter is the proper starting point because it is only from here that the institute begins to show any signs of development. Furthermore, in so far as the practical results

[44]C. 2, *de privilegiis et excessibus privilegiatorum*, V. 7, in VI°. Although the term *ad instar* is not used in this concession, it is identified as such by the glossator. Cf. Glossa on the above mentioned canon.

[45]Cf. *BRT*, III, 480, 536; IV, 157, 585, 597.

[46]Rodericus, H., *Quaestiones Regulares et Canonicae Enucleatae*, n. 41.

[47]Cf. *supra*, page 88-89.

[48]Rodericus, H., *loc. cit.*

[49]Cf. *infra*, page 96.

of communication of privileges in favor of religious institutes are concerned, there is little reason for further speculation about the precise date of the introduction of the institute of communication in favor of religious. There is little reason for speculation about this point because the certain operation of communication of privileges between religious institutes from the fifteenth century eventually included those institutes which might have enjoyed an indefinite form of communication and all those privileges which were previously granted, provided they had not been lost.

If concession *ad instar* was introduced, as suggested above,[50] into the administrative policy of the church in order to expedite grants to the Universities and to bring about some equality between them in this respect, then there was certainly a more urgent need for some such expedient instrument in order to meet the demands of the situation created by the rapid multiplication and spread of religious orders throughout the world.[51] There can be little doubt that this rapid development, and the wide difference between orders, and even within orders, in the matter of privileges customarily granted by direct concession influenced the pontiffs to permit communication of privileges in order to offset the slackening of zeal and the heightening of jealousy which are bound to arise when there is too much distinction between organizations working for the same end. Moreover, just as the general law of the church had assimilated under a single class four

[50]Cf. *supra*, page 93.

[51]This development and spread of religious establishments was acknowledged by the II General Council of Lyons (1274), when it issued a decree forbidding the establishment of new orders: "Sed quia non solum importuna petentium inhiatio, illarum postmodum multiplicationem extorsit, verum etiam aliquorum praesumptuosa temeritas diversorum ordinum, praecipue mendicantium, quorum nondum approbationis meruere principium, effrenatam quasi multitudinem adinvenit, repetita constitutione districtius inhibemus, ne aliquis de cetero novum ordinem aut religionem inveniat. . . . "—Canon 23,—Hardouin, VII, 705-719.

mendicant orders—Dominicans, Franciscans, Hermits of St. Augustine, and Carmelites—in order to effect a uniformity among them in matters pertaining to the administration of sacraments,[52] so now there appeared a tendency to accomplish the same purpose in the matter of privileges which were granted to individual orders or establishments by special concession outside of law. By virtue of the above mentioned assimilation of the mendicant orders by provision of law, legislation pertaining to Mendicants in general was applicable to all of these orders. The same results were effected when privileges were granted to the Mendicants in general. However, this assimilation did not permit the respective orders to claim those privileges which were granted to a specific order, because, prior to the introduction of communication of privileges, there was no lawfully constituted method by means of which this could be done.

In the year 1474, Pope Sixtus IV provided for such an eventuality by permitting reciprocal communication of privileges between the Franciscans and Dominicans[53] in order that "those who are engaged in the same work may enjoy the same merits."[54] By virtue of such a communication of privileges these two mendicant orders were permitted to acquire all the privileges which had been given or would be given to either order, and the privileges thus acquired were to have the same force as those which were expressly granted to a specific beneficiary.[55] Thus, an

[52]C. un. *de iudiciis,* II, 1, in Extrav. Comm.

[53]Const. *Regimini universalis Ecclesiae,* 31 aug. 1474—*BRT,* V. 212.

[54]" . . . ut quos par labor pariaque merita coniungunt, paria coniungant privilegia et favores . . . "—*Loc. cit.*

[55]" . . . ac si nominatim exprimerentur, haberi hic volumus pro expressis et nostrae approbationis munimine solidamus, ac decernimus robur perpetuae firmitatis obtinere, potiri et gaudere possint, et debeant, perpetuis futuris temporibus, in omnibus et per omina prorsus sine ulla differentia." —Sixtus IV, Const. *Regimini universalis ecclesiae,* 31 aug. 1474—*BRT,* V, 212.

equality was effected between the Dominicans and Franciscans alone in respect to privileges which were granted outside of law, but though this perfect form of communication was restricted to these orders alone, reciprocal communication of privileges was eventually permitted to all the orders and other religious institutes.

Further provisions of the constitution issued by Sixtus IV permitted the nuns subject to the respective orders to acquire the privileges which were expressly given to the orders of men; reciprocal communication of privileges was permitted between the orders of nuns; privileges vested in the offices of the Dominican and Franciscan superiors were included within the scope of this communication of privileges with directions which were none too precise.[56] In the same year, another constitution similarly entitled,[57] and differing from it only by virtue of added privileges, was issued to the Dominicans. A few years later, the same pontiff enriched this fund of privileges by permitting the Dominicans and Franciscans to acquire the privileges of the Carmelites, Augustinians, and Servites "so that they (the Franciscans and Dominicans) would not seem to be inferior to these orders."[58] Thus, Pope Sixtus, who himself was a former general of the Franciscans, expressed his predilection for the Franciscans and Dominicans not only by his statement, but also by preventing the other orders from acquiring the privileges of the Franciscans and Dominicans through reciprocal communication.[59] By showing special favor to the Dominicans and Franciscans,

[56]Cf. *infra*, pages 150-153.

[57]Sixtus IV, Const. *Regimini Universalis* (exact date is not given) 1474—*BRT*, V, 224.

[58]Sixtus IV, Const. *Sacri Praedicatorum*, 26 iul., 1479—*BRT*, V, 280.

[59]" . . . convenit ut ipsi prae caeteris ampliores favores et gratiarum praerogativas a praefata Sede recipiant et reportent . . . "—*Loc. cit.*

particularly the latter,[60] Pope Sixtus IV hardly employed the institute of communication in accord with the purpose for which it was introduced in favor of the religious institutes.[61]

Although the express terminology of the Constitution "*Sacri Praedicatorum*" seems to exclude reciprocal communication of privileges between the interested mendicant orders, Pope Julius II acknowledged it as such in two later constitutions,[62] by virtue of which the Minims of St. Francis de Paul were included within the scope of this communication of privileges. By virtue of the first constitution Pope Julius II referred to the previously acquired privileges of all these orders as the *Mare Magnum*,[63] which he con-

[60]"To enumerate the good things bestowed on the Mendicant Friars and more particularly on the Franciscans during this long Pontificate would be an endless task." Pastor, *The History of the Popes from the Close of the Middle Ages* (29 vols., translation, Vols. I-IV ed. by Antrobus; Vols. VII-XXIV, ed. by R. Kerr; Vols. XXV-XXIX, ed. by Dom Ernest Graf, St. Louis: Herder, 1906-1938), IV, 390.

[61]Commenting on the Constitution *Dudum ad nos*, issued by Pope Leo X, 10 dec. 1519—*BRT, V*, 732, Pignatelli writes: "Quod quidem constitutio cum respiciat bonum commune Religionum Mendicantium et habet pro fine eas reducere ad aequalitatem quoad participationem gratiarum Sedis Apostolicae . . . habet vim legis ordinatae ad moderationem communitatis et ad tollendam illam particularitatem affectus Romanorum Pontificorum erga hanc vel illam religionem et ad inducendam debitam aequalitatem . . . "—*Consultationes Canonicae*, X, Consult. 1, n. 26. "[Per communicationem] artificiali quoddam modo atque automatice equalitas iuridica inter diversas religiones conservabatur." Pejska, *Ius Canonicum Religiosorum*, 31.

[62]Const. *Dudum ac sacrum*, 28 iul. 1506—*BRT*, V, 421; Const. *Etsi ad benemerendum*, 17 iun. 1508—*BRT*, V, 471.

[63]"Mare magnum dicunt diplomata, seu pontificias, constitutiones quibus ampliantur et firmantur privilegia regularium," Icard, *Praelectiones Iuris Canonici Habitae in Seminario Sancti Sulpitii* (2 vols., Lutetiae Parisiorum, 1859) I, 318, n. 1.

It is interesting to note, that Pope Julius II was the first to use the rather expressive phrase—"*Mare magnum*"—in reference to the fund of privileges enjoyed by the religious. Cf. Const. *Etsi ad benemerendum*—*Loc. cit*.

firmed with a specific confirmation.[64] Through the medium of the latter constitution,[65] the Minims of St. Francis de Paul were permitted to acquire the privileges which would be granted to the Mendicants in the future. Later on, Pope Julius II introduced another change in the documents of communication by permitting the beneficiaries to transcribe all previous documents by virtue of which privileges had been granted.[66] Regarding this point, Pope Paul III made a further concession by permitting the beneficiaries to substitute his name for the names of the pontiffs affixed to the originals, and to change the name of the addressee accordingly.[67] He further prescribed that a transcribed copy of any of these documents would have the same force as the original only when it was signed by a notary and sealed with the stamp of any ecclesiastical prelate, whereupon such a transcribed copy was to have the same force as the original both judicially and extrajudicially.[68]

As a result of the far-reaching, unlimited terminology of previous documents, and the absence of precise rules and restrictions concerning the efficacy of communication, untold confusion and misinterpretation resulted.[69] In order to remove the doubts that were bound to arise from the general terminology of previous documents of communication, Pope Julius II issued another constitution to

[64]A specific confirmation of privileges, or more precisely "confirmatio in forma specifica", is an official approval which sanates the defects of previously acquired privileges, thus approximating a new concession. Cf.. Suarez, *De Legibus, lib.* 8, cc. 18-20. Cf. also *infra*, page 191, note 74.

[65]Iulius II. Const. *Etsi ad benemerendum—Loc. cit.*

[66]Const. *Dudum ac sacrum*, 28 iul. 1506—*BRT*, V, 421.

[67]Const. *Ratione Congruit*, 3 nov. 1534—*BRT* VI, 173-182.

[68]"Necnon quod litterarum desuper conficiendarum transumptis, manu notarii publici subscriptis et sigillo alicuius praelati ecclesiastici munitis, ubique staretur, prout originalibus litteris staretur, et plena fides in iudicio et extra iudicium adhibetur."—*Loc. cit.*

[69]Thomassinus, L., *Vetus et Nova Ecclesiae Disciplinae circa Beneficia et Beneficiarios* (10 vols., Moguntiae, 1787), I, par. 1, lib. 3, c. 39, p. 306, n. 8.

clarify some of these matters.[70] In this constitution, applicable only to the Dominicans and Franciscans, the pontiff matched the offices of the respective superiors of these orders and prescribed that the privileges of a Dominican superior could be communicated only to a Franciscan superior of corresponding rank, regardless of the title. In the same way the privileges of the Franciscan superiors were to be communicated to the Dominican superiors. Further regulations contained in this constitution permitted reciprocal communication of privileges between congregations (lay societies) erected and incorporated by each order, communication of privileges granted to private members, and communication of privileges attached to the feast days of either order.[71] Except for the appearance of another constitution issued in favor of the Canons Regular of the Blessed Savior,[72] to whom the privileges of the Lateran Congregation, the Servites, and Cassinese Benedictines were communicated, there were no added changes or developements affecting the institute of communication before the convocation of the V General Lateran Council. (1512-1517).

ARTICLE 1. COMMUNICATION OF PRIVILEGES IN FAVOR OF NUNS

By including the nuns among the beneficiaries of communication in the Constitution "*Regimini universalis ecclesiae*", Pope Sixtus IV started a trend which eventually would permit the principal orders of nuns to acquire the

[70]" . . . ad tollendam quamcumque haesitationem et inde forte ortum scrupulum, auctoritate et tenore praefatis declaramus."—Const. *Alias ad supplicationem*, I iun. 1509—*Bullarium Ordinis Praedicatorum*, (ed. a Th. Rippoli, 8 vols., Romae: 1729-1740), IV, 258.

[71]Concerning the proper interpretation of these provisions, see pages *infra*, 150-155.

[72]Julius II, Const. *Inter caeteros*, 2 apr. 1512—*BRT*, V, 516.

privileges of the orders of men by virtue of communication.[73] As a general rule, communication of privileges is effected expressly in favor of the orders of men, and unless mention is made in the documents of communication, neither the nuns nor any other subjects besides the professed members can enjoy the benefits of communication.[74] However, notwithstanding this general rule, the nuns affiliated with the mendicant and monastic orders were gradually included within the scope of communication of privileges so that by the end of the seventeenth century the privileges granted to the religious orders of men were acquired by the corresponding orders of nuns.[75] Privileges were acquired by them in accessory form when the privileges of the orders of men were communicated to them,[76] whereas equal communication took place when communication of privileges was permitted between the distinct orders of nuns.[77] In view of the fact that privileges acquired through communication were not adverse to future communication before the promulgation of the Code,[78] nuns who were favored with equal communication with other orders of nuns could acquire privileges first acquired in accessory form by the order of nuns with whom they enjoyed equal communication. The former beneficiaries thus acquired independent privileges while the latter retained their privileges only in accessory form. Whenever the privileges of the orders of

[73]Rodericus, H., *Questiones Regulares et Canonicae Enucleatae*, p. 834, nn. 46-48.

[74]Petra, *Commentarium ad Constitutiones Apostolicas*, II, p. 111, n. 25; Rodericus, E., *Quaestiones Regulares et Canonicae Enucleatae, sive Resolutiones Questionum Regularium* (3 vols. in 1, Antverpiae: 1628), III, q. 52, art. 12. Hereafter cited *Quaestiones Regulares et Canonicae*.

[75]Tamburini, A., *De Iure Abbatum*, I, dist. 17, q. 1, n. 43.

[76]Piatus Montensis, *Praelectiones Iuris Regularis*, II, p. 111, n. 4.

[77]Cf. Clemens VII, Const. *Cum ex corpore*, 13 aug. 1525—*BRT*, VI, 93.

[78]Cf. for example, Gregorius XIV, *Romanus Pontifex*, 18, febr. 1591—*BRT*, IX, 289, which is one of the many papal documents wherein privileges acquired through communication are expressly included within communication of privileges.

men were communicated to the nuns, the extent of communication was always limited by one principal restriction, which was always implied and at times expressed. Manifestly, the nuns cannot acquire any privileges which are contradictory to their sex and their state in life.[79]

There is abundant evidence to prove that nuns were permitted to acquire the privileges of the corresponding order of men and of other orders with whom they were not affiliated either by juridic dependence or by similarity of rule of life. Though the acquisition of privileges through communication cannot be denied the nuns when they are expressly mentioned in papal documents of communication, pre-Code authors are not agreed concerning the implicit or virtual inclusion of nuns within the scope of communication of privileges. Thus, Barbosa maintains that they are not included because it is useless for them to claim the privileges of the orders of men through communication,[80] which they frequently did.[81] It is generally agreed that the nuns can acquire the privileges of the corresponding order of men under a virtual inclusion in a direct concession or in communication of privileges.[82] However, the nuns are capable of acquiring the privileges of the corresponding order of men not by virtue of communication, strictly socalled, but by virtue of a lawful, comprehensive interpretation,[83] which is permissable when the privileges are not contrary to law or prejudicial to a third party[84] and are not expressly restricted to the orders of men.[85]

[79]Cf. Sixtus IV, Const. *Sacri Praedicatorum*, 26 iul. 1479—*BRT*, V, 280.

[80]*Iuris Ecclesiastici Universi Libri III* (Lugduni: 1660), I, c. 42, n. 217.

[81]Cf. Tamburini, A., *op. cit.*, I, dist. 8, q. 10, n. 7.

[82]Suarez, *De Legibus*, lib. 8, c. 10, n. 7; Didacus ab Aragonia, *Dilucidatio Privilegiorum*, tract. 1, n. 8; Tamburini, A. *op. cit.*, I, dist. 17, q. 1, n. 49.

[83]Cf. Schmalzgrueber, *Ius Canonicum Universum*, lib. V, tit. 33, n. 131.

[84]Petra, *Commentarium ad Constitutiones Apostolicas*, II, 111, n. 28.

[85]Suarez, *De Legibus*, lib. 8, c. 10, n. 7.

In accord with the above mentioned regulations, then, nuns continued to enjoy communication of privileges with the orders of men with which they were affiliated. No doubt, they were originally permitted to acquire the privileges of the orders of men because they were subject to the jurisdiction of the superior of the religious orders of men. Their withdrawal from the jurisdiction of the superior of the religious order of men, however, did not prevent them from enjoying the benefits of communication which was originally permitted for the above mentioned reason. According to Piatus Montensis, there were some authorities who maintained that subjection to the jurisdiction of the superior of the religious orders of men is a necessary condition for enjoying the benefits of communication of privileges with that order.[86] However, this same canonist asserts that it is the more probable opinion that nuns enjoy the privileges of the male religious whose rule they profess, even though they have been placed under the authority of bishops.[87] This opinion is substantiated by a pronouncement issued by the Sacred Congregation of Indulgences,[88] which declared:

> "Eadem S. Congregatio, re mature discussa, die 20 Aprilis, 1711, declaravit, monasteria omnia sanctimonialium, quae a cura et gubernio fratrum suorum ordinum sub immediatam iurisdictionem episcoporum translata sunt, seu in posterum transferri aliqua ratione contigerit, non ideo privilegia et indulgentias, quibus antea gaudebant, amisisse seu amissura fore, sed eodem modò cunctis praedictis privilegiis et indulgentiis uti et frui debere, ac si sub gubernio fratrum suorum ordinum actu existerent. Quam Sacrae Congregationis sententiam SSmus D. N. die 22 eiusdem mensis approbavit."[89]

[86] Piatus Montensis, *op. cit.*, II, q. 153, sub (b).

[87] *Loc. cit.*

[88] S. C. Indulgentiarum, 22 apr. 1711—*Fontes*, n. 4954.

[89] *Loc. cit.*

This same situation prevails by virtue of Code law which permits nuns to acquire the privileges of the corresponding order of men without requiring their subjection to the order of men whose privileges they are permitted to acquire through communication.[90]

ARTICLE 2. COMMUNICATION OF PRIVILEGES IN FAVOR OF SECULAR THIRD ORDERS.

With the issuance of the Constitution *"Sacri praedicatorum"*[91] the members of the third order of seculars[92] affiliated with the Franciscans and the Dominicans were permitted to acquire the privileges of those orders through communication. When the privilege of establishing third orders was given to other orders, it became the common practice for subsequent pontiffs to include members of the third orders within the scope of communication of privileges. As beneficiaries of communication, the members of the third orders are bound by the same restriction as the nuns in regard to capacity,[93] and privileges are acquired by them in accessory form. By virtue of the above mentioned constitution only those members of the third order of seculars profitted by communication who lived in a community and followed the rule prescribed for them. According to the testimony of Emmanuel Rodericus, Innocent VIII (1484-1492) is supposed to have communicated all the privileges of the tertiaries living in common to those

[90]Canon 613, § 2.

[91]Sixtus IV, Const. *Sacri Praedicatorum*, 26 iul. 1479—*BRT*, V, 280.

[92]It is quite certain that St. Francis of Assisi founded the third order of seculars in the early thirteenth century (1221). The privilege of establishing third orders was later acquired by the Premonstratensians, Carmelites, Dominicans, Augustinians, Servites, Trinitarians, Minims of St. Francis de Paul, and Benedictines. Cf. (Bachofen) Charles Augustine, *Religious*, pp. 443-444; Vermeersch—Creusen, *Epitome Iuris Canonici*, I, 857.

[93]" . . . quatenus earum sexui et statui non contradicant." Rodericus, H., *Quaestiones Regulares et Canonicae Enucleatae*, p. 843, n. 46. " . . . in quantum earum capacitas permittit." Rodericus, E., *Quaestiones Regulares et Canonicae*, I, q. 55, art. 14.

living alone.[94] That such a communication of privileges was permitted is quite certain in view of the fact that the V General Lateran Council prescribed that "Brothers and sisters of the third order...living in their own homes, are free to choose their place of burial, but communion on Easter Sunday, Extreme Unction, and the other sacraments, the sacrament of penance excepted, they must receive from their proper pastor."[95] Obviously, the privileges which were denied to the tertiaries living at home were still available to those living in common. Except for this one restriction on communication of privileges imposed by universal law, the members of the third orders of seculars continued to acquire communicable privileges of the religious through the institute of communication until the promulgation of the Constitution "*Misericors Dei Filius*",[96] whereby Pope Leo XIII reorganized their rule of life, revoked all former privileges,[97] and granted new ones by direct concession.[98] As a result of this revocation of privileges previously enjoyed through communication by the third orders of seculars, the benefits of communication are no longer available to them. The Franciscan Third Order of Seculars, however, enjoys a special communication of favors permitted between the first, second, and third orders by Pope Pius X.[99]

[94]Rodericus, E., *loc. cit.*

[95]V General Lateran Council, Ex Bulla Leonis X, *Dum intra mentis arcana,* Sessio IX, 19 Dec. 1516—Hardouin, IX, 1834. English translation is taken from Schroeder, *Disciplinary Decrees of the General Councils* (St. Louis: Herder, 1937), p. 508.

[96]Leo XIII, Const. *Misericors Dei Filius,* 30 maii 1886—*Fontes,* n. 588.

[97]" . . . sublatis penitus indulgentiis privilegiisque universis, quae eidem sodalitio haec Apostolica Sedes quocumque vel tempore vel nomine, vel forma ante hanc diem concesserat."—*Loc. cit.*

[98]For a list of specific privileges enjoyed by the members of the third orders of seculars, consult Coronata, *Institutiones,* I, n. 691.

[99]Cf. Coronata, *Institutiones,* I, n. 691, c.

CHAPTER V

HISTORY OF THE INSTITUTE OF COMMUNICATION FROM THE V LATERAN COUNCIL UNTIL THE EIGHTEENTH CENTURY

It would be beyond the scope of this dissertation to treat of the details of the legislation of the V. General Lateran Council 1512-1517 especially since it does not directly affect the institute of communication. However, in view of the fact that the background of one of the sessions pertains to communication of privileges, it merits some attention.[1] If the wishes of some of the bishops had been put into effect, perhaps the institute of communication would have ceased to be such a prodigious source of privileges for the religious institutes and those affiliated with them.[2] Before the tenth session of the Council in 1515, the bishops insisted that they would not attend further sessions unless the mendicant orders were subjected to the provisions of common law in all matters.[3] As a result of this bitter antagonism and opposition on the part of the bishops, the General of the Dominicans[4] and the General of the Augustinians,[5] together with the Cardinal protectors of these orders, petitioned the Pope not to be so severe. Thereupon,

[1]Cf. Thomassinus, L., *Vetus et Nova Ecclesiae Disciplina*, I, pars I, lib. 3, c. 39, p. 304, n. 5; Hefele-Leclercq, *Histoire des Conciles* (10 vols. in 18, Paris: 1907-1921), VIII, première parte, pp. 451-464.

[2]"The episcopate was gathering together all its strength to make an end, once and for all, of the privileges, especially the *mare magnum* . . . " Pastor, X., *History of the Popes*, VIII, 394.

[3]" . . . nisi ante pontifex revocasset . . . mare magnum . . . et ad ius commune reduxisset Mendicantes omnes, quorum privilegia episcopi experti erant, scatebras esse inexhaustas abusuum et dissensionum."—Thomassinus, *loc. cit.*

[4]Thomas de Vio (Cajetan) (1469-1543).

[5]Aegidius Canisius de Viterba (1465-1532).

the pontiff issued the Bull "*Regimini universalis ecclesiae*"[6] and the Bull "*Dum intra mentis arcana*"[7] which were designed to settle some of the difficulties that came to the fore. The former bull asserted the principles of ecclesiastical liberty and episcopal dignity, and condemned the abuses of certain religious who enjoyed the privilege of exemption from episcopal jurisdiction; the latter curtailed some of the privileges of the regulars. Although some of the privileges flowing from the *Mare Magnum* were abolished during the V General Lateran Council, and others curtailed, the channels of communication were not blocked. The institute which was so fruitful a source of privileges before the Council, continued to operate in full vigor after the cessation of the Council.

In 1519, Leo X issued a constitution[8] which was modeled after a previous constitution issued by Julius II,[9] permitting reciprocal communication of privileges among six mendicant orders.[10] The constitution which was issued "*motu proprio et ex mera scientia*," permitted equal communication, which source was to be available for privileges already granted and those that would be granted. For the rest, the constitution follows the same plan of the Julian constitution enumerating the specific subjects who are included within the scope of communication of privileges.

Shortly afterwards, Clement VIII[11] communicated the privileges of the non-mendicant orders to the Carmelites, prescribing that those privileges which are not contrary to the mendicant rule of life cannot be acquired through communication.[12] Quite obviously, privileges, whether contrary

[6]Sessio X, 4 maii 1515—*BRT*, V, 617-621; Hardouin, IX, 1775-1779.

[7]Sessio XI, 19 dec. 1516—Hardouin, IX, 1832-1835.

[8]*Dudum per nos*, 10 dec. 1519—*BRT*, V, 732.

[9]Cf. *supra*, page 99.

[10]Franciscans, Dominicans, Augustinians, Carmelites, Servites, and Minims of St. Francis de Paul.

[11]Const. *Ex clementi sedis*, 12 aug. 1530—*BRT*, VI, 144.

[12]" . . . suae professioni non contrariis."—*Loc. cit.*

to the general law or beyond it are granted in order to encourage and foster a more zealous religious life, not to destroy it.[13] Some time later, Sixtus V emphasized the restriction by prescribing that only these privileges can be communicated which are not contrary to the purity of the rule of St. Francis.[14] By virtue of the above mentioned constitution issued by Clement VIII, the privileges of the non-Mendicants were communicated to the Carmelites. Before the issuance of this constitution, the non-mendicant orders were not permitted to acquire the privileges of the Mendicants. Hence, until this time communication of privileges was permitted only between those institutes which exhibited close similarity. Before long, however, even this requisite was waived as communication of privileges was instituted in favor of both mendicant and non-mendicant orders. Pope Paul III was the first to permit communication of privileges between organizations which were not identical. Thus, he permitted the Hermits of St. Romuald to enjoy communication of privileges with every order living under an approved rule of life.[15]

Between the publication of the constitution *"Ratione congruit"* and the next document of communication, the Council of Trent intervened. The twenty-fifth reform session of the Council, which was devoted exclusively to the reorganization and reformation of the religious life,[16] incorporated much legislation relative to privileges, and revoked many which had fallen into desuetude, or had become harmful, or useless.[17] Although the Council carried no specific legislation relative to the institute of communication, it did affect its products by specifically referring to the

[13]Suarez, *De Legibus*, lib. 8, c. 17, n. 3.

[14]Const. *Apostolici muneris*, 15 oct. 1587—*BRT*, VIII, 235.

[15]Paulus III, Const. *Ratione congruit*, 3 nov. 1534—*BRT*, VI, 173-182.

[16]Sessio XXV, *de regularibus Canones et Decreta Sacrosancti Oecumenici Concilii Tridentini* (Romae: ex typographia polyglotta S. C. de Propaganda Fide, 1882).

[17]Sessio XXV, *de regularibus*, c. 22.

Mare Magnum when it revoked certain privileges.[18] Moreover, the Council of Trent influenced the institute of communication to such an extent that subsequent documents permitting communication of privileges usually prescribed that only those privileges can be acquired through communication which are not contrary to the legislation of the Council.[19] A year following the council, Pius IV issued a constitution addressed to all religious institutes whereby he confirmed all their privileges *"ex certa scientia,"*[20] and to prevent any religious orders from claiming the privileges revoked by the Council of Trent on the strength of this confirmation, he repeated the revocations of the Council.[21] Instead of abolishing all doubt concerning the revocations of the Council of Trent, Pope Pius IV's constitution was the cause of further disagreement. Thus, Tamburini maintains that, since the constitution was issued to supplement the decrees of the Council, only those privileges were abolished which the Council of Trent revoked expressly and all those which were contrary to the decrees of the twenty-fifth session.[22] Hence, according to the traditional law that a legislator does not revoke any particular privileges or customs without an express revocation,[23] privileges contrary to any other decrees of the council are retained.[24] Commenting on this constitution, E. Rodericus records that it was the common practice of his day to interpret the constitution as

[18]*Loc. cit.*

[19]Cf. for example, Pius IV, *In principis apostolorum,* 17 febr. 1565—*BRT,* VII, 277; Gregorius XIV, *Illius qui,* 21 sept. 1591—*BRT,* IX, 479.

[20]Although a specific confirmation revalidates all invalid privileges, it by no means restores those privileges revoked by a general council. Cf. Suarez, *De Legibus,* lib. 8, c. 19, n. 5.

[21]" . . . in his omnibus et singulis, in quibus illa statutis et decretis concilii huiusmodi contrariantur, ipso iure revocata, cassata, et annullata, ac ad ipsius concilii terminos atque limites reducta sint . . . " Sessio XXV, *de regularibus,* c. 22.

[22]*De Iure Abbatum,* disp. 17, quest. 6, claus. 1, n. 3.

[23]C. 1, *Licet, de constitutionibus,* 1, 2, in VI°.

[24]Tamburini, *loc. cit.*

excluding all privileges which were contrary to any of the decrees of the Council of Trent.[25] This, however, is hardly the correct opinion because a later constitution issued by the same pontiff excluded only those privileges from communication which were expressly contrary to the decrees of the Council.[26] By adding the word 'expressly' and by stating that he wished the revocation to be understood differently from the connotation attached to the terminology of the previous constitution,[27] Pope Pius IV sanctioned the validity of those privileges which were not expressly abrogated by the Council.[28] Besides clearing up the doubts on this point Pope Pius IV approved and confirmed all of the privileges of the religious, including privileges received by direct concession, written or oral, and by communication.[29] By confirming orally granted privileges and including them within the scope of communication, Pope Pius IV prepared the way for added confusion and uncertainty which was later acknowledged by Popes Gregory XV[30] and Urban VIII,[31] both of whom drastically reduced the force of these privileges. Thus, Gregory XV revoked all the orally granted privileges, except those which had been granted to the religious at the request of kings and

[25]*Questiones Regulares et Canonicae,* I, quest. 8, art. 6.

[26]" . . . quae decretis Concilii Tridentini, alias quam ut superius est dictum, concessum et declaratum, non contrariantur expresse . . . " Const. *Etsi mendicantium,* 16 maii 1567—*BRT,* VII, 573.

[27]" . . . alias quam ut superius est dictum . . . "—*Loc. cit.*

[28]Cf. Reiffenstuel, *Ius Canonicum Universum,* lib. V, tit. 33, n. 139; Schmalzgrueber, *Ius Ecclesiasticum Universum,* lib. V, tit. 33, n. 236.

[29]" . . . omnia et singula privilegia . . . eisdem fratribus . . . ac illorum ecclesiis, domibus, et personis, etiam vivae vocis oraculo, in genere vel in specie . . . quomodolibet concessa . . . perpetuo approbamus et confirmamus . . . necnon privilegia . . . favores et gratias, tam spirituales quam temporales, modo et forma quibus concessa sunt, etiam per viam communicationis, active et passive inter se et alios quoscumque ordines respective, de novo concedimus . . . " Const. *Etsi mendicantium,* 16 maii 1567—*BRT,* VII, 573.

[30]Const. *Romanus pontifex,* 2 iun. 1622—*BRT,* XII, 706.

[31]Const. *Alias felicis,* 20 dec. 1631—*BRT,* XIV, 258.

cardinals.[32] Pope Urban VIII revoked even these, but later modified the force of this revocation by confirming those orally granted privileges, which had been expedited by the officials delegated by the pontiffs who granted the privileges in this manner.

The operation of the institute of communication, since its introduction in favor of religious, had accomplished one principal result. It had abolished all distinctions between mendicant orders in the matter of privileges, thereby effecting what had been done some time previously by general law.[33] The efficacy of the institute permitted the Mendicants to acquire not only the privileges of every other mendicant order, but also the privileges of all non-mendicant orders, which except for the Order of the Hermits of St. Romuald,[34] and the Theatines,[35] were excluded from reciprocal communication with the Mendicants. Before long, however, the extent of reciprocal communication between religious orders began to spread far beyond these limits. The first step toward the widening of the channels of communication occurred in the latter part of the sixteenth century, when at the request of a group of non-mendicant orders, reciprocal communication of privileges was permitted.[36] The orders which benefited by this constitution were: the Canons Regular of the Lateran Congregation, the Canons Regular of the Blessed Savior Congregation, the Cistercians, the Carthusians, the Benedictine Congregations of Mount Olivet and Vallombrosa, and the Spanish Congregation of the Jesuits of St. Jerome. By virtue of this constitution, the non-mendicant orders were permitted to acquire all the privileges of the Mendicants except the privilege of exemption from the obligation of paying the seminary tax and the privilege of begging

[32]*Loc. cit.*
[33]Cf. *supra*, page 95.
[34]Cf. *supra*, page 108.
[35]Clemens VII, *Dudum pro parte*, 7 mart. 1533—*BRT*, VI, 160.
[36]Pius V, Const. *Ex supernae*, 16 aug. 1567—*BRT*, VII, 584.

alms.[37] In 1571, Pope Pius V assimilated the members of the Society of Jesus to the Mendicants,[38] and included them within the scope of reciprocal communication with the other orders. Shortly afterwards, however, Pope Gregory XIII ruled that the other orders could not enjoy the privileges of the Jesuits by virtue of communication.[39] The force of this prohibition could hardly be misunderstood, but the publication of a later constitution, issued by Pope Clement VIII,[40] apparently revoked this prohibition.[41] Notwithstanding the manifest meaning of this revocation which was directed against all previous prohibitive clauses, canonists do not agree concerning its effects. Thus, some maintain that the privileges of the Jesuits cannot be acquired through communication by other orders because no special mention of the previous prohibition is made in this constitution.[42] Others maintain that the privileges of the Jesuits can be acquired through communication because the derogatory clauses of this constitution are forceful enough to revoke any previous restrictions.[43]

[37]*Loc. cit.* Cf. Conc. Trident., Sessio XXIII, *de ref.*, c. 18, where all religious institutes, with the exception of the Mendicants, are effectively deprived of the privilege of exemption from the obligation of paying the seminary tax.

[38]Const. *Romanus pontifex privilegia*, 18 nov. 1571—*BRT*, VII, 636.

[39]Const. *Pium et utile*, 22 sept. 1582—*BRT*, VIII, 397.

[40]Const. *Ratio pastoralis*, 10 dec. 1595—*BRT*, X, 386.

[41]"Non obstantibus praemissis . . . aliisque Apostolicis constitutionibus, ac provincialibus, et capitularibus statutis . . . cum quibusvis irritativis, annulativis, restrictivis, reservativis, exceptivis, restitutivis, declarativis, mentis attestativis, ac derogatorium derogatoriis, aliisque efficacioribus, efficacissimis, et insolitis clausulis, quomodolibet etiam pluries concessis, firmatis et innovatis . . . "—*Loc. cit.*

[42]Reiffenstuel, *Ius Canonicum Universum*, lib. V, tit. 33, n. 33; Rodericus. E., *Quaestiones Regulares et Canonicae*, I. q. 55, n. 17; Vasto, *De Communicatione Privilegiorum*, n. 87.

[43]Ferraris, *Prompta Bibliotheca*, s. v. "privilegium," art. 1, n. 27; Parma, *Collectio Indulgentiarum*, n. 1366; Rodericus, H., *Quaestiones Regulares et Canonicae Enucleatae*, p. 836, n. 50; Suarez, *De Legibus*, lib. 8, c. 17, n. 1.

The Council of Trent also restricted the efficacy of communication as a source of privileges for lay persons who were permitted to acquire the privileges of the religious because of their affiliation with the religious by virtue of employment,[44] generosity towards the religious orders, or enrollment as oblates.[45] In order to prevent lay people from claiming any exemptions which might prejudice the bishop's power over them, the Council of Trent prescribed that only those lay persons who took the vows of the military orders, and lay persons who were in the actual service of any religious orders and at the same time residing within the precincts of the monastery could enjoy the privileges of the religious. However, the only privileges which even these persons could enjoy were restricted to those which did not deprive the bishop of any jurisdiction which he had over these lay people.[46] Although the Council of Trent deprived all lay people of privileges which might prejudice the bishop's power over them[47] some canonists began to teach that the privileges revoked by the Council of Trent could be validly used in the internal forum by the regulars and the lay persons who had acquired their privileges through communication.[49] This teaching, however, which seems to have become popular,

[44]Thus, Clement VII had communicated the privileges of the Dominicans to the procurator, servants, other employees, and their families. Cf. Const. *Dum consideramus*, 16 apr. 1526—*BRT*, VI, 106.

[45]Popes Leo X and Adrian VI had communicated the privileges of the Trinitarians to lay people who were invested in the scapular of the Trinitarians without taking vows and to the benefactors of the order. Cf. Rodericus, H., *Quaestiones Regulares et Canonicae Enucleatae*, p. 836, n. 49.

[46]Conc. Trident., Sessio XXIV, *de ref.* c. 11.

[48]*Loc. cit.*

[49]"Verum est tamen quod in foro conscientiae sunt omnia privilegia revalidata, etiamsi sint contra Concilium Tridentinum . . . et per consequens in foro conscientiae possunt dicti servitores et familiares frui ipsis." Rodericus, E., *Questiones Regulares et Canonicae*, I, q. 55, art. 2; Rodericus, H., *Quaestiones Regulares et Canonicae Enucleatae*, p. 865, n. 53.

was condemned as scandalous by two decrees.[50]

Together with the inclusion of additional religious orders within the scope of reciprocal communication of privileges during this period,[51] one other significant development concerning the institute of communication occurred during this time. In the year 1604 Pope Clement VIII issued a constitution designed to regulate the establishment of arch-confraternities, confraternities, and lay societies.[52] Within the limits of this document were also included regulations relative to the force of communication of privileges which these societies enjoyed. Late in the sixteenth century, lay societies had already received permission to enjoy communication of privileges both among themselves and through the religious orders with which

[50]The following proposition: "Regulares possunt in foro conscientiae uti privilegiis suis quae sunt expresse revocata per Concilium Tridentinum." was condemned by Decrees issued on the 24th of September, 1665 and 18th of March, 1666. "Omnes damnatae et prohibitae ut minimum tamquam scandalosae." Denziger—Bannwart—Umberg, *Enchiridion Symbolorum, Definitionum, et Declarationum de Rebus Fidei et Morum* (21-23 ed., Friburgi Brisgoviae: Herder, 1937), n. 1136.

[51]The following list enumerates the other religious orders to whom communciation of privileges was permitted during this period and the documents whereby this communication was permitted. (1) Barnabites: Paulus III, Const. *Dudum*, 25 iul. 1535—*BRT*, VI, 190; (2) Order of St. Jerome of the Congregation of Blessed Peter de Pisis: Pius V, Const. *Religionis zelus*, 3 mart. 1571—*BRT*, VII, 908; (3) Hospitalers of St. John of God: Pius V, Const. *Licet ex debito*, 1 jan. 1572—*BRT*, VII, 959; (4) Order of Holy Cross, O. S. Cr.: Gregorius XIV, *Romanus Pontifex*, 12 jul. 1591—*BRT*, IX, 444; (5) Clerics Regular *Ministrantes Infirmis*: Gregorius XIV, *Illius qui*, 21 sept. 1591—*BRT*, IX, 479; (6) Order of Clerics Regular Minors, CC.RR.MM.: Gregorius XIV, Const. *Romanus Pontifex*, 18 febr. 1591—*BRT*, IX, 289; (7) Order of Clerics Regular de Somascha: Paulus V, Const. *Ex quo divina*, 9 nov. 1607—*BRT*, XI, 479; (8) Order of Clerics Regular of the Poor: Gregorius XV, Const. *Ad uberes fructus*, 15 oct. 1622—*BRT*, *XII*, 749; (9) Bavarian Congregation of Benedictines: Innocentius XII, Const. *Creditae nobis*, 11 aug. 1691—*BRT*, XX, 218.

[52]Const. *Quaecumque*, 7 dec. 1604—*Fontes*, 192.

they were affiliated.[53] Now, Pope Clement VIII revised the laws which formerly governed the erection and administration of these lay societies and prescribed that the regulations contained in the constitution *"Quaecumque"* were to be observed in the future not only in regard to their establishment and administration but also in regard to communication of privileges. All religious superiors—major and minor—were given permission to erect and aggregate only one confraternity and congregation to each institute of the religious order. The term "institute" included the monasteries, churches, or colleges of the aggregating religious order. After a confraternity had been validly established, which could not be done without the local ordinary's permission, the privileges, indults, faculties and other spiritual favors, received by the religious order through direct concession,[54] were to accrue to the confraternity or congregation through communication. By virtue of the same constitution, arch-confraternities and congregations established with the permission of the Holy See or the local bishop, were permitted to establish and aggregate only one confraternity and congregation, which, in turn, was favored with the privileges of the aggregating organization in accordance with the same rules concerning communication of privileges.[55] The constitution *"Quaecumque"* introduced two important changes relative to the institute of communication. Thus, for the first time it was prescribed by law that only those privileges of the primary grantee were subject to communication which had been granted directly to the primary grantee. Undoubtedly, the provisions of the constitution on this point

[53]Cf. Gregorius XIII, Breve, *Pastoris aeterni*, 5 maii 1582—*BRT*, VIII, 145; Sixtus V, Breve, *Dum ineffabilia*, 30 ian. 1586—*BRT*, VIII, 659.

[54]" . . . ea tantum privilegia, indulgentias, facultates, aliasque spirituales gratias, et indulta, quae ipsi ordini . . . nominatim ac in specie, non autem extensionem, vel communicationem sibi quovis modo concessa sunt . . . " Const. *Quaecumque*—*Fontes*, 192.

[55]*Loc. cit.*

inspired the provision contained in Canon 64.[56] The second innovation concerning the institute of communication prescribed that privileges could not be communicated to these societies unless the specific privileges which had been acquired through direct concession were set down in writing and presented to the ordinary of the place, who, upon consulting two members of the cathedral chapter, was to approve, modify, or correct them if necessary. After fulfilling these regulations, the bishop himself was to present the document of communicated privileges to the lay society. Moreover, any violation of these laws was punishable by a penalty reserved to the Holy See. The law of this constitution, with the exception of the penalty contained therein, is incorporated into the Code of Canon Law in Canons 720-724. There can be no doubt that the regulations contained in this constitution relative to the institute of communication were highly desirable and were undoubtedly introduced to offset any unrestrained claim of the primary grantee's privileges. Until the issuance of this constitution, communication of privileges always implied that the beneficiary of this source was charged with the responsibility of ascertaining the nature of the privileges which were to accrue to him through communication. The desirability and necessity of the regulations contained in the constitution issued by Pope Clement cannot be underestimated. Similar changes would have been very profitable for the institute in general whenever and to whomsoever it was made available, but, desirable as they might have been, no such regulations were introduced to regulate the operation of the institute in general. Thus the regulations contained in the above mentioned constitution affected the institute of communication only when it served as a source of privileges for the organizations in consideration of which the constitution was

[56] "Per communicationem privilegiorum . . . ea tantum privilegia impertita censentur, quae directe . . . concessa fuerant primo privilegiario . . . "

published. In all other instances communication still served as a source of privileges with comparatively few legal regulations or restrictions.

CHAPTER VI

HISTORY OF THE INSTITUTE OF COMMUNICATION FROM THE EIGHTEENTH CENTURY UNTIL THE PROMULGATION OF THE CODE

ARTICLE 1. REACTION AGAINST THE INSTITUTE OF COMMUNICATION

From the beginning of the eighteenth century until the promulgation of the Code, the institute of communication continued to serve as a source of privileges for former beneficiaries and was invoked on a number of occasions especially in favor of the newly established religious organizations. It is not so much from this aspect that the present period is so important. Much more significant are the various modifications which curtailed the pristine vigor of the institute.

It was during the reign of Pope Clement XII (1730-1740) that the institute of communication, or rather its products, suffered its most severe setback. Clement XII showed himself very unfavorable toward communication as a source of privileges. This is not to say that he departed from the traditional benevolence of the pontiffs toward religious institutes and other pious organizations. Following the example of his predecessors, he continued to grant privileges to religious, but he did depart from the accepted practice of granting privileges by means of communication, which, in his own words, was a source of confusion and controversy.[1] Accordingly Pope Clement XII employed direct concession whenever he granted privileges to any beneficiaries. However, in spite of his personal dislike

[1] *Romanus Pontifex*—*BRT*, XXIII, 324.

for communication of privileges, he never prohibited the beneficiaries of communication to acquire the newly granted privileges through communication. Hence, in the absence of any such express prohibitions, all former beneficiaries of communication were still able to claim the privileges of those with whom they enjoyed a communication of privileges.

In the year 1732, Clement XII dealt the institute of communication, and especially its products, a most damaging blow, when he issued the Decree *"Romanus Pontifex,"* wherein, in unmistakable terms, he revoked fifteen specific privileges enjoyed by the regulars and other religious institutes.[2] In order to obviate any misunderstanding of the revocation, he proceeded with the decree by mentioning as subject to it the specific and general beneficiaries of those privileges.[3] After these effective preliminaries, Clement XII listed the specific privileges, and then concluded with a repetition of the uncompromising force of the revocation. In the following month, Clement XII issued another decree by means of which he revoked those

2" . . . omnia et singula infrascripta indulta, facultates, et gratias, quae tam ad supplicationem partium, quam motu proprio, scientia, et potestatis plenitudine similibus, a Romani pontificibus praedecessoribus nostris, vivae eorum vocis, vel per rescripta illorum, aut de eorum mandato . . . "—Clemens XII, Const. *Romanus pontifex*, 12 febr. 1732—*BRT*, XXIII, 316.

3" . . . quibuscumque utriusque sexus personis, saecularibus, et regularibus, cuiuslibet status, gradus, conditionis, praeeminentiae ac dignitatis, sive ecclesiasticae, sive temporalis existentibus, etiamsi de iis specialis ac individua mentio necessario facienda foret, communitatibus quoque, universitatibus, capitulis, collegiis, confraternitatibus, conventibus, et monasteriis cuiusve ordinis, congregationis, militiae, etiam S. Ioannis Hierosolymitani, ac instituti et societatis etiam Jesu, tam mendicantium quam non mendicantium exemptorum ac non exemptorum, ac quovis tamen privilegio suffultorum, nullis prorsus exceptis, quandocunque et qualitercunque concessa fuerunt, tenore praesentium revocamus, cassamus, tollimus, abrogamus, irritamus, et annullamus, viribusque et affectu vacua esse ac perpetuo fore, neque de cetero cuiquam suffragari posse vel debere, decernimus et declaramus."—*Loc. cit.*

privileges of the Regulars and Mendicants, which had been granted them by Benedict XIII. Only those privileges, however, which were mentioned in this decree were revoked.[4] Thus, religious and their affiliates were deprived of many treasured privileges during the pontificate of Clement XII, but those privileges which were not expressly abrogated still remained in force, and communication still served as an effective source both for these privileges and for those which would be granted in the future.

Following this stormy period, communication was again revived after Clement XII's reign in favor of the newly founded religious congregations. Those congregations which existed in the previous century were able to acquire privileges through communication, but the benefits of this source were restricted to the privileges of the congregations.[5] One of the first congregations to benefit by a wider communication of privileges was the Congregation of Discalced Passionists, to whom were communicated the privileges of all Congregations, both clerical and lay, and the privileges of the Regulars.[6] Not long afterwards other Congregations, namely, the Marian Congregation, the Redemptorists, the Pious Workers, the Congregation of Christian Doctrine, and the Passionists were favored with reciprocal communication of privileges among themselves

[4] "Non obstantibus praemissis, nec non nostrae et Cancellariae Apostolicae regula de iure quaesito non tollando, nec non omnibus et singulis Benedicti decessoris, ac declarationibus apostolicis, nec non omnium et singulorum ordinum praedictorum, statutis et consuetudinibus, privilegiis quoque indultis, etiam Mare Magnum vel alias quomodolibet nuncupatis, litterisque apostolicis, sub quibuscumque formis et tenoribus, ac quibuscumque derogatoriis, aliisque efficacioribus et insolitis clausulis, irritantibus aliisque decretis . . . latissime ac plenissime hac vice dumtaxat specialiter et expresse derogamus; caeterisque quomodolibet contrariis quibuscumque." —Const. *Romanum pontificem*, 29 *Mart.* 1732—*BRT*, XXIII, 325.

[5] In 1632, Pope Urban VIII had permitted the Congregation of the Missions to acquire the privileges of other Congregations through communication.—Const. *Salvatoris nostri*, 12 ian. 1632—*BRT*, XVI, 67.

[6] Clemens XIV, Const. *Supremi Apostolatus*, 16 nov. 1769—*BRC*, V, 73.

and with the Regulars.[7] The communication of privileges which was permitted to these congregations gave rise to a great deal of disagreement concerning the effectiveness of the institute as a source for the privilege of exemption from episcopal visitation. When Pope Clement XIV issued a rescript in which he expressly stated that a modified form of exemption from episcopal jurisdiction was included within the scope of communication in favor of the Passionists,[8] other Congregations enjoying reciprocal communication of privileges with the Passionists claimed the privilege by virtue of communication of privileges. Without attempting to analyze the legal intricacies of this question, it may be noted that it is the consensus of canonists that the Congregations are incapable of acquiring

[7]Communication of privileges in favor of the Marian Congregation was permitted by Pope Pius VI, Const. *Iniuncti nobis*, 27 mart. 1787—*BRC*, IX, 1795. The Redemptorists, the Pious Workers, the Congregation of Christian Doctrine, and the Passionists were favored with communication of privileges by the same pontiff. Const. *Sacrosanctum*, 21 aug. 1789—*BRC*, 211. In 1826, Pope Leo XII included the Oblates of the Blessed Virgin Mary in the reciprocal communication of privileges with the other congregations. Cf. *Analecta Iuris Pontificii*, XII (1870), col. 1019, n. 863.

[8]The privilege of exemption was limited with these restrictions: " . . . exceptis tum iis, quae ad curam animarum et sacramentorum administrationem pertinent, tum casibus, in quibus episcopis, atque ordinariis iure ordinario competit iurisdictio ad forman sacrorum canonum concilii Tridentini (Sessio XXV, *de regularibus*, c. 11) et constitutionum apostolicarum, atque ita sanctitas sua in perpetuum servari, atque exequi mandavit."—"Traité des Congregations Séculières."—*Analecta Iuris Pontificii*, V (1862), col. 160. "L'original (rescrit) est conservé aux archives de la maison de S. Jean et Paul. Depuis ce rescrit, le privilège de l'exemption n'a plus été mis en question."—*Loc. cit.*

the privilege of exemption on the strength of communication of privileges.[9]

ARTICLE 2. OPINIONS OF PRE-CODE CANONISTS CONCERNING THE EFFICACY OF COMMUNICATION

In view of the abundance of the positive evidence which exists, it cannot be denied that the institute of communication was long considered a legitimate source of privileges. That it was also the richest source, especially for religious institutes and their affiliates, is unmistakable. But, just as it was a legitimate and fruitful source of privileges, so too, it was a fruitful source of antagonism, controversy, confusion, and uncertainty.[10] From the introduction of the institute of communication into the Church's system of privileges until its clearer development in the fifteenth century, the predominant characteristic of the

[9]Cf. *supra,* page 76-79, where the question is treated in greater detail. Concerning the possible acquisition of the privilege of exemption by Congregations enjoying reciprocal communication with the Passionists or with Regulars the following opinions prevail. " . . . privilegia tam Jesuitarum quam aliorum ordinum mendicantium, quae . . . iurisdictioni ordinariae episcoporum sunt laesiva, non conferuntur per solam communicationem, sed indigent speciali et expressa concessione non obstante quod communicatio habeat clausulas praegnantes." "Congrégation de Prêtres professant des voeux simples."—*Analecta Iuris Pontificii,* IX (1867), col. 385. "Nul canoniste n'admet que la communication des privilèges des réguliers suffise pour exempter une congrégatione de l'autorité, épiscopale."—*Analecta Iuris Pontificii,* VII (1864), col. 1095. " . . . sententia magis consentanea est tum SS. Pontificum decisionibus, ut videre est in Const. Benedicti XIV, *Impositi nobis,* 27 feb., 1747, . . . tum religiosorum agendi rationi, qui licet gaudeant communicatione privilegiorum . . . tamen privilegium exemptionis a Sede Apostolica speciatim expostulant."—Vecchiotti, S., *Institutiones Canonicae ad usum seminariorum accomodatae* (5 vols., 10 ed., Augustae Taurinorum: 1886), I, pp. 351-355, § 93, especially p. 355.

[10]Cf. Thomassinus, L., *Vetus et Nova Ecclesiae Disciplina,* I, lib. 3, c. 39; Schroeder, H., *Disciplinary Decrees of the General Councils,* 382-386.

institute was the one which permitted a wholesale communication of privileges. The terminology of most of the documents of communication cannot but leave the impression that all of the privileges of the primary grantee are liable to communication, with the exception of those which are always implicity excluded because of the incapacity of the beneficiaries of communication. However, while the institute of communication continued to serve as a source of privileges, its apparently unlimited efficacy began to be curtailed to a great extent. Thus, on a number of occasions the pontiffs inserted express regulations concerning the incommunicability of certain privileges.[11] On a number of occasions, the various Sacred Congregations ruled that privileges which seemed to be liable to communication could not be acquired through this source.[12] Finally, all canonists unanimously agreed that certain privileges

[11]Cf. for example, Pius V, Const. *Ex supernae*, 16 aug. 1567—*BRT*, VII, 584. Clemens XII, Const. *Quaecumque*, 7 dec. 1604—*BRT*, XI, 138-143.

[12]Cf. *supra* page 76, where references are given to two Rota decisions which denied the validity of communication for the acquisition of privileges that are rarely granted by the Holy See. The Sacred Congregation of Indulgences forbade the beneficiaries of communication to acquire the privilege of a privileged altar through this source. Cf. S. C. Indulg., 27 nov. 1764—*Decreta Authentica Sacrae Congregationis Indulgentiis Sacrisque Reliquiis ab anno* 1668 *ad annum* 1882, edita iussu et auctoritate Sctissimi D. N. Leonis P. P. XIII (Ratisbonae, Neo-Eboraci, Cincinattis: 1883), n. 233. The Sacred Congregation of Rites proscribed the acquision of privileges pertaining to the recitation of special offices by religious. "Rev. mus Joseph Ximinez Samaniego Minister Generalis Ordinis Minorum sequentia dubia circa extensionem officiorum S. Rituum Congregationi proposuit solvenda. 1) An communicatio etiam amplissima privilegiorum unius religionis alteri facta, se extendat ad Officia Sanctorum? 2) An facultas recitandi officium de aliquo sancto, concessa specialiter Minoribus Conventualibus, vel Capuccinis, vel Fratribus Tertii Ordinis S. Francisci, vel Monialibus S. Clarae, S. Elisabeth, Conceptionis aut Annuntiatae, se extendat ad Fratres Minores de Corpore Observantiae, sive de Familia, sive Reformati, sive Excalceati, sive Recollecti dicantur, ita ut isti licite illa uti possint? 3) An facultas recitandi aliquod Officium concessa specialiter fratribus Minoribus Reformatis Italiae, sub hoc nomine se extendat ad Observantes de Familia, vel excalceatos His-

were always excluded from communication even though they were not expressly proscribed.[13] As a result of this accumulation of restrictions, whereby the efficacy of communication was drastically curtailed, the practical effects of this source of privileges was seriously questioned during

paniae, vel recollectos Galliae et e converso? 4) An eadem facultas concessa specialiter Fratribus Minoribus de Observantia familiae Cismontanae, se extendat ad Fratres eiusdem Ordinis familiae Ultramontanae, et e converso? 5) An facultas recitandi aliquod officium concessa specialiter alicui provinciae, se extendat ad alias provincias eiusdem Ordinis et instituti, aut concessa alicui conventui se extendat ad alios conventus eiusdem Ordinis, vel saltem eiusdem provinciae? 6) An concessio recitandi singulis mensibus una die, festo novem lectionum non impedita, Officium S. Clarae a Clemente X Fratribus Minoribus Regularis Observantiae absolute facta, sit intelligenda cum moderatione similibus officiis ab eadem S. Congregatione posita, nempe exceptis Quadraginta Dierum, Adventu, Quattuor Temporibus, et Vigiliis, vel absolute, ut sonat. Responsum: Negative ad 1, 2, 3, 4, et 5. Quoad 6, intelligendum cum moderatione. Ordinis Minorum S. Francisci de Observantia, 16 dec. 1679. *Decreta Authentica Congregationis Sacrorum Rituum* (6 vols., Romae: 1898-1927), I, p. 17, n. 2906. On another occasion, the same Sacred Congregation of Rites restricted the force of communication when it was asked: "An Regulares, absque speciali privilegio, sed sola communicatione privilegiorum aliarum religionum, possint addere nomen S. Fundatoris in Litaniis et Confiteor, itemque recitare officia et missas concessas aliis Religionibus? R. Negative in omnibus.—*Op. cit.*, II, p. 244, n. 3741 ad 3. The Sacred Congregation of the Council deprecated the efficacy of communication when it was asked whether the Superiors of the Congregation of St. Maur, O.S.B., which enjoyed communication of privileges with other congregations and orders, could acquire the privilege of dispensing from certain irregularities through communication of privileges. "An Superiores dictae Congregationis licite valideque possint absolvere in utroque foro, ac dispensare super irregularitatibus et censuris suorum monachorum per homicidia vel in bello, vel in jurgiis, aliisque motibus quasi indeliberatis contractis? An eas possint rehabilitare ad susceptionem ordinum, dignitatum, et prioratuum, seu cappellarum regularium? S. C. C. respondit: Negative ad utrumque."—*Analecta Iuris Pontificii*, IV (1861), col. 755.

[13]Cf. *infra*, pages 155-157.

the latter part of the last century,[14] and it was admitted that the Holy See permitted communication of privileges rarely and reluctantly.[15] However, despite the fact that the institute of communication had lost much of its original force, it continued to serve as a source of privileges for the beneficiaries who were favored with its advantages. Moreover, the privileges which were acquired through communication retained their force as long as they were not revoked. Finally, while the efficacy of communication as a source of privileges continued to be the object of controversy and disagreement, the institute itself was affected by general law for the first time when the Code endorsed this source of privileges.[16] Besides giving official approbation to the institute of communication, the Code also issues regulations which are to guide its operation.[17] While the Code preserves communication as a source of privileges and provides that certain persons may enjoy its benefits,[18] it also prescribes that religious institutes shall no longer be able to acquire privileges through communication.[19]

[14]"Haec omnia revera ostendunt, communicatio privilegiorum inter ordines regulares, si adhuc valet aliquid, valde angustiis limitibus modo esse circumscriptum . . . "—Parma, *Collectio Indulgentiarum*, n. 1368. "Si vigor et extensio communicationis privilegiorum . . . desumi et mensurari debeat ex ipsorum ordinum regularium usu et praxi, nos in tali hypothesi non hesitamus asserere predictum communicationis privilegium iamdiu cessasse."—*Op. cit.*, n. 1383.

[15]"Etant reconnu que la communication des privilèges engendre la confusion, le St. Siège procède avec circonspection surtout de nos jours."—"Congrégations Seculieres," *Analecta Iuris Pontificii*, VII (1864), col. 758. Cf. also *Collectanea in Usum Secretariae Sacrae Congregationis Episcoporum et Regularium*, p. 478.

[16]Canon 63.

[17]Canons 64, 65.

[18]Cf. Canons 613, § 2, 713, § 1, 722, § 2.

[19]Canon 613, § 1.

By forbidding communication of privileges between religious organizations,[20] the Code inspired further disagreement among canonists concerning communication of privileges. Since the clause *"exclusa in posterum qualibet communicatione"* is none too clear, some canonists maintained that the Code intended to revoke all the privileges which had been acquired through this source. An equally impressive array of ranking canonists held the opposite opinion, maintaining that the clause *"exclusa in posterum"* abolished communication of privileges only for the future without affecting those privileges which had been acquired through this source before the promulgation of the Code.[21] While this controversy was in progress, Pope Pius XI approved the validity of pre-Code communication when he confirmed the privileges of the Jesuits, specifically mentioning those received through communication.[22] The importance of this confirmation cannot be underestimated[23] for it undoubtedly paved the way for the response which approved the validity of the privileges acquired through communication before the promulgation of the Code. Thus, in the year 1937, the Pontifical Commission for the Authentic Interpretation of the Code issued a negative answer to the following question:

"An verba canonis 613, § 1: 'exclusa in posterum

[20]"Quaelibet religio iis tantum privilegiis gaudet, quae vel hoc in Codice continentur, vel a Sede Apostolica directe eidem concessa fuerint, exclusa in posterum qualibet communicatione."—Canon 613, § 1.

[21]For an analysis of the opinions proposed by canonists concerning the force of this canon, the reader is referred to the following works, where the authorities are enumerated and the opinions are analyzed. Larraona, "Questio Canonica," *Commentarium pro Religiosis* (Romae, 1920—after 1935 entitled *Commentarium pro Religiosis et Missionariis*), III (1922), 205-213; Roelker, Principles of Privilege, pp. 52-59; Vasto, *De Communicatione Privilegiorum*, pp. 81-94; Tatjer, "De Communicatione Privilegiorum inter Religiones," *Apollinaris*, V (1932), 458-486.

[22]Pius XI, Acta, *Paterna caritas*, 12 mart. 1933—*Acta Apostolicae Sedis* (*AAS*) (Romae, 1909—), XXV, 245.

[23]Cf. Creusen, "Privileges par communication," *Revue des Communautes Religieuses* (Louvain: 1925—), IX (1933), 113.

qualibet communicatione' ita intelligenda sint ut revocata fuerint privilegia a religionibus ante Codicem Iuris Canonici per communicationem legitime acquisita et pacifice possessa."[24]

[24]Responsum P.C.I., 30 dec. 1937, *AAS,* (1938), 73. A brief commentary on this answer was published in the *Apollinaris* by Goyeneche, "Commentarium in Responsum ad Can. 613, § 1," *Apollinaris,* XI (1938), 178-180.

PART THREE
CANONICAL COMMENTARY

CHAPTER VII

COMMENTARY ON CANON 64

ARTICLE 1. THE MATERIAL OBJECT OF COMMUNICATION ACCORDING TO THE CODE

In accord with its established policy of preserving the greater part of pre-Code discipline,[1] the Code of Canon Law endorses the institute of communication as a lawful source of privileges.[2] Immediately after sanctioning this source of privileges, the Code sets forth the rules according to which a communicable privilege is to be determined.[3] Before considering the rules which the Code prescribes for the proper interpretation of this source of privileges, it is important to note that the norms pertaining to the institute of communication are inclosed within the Code's treatise on privileges. The significance of this feature lies in this that by enclosing the provisions pertaining to communication in its treatise on privileges, the Code implicity limits the material object of communication to privileges as such. Although there might have been some foundation in fact for claiming other favorable concessions, which were frequently identified with a privilege[4] through

[1]Canon 6.

[2]Canon 63.

[3]"Per communicationem privilegiorum, etiam in forma aeque principali, ea tantum privilegia impertita censentur, quae directe, perpetuo et sine speciali relatione ad certum locum aut rem aut personam concessa fuerant primo privilegiario, habita etiam ratione capacitatis subiecti, cui fit communicatio." —Canon 64.

[4]Cf. *supra*, pages 33-49.

communication of privileges because of the indiscriminate use of the word privilege or because documents of communication frequently list the various favorable concessions, the Code leaves no room for such a careless use of the word privilege. It is true that the Code offers no definition for a privilege whereby it might be more easily distinguished from other favorable concessions; such as favors, rescripts, indulgences, and dispensations. But despite the absence of an official definition, it can reasonably be presumed that the Code sanctions the more advanced juridic opinion on this point. According to this more advanced opinion, a privilege is a special normative right created by law or by a special act of the competent superior outside of law. As a juridic entity a privilege is endowed with special characteristics,[5] which serve to distinguish it from other favorable concessions with which it was formerly identified. According to the law of the Code the material object of communication is restricted to special normative rights, just as the other sources listed in Canon 63 refer only to these rights. It cannot be maintained that other favorable concessions which beneficiaries of communication of privileges were wont to claim through this source are implicitly included in the term privilege, any more than it can be maintained that custom and prescription may serve as sources for the acquisition of indulgences, rescripts, or dispensations. Now, it is not to be inferred that communication cannot serve as a source for the acquisition of other favorable concessions. It is merely implied that communication of privileges alone, whether permitted by law or outside of it, does not implicitly extend to other favorable concessions which cannot be classified as privileges. The Code itself permits the communication of other favorable concessions besides privileges[6]. In this instance, as well as in others when

[5]Cf. *supra*, pages 37-38.

[6]"Per aggregationem communicantur omnes indulgentiae, privilegia, et aliae gratiae spirituales . . . "—Canon 722, § 2.

communication is permitted by means of a special document, other favorable concessions are acquired through communication. Strictly speaking, however, they are not acquired through communication of privileges. But in the absence of any specific rules pertaining directly to communication of other favorable concessions, the rules concerning communication of privileges may, by analogy, be followed in determining the communicability of other favorable concessions when their acquisition through communication is permitted in particular cases.

Restricting the material object of communication to privileges alone, the Code prescribes that the only privileges which can be acquired by means of communication are those which have been granted directly, perpetually, and without any special relation to a certain place, thing, or person, always presupposing the capacity of the subject who is to benefit by the communication of privileges.[7] It is understood that these directions pertain to those privileges which are given to the primary grantee. Furthermore, the characteristics which must be possessed by a communicable privilege, as well as the capacity of the beneficiary of communication, are prescribed conjunctively and unless these requirements are fulfilled for every privilege, which might become the subject of communication, it cannot be acquired through this source.

Article 2. Prerequisites Implicitly Demanded for the Efficacy of Communication

Although Canon 64 makes no mention of it, communication always presupposes another necessary condition, which must be fulfilled before there can be any thought of applying the rules prescribed in Canon 64. Thus, be-

[7]Canon 64.

cause communication of privileges always implies that another's privileges serve as a model for the origin and specification of these which are to be acquired through communication, it is absolutely necessary that the primary grantee have some privileges which might serve as a model for the beneficiary of communication.[8] However, it is not sufficient that the primary grantee merely possess some privileges. He might have acquired some privileges invalidly; and at the same time that another is permitted to acquire his privileges through communication, he might be using the invalidly acquired privileges as a norm of action. When the competent authority permits communication of privileges to any beneficiary it does not intend to include invalidly acquired privileges,[9] because such privileges have no legal existence. It is absurd to think that the competent authority would permit another to acquire privileges which that authority does not approve. The previous valid acquisition of a privilege by the primary grantee as a necessary prerequisite for the actualization of the grantor's benevolence through communication or concession *ad instar*,[10] influenced authors to speculate further about the efficacy of either source when the primary grantee is deprived of his privileges through misuse, or when he has lost them through non-use or renunciation. In answer to this hypothesis, canonists agree that the privileges are most probably acquired through communication (i.e., equal communication) or concession *ad instar* even under these circumstances. Such privileges can be acquired because the grantor makes the concession in view of the previous concession or valid acquisition without considering the subsequent loss of those privileges through any of the above-mentioned

[8]Schmalzgrueber, *Ius Ecclesiasticum Universum*, lib. V, tit. 33, n. 79.

[9]Suarez, *De Legibus*, lib. 8, c. 15, n. 9.

[10]The identity between these two sources has been pointed out on pages 85-86, *supra*.

causes.[11] Such reasoning might be upheld if the grantor expressly states that he communicates to this person the same privileges which had been granted to another. However, it can hardly be sustained when the grantor communicates those privileges which another enjoys at the time the document of communication is issued. The canonists who favor the probable efficacy of communication for privileges which are lost through non-use or renunciation make no such distinction. They imply that a valid previous concession is the only thing necessary to make communication an effective source of privileges which had once been granted to a primary grantee. If such reasoning is pressed to the limit, it can be maintained that privileges which have been revoked by competent authority are included within the scope of communication by virtue of the fact that they had previously been granted to the primary grantee. It is unreasonable to think that the grantor wishes to include these. By the same token, it seems that he also wishes to exclude those which are no longer in existence regardless of the manner in which they ceased to exist because concession *ad instar* or communication always implies that there is an existing privilege from which the beneficiary of communication might ascertain the quality of his privilege.

Another hypothetical question concerning the efficacy of communication pertains to the value of this source for the acquisition of privileges which are specifically mentioned when the primary grantee does not possess such

[11]Castro Palao, *Opus Morale*, I, tract. 3, disp. 4, punct. 2, § 8, n. 2: Barbosa, A., *De Clausulis Usufrequentioribus*, clausula 5, p. 6. " . . . valiturum probabiliter privilegium tuum, si hoc tibi concessit princeps ad instar illius quod habet Petrus, etsi illud Petrus non usu, vel renuntiatione amiserit, modo privilegium Petri aliquando fuerit validum, et firmum; . . . videtur facta concessio privilegii ad similitudinem illius, quod Petro aliquando concessum est, neque censetur princeps alligare velle valorem recens concessi privilegii valori praesenti, quem habet privilegium Petri, sed praeterito."—Schmalzgrueber, *Ius Ecclesiasticum Universum*, lib. V, tit. 33, n. 81.

privileges. If, for example, the grantor communicates privileges in this way: "The Franciscans are hereby given the same privilege of dispensing from private vows as that which is enjoyed by the Dominicans." Since communication implies that the quality of a privilege is to be determined by the quality of another, it is asked whether Franciscans in the above-mentioned hypothesis would acquire any privilege if the Dominicans do not have such a privilege. According to the consensus of canonists consulted on this point, there is no doubt that the beneficiary of such a communication acquires the privilege in question because the specific mention of the privilege renders the communication efficacious whether the primary grantee, to whose privilege it is likened, possesses such a privilege or not. In such a communication, the primary grantee's privilege is used demonstratively and not conditionally, i.e., the primary grantee's privilege is not a necessary condition for the creation of the privilege which is communicated.[12]

Finally, many documents of communication explicitly demand that only those privileges of the primary grantee which are in use at the time of the concession can be acquired through communication. This requirement, however, does not demand that the privilege be in actual use by the primary grantee. According to the common teaching of pre-Code canonists,[13] acknowledged by present day

[12]Schmalzgrueber, *Ius Ecclesiasticum Universum*, lib. V, tit. 33, n. 82; Suarez, *De Legibus*, lib. 8, c. 16, n. 7; Castro Palao, *Opus Morale*, I, tract. 3, disp. 4, punct. 2, § 8, n. 4. Suarez states that there were some authors, like Mandosius, who were under the opinion that communication would be ineffective even under such circumstances. Suarez discards this opinion by stating: " . . . non video fundamentum urgens, et ideo illos omitto."—*Loc. cit.*

[13]Rodericus, H., *Quaestiones Regulares et Canonicae Enucleatae*, p. 839, nn. 57-58; Salmanticenses, *Cursus Theologiae Moralis*, II, tract. 18, c. 1, punct. 7, § 1, n. 99; Tamburini, *De Iure Abbatum*, III, disp. 17, q. 5, n. 3; Piatus Montensis, *Praelectiones Iuris Regularis*, II, p. 103.

canonists,[14] potential use suffices to make a privilege liable to communication. All that is necessary is that the subject whose privileges are communicated is able to use the privilege at the time that another is favored with communication of privileges, because ability to use the privilege is comparable to actual use.[15] A privilege is to be presumed actually in use in order that a beneficiary of communication might acquire the privilege if it is apparent that it is being used by the primary grantee. If, however, it is not evident that the privilege is still in use, but it is well known that it was in use before a person is favored with the benefits of communication, its use at the time of the concession can also be presumed.[16] If it is evident that the privilege was never in use, obviously its non-use is to be presumed. If the beneficiary of communication might attempt to claim a privilege whose past use is not manifest, it is necessary for him to prove that it is still potentially available to the primary grantee.

Only when the above-mentioned conditions are fulfilled can there be any question of applying the rules prescribed by Canon 64 to determine whether a particular privilege or privileges are available to the beneficiary of communication. In the analysis of Canon 64 which is to follow, the characteristics of a communicable privilege will be considered separately. In this process only that part of the Canon will be cited which refers to the characteristic which is being treated.

[14]Van Hove, *De Privilegiis*, n. 147; Tatjer, "De Communicatione Privilegiorum inter religiones," *Apollinaris*, V (1932), 466.

[15]" . . . haec potentia propinqua actui, habetur pro actu, et vix inveniri poterit aliquod privilegium, quod actualiter sit in usu . . . "—Rodericus, H., *op. cit.*, p. 839, n. 57.

[16]*Loc. cit.*

Article 3. Characteristics of Communicable Privileges according to the Code

A. *Communicable Privileges Must Have Been Conceded Directly*

"Per communicationem privilegiorum . . . ea tantum privilegia impertita censentur, quae DIRECTE . . . concessa fuerant primo privilegiario."

By prescribing that a privilege must be conceded directly to the primary grantee, in order to be communicable, the Code introduces a new requirement for privileges which might be acquired through communication by any beneficiaries. Except for the provisions contained in the Constitution *"Quaecumque,"*[17] which regulated communication of privileges for lay societies, the mode of acquisition did not affect the communicability of a privilege as long as other legal or doctrinal restrictions did not prevent its acquisition through this source. It was not at all uncommon for the pontiffs to permit the beneficiaries of communication to acquire the privileges of another regardless of the manner in which they were acquired by the primary grantee.[18] The restriction imposed by Canon 64 seems to be self-evident, but actually it is open to a variety of interpretations arising from the meaning of the word *"concessa"*... Understanding the word "conceded" in an accommodated sense for the time being, thus not excluding

[17]Cf. *supra*, pages 114 ff.

[18]The following terminology appears in many documents of communication: " . . . omnia et singula privilegia . . . etiam per viam communicationis aut quomodolibet concessa."—Gregorius XIV, Const. *Romanus pontifex*, 18 febr. 1591—*BRT*, IX, 289. Cf. also, Gregorius XV, Const. *Ad uberes fructus*, 15 oct. 1622—*BRT*, XII, 749.

privileges which are acquired through custom or prescription, the phrase "directly conceded" signifies that the beneficiary of such a concession is the immediate beneficiary of the grantor's benevolence. Furthermore, the word "directly" admits of no dependence of a concession upon the pre-existing privileges of another subject, but it demands that the privilege be granted directly or immediately to a determined grantee.

Relative to the acquisition of a privilege, the word "concede", considered alone, has a two-fold connotation. First of all, it signifies a special and distinct act of competent authority from which a privilege derives its existence. Considered in this sense, the concession, either in law or outside of it, is the immediate as well as the final cause of the privilege, whose essence can be defined directly or indirectly. As such, concession is the genus of which direct and indirect concession (communication) are species. In both instances, the existence of the privilege depends upon the positive act of competent authority. In one instance, however, the essence of the privilege is specified by that positive act, while in the other the essence of the privilege depends upon a pre-existing privilege. Secondly, the final cause or the legal consent which sanctions the privileges acquired through custom or prescription can be called a concession, and properly so, because without that consent, privileges cannot have lawful existence even though the privilege originates with the action of the subject. Hence, privileges acquired by direct concession or communication derive their origin and existence in the special act of competent authority who makes a concession by specifying a privilege or permits communication implying that the privilege will derive its specification from another. Privileges acquired through custom or prescription receive their origin through the acts of a subject in accord with the provisions of law, which, by permitting the acquisition of privileges through these sources, makes a concession. In the last analysis, privileges acquired through any source are the products of a concession emanating from the benevolence of competent authority. If concession is understood in this sense, then direct concession or the phrase "directly conceded" is opposed only to communication and not to custom or prescription, which, in turn, would imply that privileges acquired through these sources are not excluded from communication of privileges.

There is no present day canonist who questions the obvious exclusion of communicated privileges from further communication in view of the fact that the Code prescribes that the communicable privileges must be conceded directly.[19] Although all canonists agree on this point, not all canonists agree about the implications of the phrase "directly conceded" in so far as privileges acquired through custom and prescriptions are concerned. Thus, some maintain that the phrase "directly conceded" unequivocally prohibits the further communication of privileges acquired by means of communication, custom, and prescription.[20] Of these canonists, Toso alone indicates that privileges acquired by means of custom and prescription are excluded from communication not because they are granted indirectly, but because they are not constituted by a special act of competent authority.[21] Although other authors who sponsor the opinion that privileges acquired through custom and prescription are proscribed by the phrase "directly conceded" offer no explanation for their stand, it may be inferred that their opinion is based on the same interpretation. Otherwise, it would have no solid foundation.

[19]Sipos, S., *Enchiridion Iuris Canonici* (3 ed., Pecs: 1936), 44; Vasto, *De Communicatione Privilegiorum*, p. 60; Cicognani, Canon Law, 795; Toso, *Ad Codicem Iuris Canonici Commentaria* Minora (5 vols. Romae: Marietti, 1920-1934. Vol. I, 2 ed., 1921), I, 154; Van Hove, *De Privilegiis*, p. 143, n. 143.

[20]Vasto, *op. cit.*, p. 60; Michiels, *Normae Generales*, II, p. 362; Toso, *ibid.*, 154; Roelker, *Principles of Privilege*, p. 49.

[21]Toso, *Loc. cit.*

Basically, the same opinion is sponsored by other canonists,[22] but they qualify it to the extent that they admit the communicability of privileges acquired through custom or prescription if they have centenary or immemorial existence, because Canon 63, § 2 provides that centenary or immemorial possession gives rise to the presumption that such privileges have been granted directly. Since such privileges enjoy the presumption of having been granted directly, they can assuredly be acquired by means of communication, providing, however, that their communication is not otherwise prohibited. However, there seems to be no solid foundation for restricting the meaning of the word "possession" to privileges acquired by means of custom or prescription. "Possession," which signifies the detention of a thing or a right,[23] does not originate with any special mode of acquisition; for a thing or a right can well become the object of possession notwithstanding the exact source of its acquisition. Undoubtedly, the law intends to favor all possessed privileges with such a presumption without any consideration of the source of its acquisition. Such a provision is not superfluous even though the privilege had originally been acquired through direct concession or communication. In actual cases the exact source of acquisition can easily become shrouded in obscurity. If, in spite of such uncertainty concerning the proximate source, a privilege has been enjoyed for a period approaching a hundred years, or from time immemorial, the law favors such privileges with the presumption that they have been granted directly as long as they were never revoked, lost, or renounced. By provision of law, privileges possessed from time immemorial, or for approximately a hundred years, are supplied with a lawful

[22]Coronata, *Institutiones*, I, n. 92; Wernz, F.—Vidal, P., *Ius Canonicum*, I, 293; Van Hove, *De Privilegiis*, n. 141.

[23]"Definitur possessio detentio rei cum animo eam retinendi ut propriam, utendi iure tamquam suo."—Van Hove, *De Privilegiis*, n. 111.

title;[24] and unless the actual mode of acquisition is conclusively proved, such privileges are assimilated to those which are acquired through direct concession. Thus, if a beneficiary enjoys immemorial or centenary possession of a privilege and the original source through which the privilege is acquired is unknown, the title is supplied by a presumption of law, which merely relieves the possessor of the burden of proving the original title. If, however, it is proved that the privilege was originally acquired through a source other than direct concession, the presumption must yield to the fact and the privilege must be judged in accord with the rules which apply to the specific source. As long as no contrary proof is adduced, the privilege which is enjoyed through immemorial or centenary possession is governed by the same rules that govern those privileges which are acquired through direct concession. Hence, by virtue of the title which is supplied by a presumption of law, privileges which fulfill the requirements of immemorial or centenary possession are not to be excluded from communication.

If the presumption provided by Canon 63, § 2 is only a presumption of law,[25] and this seems to be the more com-

[24]Cf. Michiels, *Normae Generales*, II, p. 367; Toso, *Ad Codicem Iuris Canonici Commentaria Minora*, I, p. 157; Van Hove, *De Privilegiis*, nn. 120 and 122.

[25]"Praesumptio est rei incertae probabilis coniectura, eaque alia est iuris, quae ab ipsa lege statuitur; alia hominis, quae a iudice coniicitur."—Canon 1825, § 1. "Praesumptio iuris alia est iuris simpliciter; alia iuris et de iure."—Canon 1825, § 2. *"Praesumptio iuris simpliciter"* can be contradicted both by direct and indirect proof. Hence, the presumption that a privilege was granted directly can be attacked by proving that it was acquired through some other source. A *"praesumptio iuris et de iure,"* on the other hand, cannot be attacked directly, but its foundation alone can be questioned. Hence, if the presumption contained in Canon 63, § 2 would be a praesumption *"iuris et de iure,"* the law would not admit any evidence which would prove that the privilege was granted in some other way.

mon opinion,[26] then the presumption must cede to contrary proof. Therefore, if it is proved that possession of a privilege was produced by custom or prescription, the presumption is of no value and the communicability of privileges acquired through custom or prescription depends upon the meaning of the phrase *"directe concessa"*, which will be treated presently. If it is proved that possession of a privilege originated with communication, then the further communication of such a privilege is no longer possible. If, however, no proof to the contrary can be offered but there is evidence to show that the privilege is based on centenary or immemorial possession regardless of the actual mode of acquisition, which it is presupposed cannot be proved, the law favors such privileges with the presumption that they were granted directly and thus they would be included within the scope of communication.

Other canonists maintain that the provision of Canon 64, demanding that communicable privileges be granted directly, excludes only those privileges which have been acquired by means of communication.[27] From their silence about the communicability of privileges acquired through custom or prescription, it may be inferred that such privileges are not excluded from communication. By sponsoring this opinion, these canonists maintain, implicitly at least, that privileges acquired through custom or prescription are the products of a direct concession. This implicit opinion is upheld by Larraona,[28] Wernz--Vidal,[29] Tatjer,[30]

[26]Cf. (Bachofen) Charles Augustine, *A Commentary on the New Code of Canon Law*, I (1926), 156; Roelker, *Principles of Privilege*, pp. 67-69; Vermeersch—Creusen, *Epitome Iuris Canonici*, I, n. 180, n. 854.

[27]Cicognani, *Canon Law*, p. 795; Sipos, *Enchiridion Iuris Canonici*, p. 44; Vermeersch—Creusen, *Epitome Iuris Canonici*, I, n. 152; Van Hove, *De Privilegiis*, nn. 142, 143.

[28]"Questio Canonica,"—*Commentarium pro Religiosis*, III (1922), 207.

[29]*Ius Canonicum*, III, n. 388.

[30]"De Communicatione privilegiorum inter religiones," *Apollinaris*, V (1932), 468.

and Goyneche.[31]

It has already been pointed out that a number of canonists maintain that privileges acquired through custom or prescription cannot be acquired through communication because Canon 64 prescribes that communicable privileges be granted directly.[32] Since no other explanation is offered by these canonists, it must be deduced that privileges acquired through these sources are excluded from communication because they are the objects of an indirect concession. Thus, Suarez[33] and Michiels[34] teach that privileges acquired through custom and prescription result from an indirect concession because the permission granted by law to acquire privileges in this way does not benefit any specific or particular subject. According to this explanation, then, the word "indirect" is synonymous with general or indeterminate. There is no doubt that the word "indirect" can carry such a connotation; and hence, it is possible that the legislator intends to render incommunicable those privileges which are acquired through custom or prescription by demanding that they be conceded directly. However, it cannot be conclusively proved that privileges acquired through custom or prescription are excluded from communication by using an argument which is based on a less accurate connotation of the word "indirectly."[35]

In fact, it cannot be proved conclusively that the phrase "directly conceded" implicitly includes those privileges which are acquired through custom and prescription; but the Code itself offers a negative argument to prove that it is not the legislator's intention to prohibit the communication of privileges acquired through custom and pre-

[31]"Commentarium in responsum P.C.I. ad Can. 613, § 1," *Apollinariis,* XI (1938), 178.

[32]Cf. *supra,* pages 53-58.

[33]*De Legibus,* lib. 8, c. 7, nn. 4-7.

[34]*Normae Generales,* II, 363.

[35]Primarily, the word "indirectly," used as a modifier of a causal act, signifies that the effects of the act are produced through an intermediary.

scription. Before considering the value of this argument, Toso's interpretation of the phrase "directly conceded" will be analyzed. By maintaining that the phrase "directly conceded" demands that privileges be granted to a specific subject by means of a special act, Toso implies that this phrase must be interpreted in the light of Canon 63, where direct concession is listed as a source of privileges distinct from custom, prescription, and communication.[36] Hence direct concession is to be understood as a special constitutive act, which creates a privilege in favor of a subject who is the first and immediate beneficiary of the competent authority's benevolence. Although direct concession, according to Canon 63, is distinct from custom and prescription, and must necessarily be understood in this way, the phrase "directly conceded" does not necessarily have to be interpreted thus. The phrase "directly conceded" need not necessarily imply that a privilege must be the product of a special constitutive act of competent authority, as it is when it is established by law or by an act outside of law. The permission which is granted to subjects of law to posit acts by means of which they can prescribe privileges, or introduce custom, through which privileges can be acquired, is as much of a concession as the very act which creates a privilege. It is true that such a concession is different from that which is a special source of privileges; but the difference is only accidental insofar as the former is the remote cause of a privilege, whereas the latter is the proximate cause. Essentially, the two concessions are the same insofar as both produce privileges.

The negative argument which the Code furnishes in opposition to the opinion of those authors who claim that privileges acquired through custom and prescription cannot be acquired by means of communication is found in

[36]Cicognani maintains that this is the way in which the phrase must be interpreted, but he seems to contradict himself when he says: "The grantee receives it not by communication, but by direct concession of the superior." —*Op. cit.*, p. 793.

Canon 613, § 1, wherein it is stated that religious shall henceforth enjoy only those privileges which are conceded directly, excluding any kind of communication in the future. Although the Code expressly states that religious shall enjoy only those privileges which are directly conceded, it is hardly the legislator's intention to prohibit religious from acquiring privileges by means of custom and prescription.[37] That it is not the legislators intention to prohibit religious from enjoying the benefits of these sources may be deduced from the fact that the law expressly prohibits only communication in spite of the fact that it prescribes that privileges must henceforth be conceded directly to the religious. If the legislator intended to prohibit religious from acquiring privileges through custom or prescription, it is only reasonable to expect that such a prohibition would have been expressly stated in the concluding clause of canon 613, § 1. In the absence of such an express prohibition, it seems permissible to maintain that the phrase "directly conceded" implicitly includes those privileges which are acquired through custom or prescription. It might be argued that the express prohibition of communication alone in canon 613, § 1 derogates from a restrictive interpretation which might be applied to the phrase "directly conceded", which is used in this canon. Such an explanation, however expedient as it might be, is hardly acceptable because it is unlikely that the legislator would use identical phraseology to convey entirely different connotations.

[37]Cf. Canons 25, 26, 1508-1512. Although custom and prescription are constantly used correlatively, it must be noted that there is a difference between these two sources of special normative rights. Custom is available only to a community capable of receiving law.—Canon 26. Prescription, on the other hand, is available to individuals as well as communities. If a community, acting as a body, takes away a right possessed by an individual or a community, the acquisition of the right is governed by norms pertaining to prescription. Cf. Suarez, *De Legibus*, lib. 8, c. 1, n. 11; Van Hove, *De Privilegiis*, n. 72, pp. 72-73.

It is true that the interpretation of the phrase "directly conceded", which is supported in this dissertation is based on a purely negative argument; but in the absence of an authentic interpretation, it seems to be preferable to the doctrinal interpretation which would exclude privileges acquired through custom and prescription from communication, and, if consistently followed, would imply that religious are incapable of acquiring privileges through these sources. The more liberal interpretation of the phrase "directly conceded" seems to be more consonant with the sense of many of the documents of communication, wherein it is stated that privileges acquired directly or through communication are communicated.[38] In these documents communication is placed in opposition to direct concession, not explicitly excluding custom or prescription, but implicitly including these sources, with the added implication that privileges which are conceded directly are opposed only to those that are conceded indirectly or through communication. It seems highly probable that the phrase "directly conceded", placed in opposition to communication, simply connotes that the concession as well as the acquisition of a privilege does not depend upon an intermediary as it does in the case of those privileges which are communicated. If the phrase "directly conceded" is employed in these documents merely to indicate its opposition to communication, it can lawfully be presumed that this same connotation is retained by the Code in canons 64 and 613, § 1; implicitly in the former, explicitly in the latter. Consequently, by prescribing that privileges must be directly conceded in order that they may be subject to communication, the Code excludes only those privileges which are acquired by means of communication.

38" . . . nec non omnia et singula privilegia . . . vel directe vel per communicationem concessa . . . "—Leo XIII, Breve *Dolemus inter alia,* 13 iul. 1886—*AAS,* XIX, 49; " . . . quam specialiter, ac per viam communicationis . . . concessa . . . "—Pius IV, *Inter Multiplices,* 14 dec. 1792.—*BRC,* X, 2569.

Besides excluding those privileges which are acquired by means of communication, the phrase "directly conceded" contains another restriction which is based on the tense form of the verb conceded *concessae fuerant.* Hence, communication is effective only for those privileges which had been granted prior to the issuance of the document of communication or oral notification of the permission to communicate the privileges of another. This provision, which was commonly accepted by pre-Code canonists,[39] is of importance today only when communication is permitted to those not favored by law with the benefits of this source. In those instances when the law permits subjects to acquire privileges by means of communication,[40] the restriction is not applicable because the law itself derogates from it by making communication a source for the privileges acquired by the primary grantee at any time.

Whenever any form of communication of privileges[41] is permitted to any subjects to whom the source is not made available by law, the restriction imposed by the tense form of the verb is to be observed; and unless express mention is made of privileges to be granted in the future these are not included within the scope of communication.

As a consequence of the general principle enunciated in Canon 10,[42] it follows that the provision of Canon 64 restricting communication only to those privileges which existed at the time when communication was permitted, does not apply to any pre-Code communication which was expressly extended to future privileges. If, after the pro-

[39]Castro—Palao, *Opus Morale,* tr. 3, disp. 4, punct. 2, n. 9; Suarez, *De Legibus,* lib. 8, c. 16, n. 8; Rodericus, E., *Quaestiones Regulares et Canonicae, Resol.* 116, n. 55.

[40]Cf. CC. 613, § 2; 713.

[41]Van Hove incorrectly maintains that the restriction imposed by the tense form of the verb applies only to equal communication.—*De Privilegiis,* n. 147.

[42]"Leges respiciunt futura, non praeterita, nisi nominatim in eis de praeteritis caveatur."

mulgation of the Code, any particular beneficiaries could still enjoy the benefits of communication permitted before the Code,[43] communication would still be an effective source of privileges not only for those privileges which had been granted to the primary grantee before communication was permitted, but also for those that would be granted afterwards to the primary grantee. Thus, the tense form of the verb restricting communicable privileges to those which had been conceded would not apply to communication of privileges in favor of those beneficiaries who are not deprived of the benefits of this source by the Code. Hence, the restriction contained in Canon 64 is nullified by Canon 10 in favor of those beneficiaries who still enjoy the benefits of pre-Code communication even though they are not otherwise provided with the benefits of this source by law. If the competent authority had permitted communication of privileges to a beneficiary before the promulgation of the Code in such a way that the one favored with communication was permitted to acquire not only those privileges which the primary grantee possessed at the time of the concession, but also those that would later accrue to the primary grantee, the restriction imposed by Canon 64 would not affect the efficacy of pre-Code communication on the strength of Canon 10.

It is evident that the application of the principle contained in Canon 10 is superfluous in the case of those beneficiaries to whom the advantages of communication are made available by law. By providing that certain beneficiaries can always acquire the privileges of another through communication,[44] the Code itself derogates, either

[43]In the year 1909, Pope Piux X communicated the privileges of all patriarchal basilicas and papal chapels to the Church of St. Mary of the Angels of Portiuncula, declaring: " . . . ex nunc in futurum perpetuo esse et fore decernimus." Const. *Omnipotens et misericors,* 11 apr. 1909—*AAS,* I (1909), 394.

[44]Cf. Canons 613, § 2, 722, § 1.

implicitly or explicitly,[45] from the restriction contained in Canon 64, which prescribes that only those privileges which had been conceded can be acquired by means of communication.

B. *Communicable Privileges Must Be Perpetual*

> "Per communicationem privilegiorum . . . ea tantum privilegia impertita censentur, quae . . . PERPETUO . . . concessa fuerant primo privilegiario."

In accord with the commonly accepted teaching of pre-Code canonists,[46] the Code prescribes, as a second requisite, that privileges conceded to the primary grantee must be perpetual in order that they may be acquired by another through communication. The perpetuity of a privilege cannot be called into question when significant words[47] are used by the grantor who makes the concession. If, however, the perpetuity of a privilege cannot be proved in this way, recourse must be had to the traditional juridic principle[48] incorporated into Canon 70, where it is stated

[45]Canon 613, § 2 makes an implicit derogation of the restriction imposed by Canon 64, whereas Canon 722, § 1 makes an explicit derogation of this restriction. The explicit derogation of the restriction is necessitated by the very composition of canon 722, § 1, for the restriction would imply that communication of privileges is restricted to those privileges and favors which are possessed by the aggregating confraternity at the time of the aggregation. Communication of spiritual favors permitted to confraternities and pious unions by Canon 713, § 1 is circumscribed by this restriction.

[46]Cf. Schmalzgrueber, *Ius Canonicum Universum*, lib. V, tit. 33, n. 92; Didacus ab Aragonia, *Dilucidatio Privilegiorum*, tract. 1, art. 8, n. 5; Antonius a Spiritu Sancto, *Directorium Regularium*, tract. 1, disp. 1, sect. 3, n. 44.

[47]E. g., in saecula saeculorum, in perpetuum, etc. Cf. Barbosa, *Variae Tractationes Iuris*, vol. V, *De Dictionibus Usufrequentioribus*, dict. 254, n. 193.

[48]"Decet beneficium concessum a principe esse mansurum."—Regula 16, R. J. in VI°.

that every privilege is perpetual unless the contrary is evident.

It is Vermeersch's opinion[49] that temporary privileges are excluded from communication because such privileges do not possess the nature of a true privilege. Such an explanation, however, is hardly a reasonable one, because the essence of a true privilege is not determined by the note of stability.[50] A special normative right is a true privilege whether it be permanent or temporary. Its stability depends ultimately upon the will of the competent superior, through whose benevolence the privilege is granted. It is more likely that the opinion which favored the exclusion of temporary privileges was introduced to offset the possible prorogation of privileges whose cessation was predetermined by the grantor. If communication of temporary privileges were not proscribed, it is highly probable that many privileges would have been used by subjects of communication long after their actual cessation. Although the former canonists who favored this restriction did not offer any explanation for their opinion, it can safely be presumed that they favored the restriction in order to prevent the prorogation of temporary privileges.

Van Hove explains the exclusion of temporary privileges by maintaining that all privileges which are limited in time are granted for special reasons and are incommunicable because the special reasons would not exist for the subject of communication.[51] According to this explanation temporary privileges cannot be acquired by means of communication because it is contrary to the nature of things to do so. The right order of things demands that privileges, temporary or perpetual, granted for special reasons are not liable to communication because the acquisition of such privileges through communication would contradict

[49]*De Religiosis Institutis et Personis*, I, n. 354.
[50]Cf. *supra*, page 38, note 11.
[51]*De Privilegiis*, n. 144.

the original purpose of the privilege and deprive the primary subject of the singular distinction that the grantor wishes him to enjoy. Although it must be admitted that some privileges are incommunicable *"per se"*, it cannot be alleged that temporary privileges are excluded on this score, because it is incorrect to assume that the temporary nature of a privilege necessarily implies that it was granted for a special reason. Even though every privilege ought to be perpetual, the grantor is by no means obliged to have a special reason for limiting the existence of any privilege. However, even if he were obliged to have a special reason or actually did have one, it does not follow that every privilege granted for a special reason is intrinsically incommunicable. A privilege is intrinsically incommunicable only when the special reason which motivates its concession is produced by the grantee. For example, a privilege to eat meat on all days of abstinence is granted to a certain community because it has no means of acquiring any other food. The special reason, which motivates this concession, is produced by the peculiar circumstances in which the community is situated. Manifestly, it would be absolutely contrary to the nature of things for other communities to invoke communication as a source for such a privilege because the circumstances which gave rise to the privilege would not exist in their case. On the other hand, the superior might have his own special reasons for granting a privilege or for limiting its existence. In such a case, it cannot be said that the privilege is absolutely excluded from communication because no particular grantee is the cause of the special reason for which the privilege was granted or for which it was granted temporarily.

In spite of the fact that Vermeersch and Van Hove attempt to explain the exclusion of temporary privileges by having recourse to juridic principles, their explanations are as untenable as the principles on which they are based. As a matter of fact, it is impossible to offer a satisfactory explanation based on juridic principles. It still seems most probable that the restriction was originally introduced in order to prevent the practical difficulties that the communication of temporary privileges might have produced.

Although temporary privileges are not intrinsically adverse to communication, the Code prohibits their acquisition through this source by prescribing that to be communicable privileges must be granted perpetually to the primary grantee. Since the Code makes no distinction in making this provision, it matters not whether a temporary privilege is granted for a special reason or not. Temporary privileges are excluded merely because they are temporary.

C. *Communicable Privileges Must Be Granted Without Special Relation to a Certain Place, Person, or Thing.*

> "Per communicationem privilegiorum . . . ea tantum privilegia impertita censentur, quae . . . SINE SPECIALI RELATIONE AUT CERTUM LOCUM AUT REM AUT PERSONAM . . . concessa fuerant primo privilegiario."

Next, the Code prescribes that only those privileges of the primary grantee are subject to communication which are granted without special relation to a certain place, thing, or person. The requirement contained in this part of the Canon is a concise summary of common pre-Code opinion, which, without a doubt, was originally advanced in order to interpret the instructions relative to communication of privileges contained in documents issued by Pope Julius II[52] and Leo X.[53] When Pope Sixtus IV had permitted the Franciscan and Dominican orders to enjoy

[52]Bulla, *Alias ad supplicationem*, iun. 1509—*Bullarium Ordinis Praedicatorum*, IV, 258.

[53]Const. *Dudum per nos*, 10 dec. 1519—*BRT*, V, 732.

a reciprocal communication of privileges,[54] he did so with terminology which admits a very liberal interpretation. He gave no specific instructions about the procedure to be followed by the favored orders in the process of acquiring privileges through communication, nor did he make any restrictions concerning the exclusion of any privileges. Most likely, it was because of the misinterpretations that could and possibly did result from the terminology of the original documents of communication that Julius II, at the request of the king of Spain, issued the instructions which prescribed that a due proportion must exist between the beneficiaries of privileges when they are acquired through communication. Hence, after naming the parallel offices of the superiors of the respective orders in order to demonstrate the procedure to be followed for communicating muneral privileges between the orders, Julius II stated that other privileges were to be communicated as follows: "*...de fratribus privatis, id est sine praelatura, ad fratres privatos; et de festivitatibus ad festivitates...ea quae in honorem Sanctorum...fratribus vel locis praedicatorum sunt concessa, omnia illa fratribus minoribus eorum locis, in festivitatibus sanctorum...intelligantur concessa...*"[55] Ten years later (1519), when Leo X permitted communication of privileges between six Mendicant orders he left no doubt that all muneral, real, local, and personal privileges granted to one order were communicated to the others.[56] Communication of privileges among these religious orders now implied that the privileges enjoyed by superiors were acquired by superiors of corresponding

[54]Const. *Sedes Apostolica*, 27 maii 1474—*BRT*, V, 212.

[55]Bulla, *Alias ad supplicationem*,—*Bullarium Ordinis Praedicatorum*, IV, 258.

[56]Const. *Dudum per nos*,—*BRT*, V, 212. "Privilegia communicantur quae respiciunt sive loca (ecclesias, oratoria, domos), sive personas seu superiores generales, provinciales, locales, fratres in genere, conversos, oblatos, nec non moniales ac sorores, insuper et utriusque sexus personas de poenitentia seu tertii ordinis."—Vasto, *De Communicatione Privilegiorum*, p. 21.

rank within the orders; privileges of private religious were acquired by private religious of other orders; privileges attached to places and things of one order were communicated to similar places and things belonging to the other orders. However, except for requiring that a similarity of rank or due proportion exist between the persons, places, and things whose privileges were communicated between the orders, the instructions contained in the documents issued by Julius II and Leo X still admitted a very liberal interpretation since they implied that all the privileges of corresponding beneficiaries were liable to communication. Hence, presupposing that the required similarity among the beneficiaries within the orders did exist, there was no explicit restricton in the instructions to prevent one order from acquiring, for example, the privileges attached to all the churches or only specific ones of another order regardless of the manner in which or the reasons for which those privileges were granted. From the terminology of the documents it could not be inferred that only the privileges common to all the churches of one order were liable to communication. In spite of the fact that some authors infer that only those privileges which were common to places, persons, or things of one order were liable to communication,[57] Leo X had stated expressly that privileges granted *"in genere"* or *"in specie"* were included within the scope of communication.[58]

Canonists have always admitted that communication of privileges between religious orders must operate in accord with the instructions of the above mentioned consti-

[57] "Communicantur tantum privilegia communia toti ordini . . . "— Schmalzgrueber, *Ius Ecclesiasticum Universum,* lib. V, pars 3, tit. 33, n. 92.

[58] " . . . privilegia . . . qualiacumque illa essent . . . in domibus et illorum ecclesiis . . . coniunctim vel divisim, in genere vel in specie concessa fuerunt, aut in posterum concedentur . . . communicavimus."— Const. *Dudum per nos,—BRT,* V, 212.

tutions;[59] but, on the other hand, they have always insisted on a less extensive interpretation of those constitutions, which, objectively, would permit the acquisition of all muneral,[60] personal,[61] and real privileges.[62] Thus, it has always been maintained that purely personal privileges (i.e., those given to particular individuals) could never be acquired by other private religious by virtue of the communication of privileges enjoyed by the orders.[63] Purely personal privileges are not included within the scope of communication permitted to the religious orders because their acquisition through this source would contradict that rule of law, which states: *"Privilegium personale personam sequitur, et extinguitur cum persona."*[64] Moreover, the unwarranted communication of purely personal privileges, which are generally, if not always, granted because of personal merits,[65] would certainly disrupt the discipline of religious institutes.[66] Although the phrase *"de fratribus privatis ad fratres privatos"* implies that all personal privileges are included within the scope of communication, actually, it permits the communication of those privileges

59 "Communicatio currit de praelatis ad praelatos, de fratribus privatis, id est sine praelatura, ad fratres privatos, de conventibus ad conventos, de festivitatibus ad festivitates."—Reiffenstuel, *Ius Canonicum Universum* lib. V, tit. 33, n. 59, p. 341; Bouix, *Tractatus de Iure Regularium*, II, pars 5, p. 77.

60 " . . . de praelatis ad praelatos . . . "—*Loc. cit.*

61 " . . . de fratribus privatis, . . . ad fratres privatos . . . "—*Loc. cit.*

62 " . . . de conventibus ad conventos, de festivitatibus ad festivitates."—*Loc. cit.*

63 Rodericus, H. *Quaestiones Regulares et Canonicae Enucleatae*, p. 836, n. 51; Antonius a Spiritu Sancto, *Directorium Regularium*, 42; Reiffenstuel, *op. cit.*, lib. V, tit. 33, n. 60, p. 341; Vasto, *op. cit.*, p. 59.

64 Regula 7, *De Regulis Iuris* in VI°; Canon 74; Reiffenstuel, *loc. cit.*

65 Schmalzgrueber, *op. cit.*, lib. V, tit. 33, n. 92, p. 93.

66 " . . . concessa religiosis privatis non communicantur aliis religiosis ordinibus . . . secus tota religionum observantia funditus everteretur." Rodericus, *op. cit.*, p. 836, n. 51.

alone which have been granted to an order for the benefit of all the private religious of the order.[67]

Although it is absolutely certain that purely personal privileges were always considered incommunicable, such absolute certainty cannot be reached when an effort is made to determine the status of commonly personal or real privileges[68] which were granted to a particular beneficiary[69] within a religious order.

Despite the fact that there were some pre-Code canonists who maintained that all privileges granted to a particular beneficiary were liable to communication[70] it was by far the more common opinion among pre-Code canonists to favor the exclusion of privileges granted to a particular beneficiary for special reasons or for a determined length of time,[71] and to consider only those privileges as communicable which were granted to a particular beneficiary for no special reason.[72] In this case, however, there must be

[67]Suarez, *De Legibus*, lib. 8, c. 17, n. 7.

[68]For a technical division of commonly personal and real privileges, cf. page 59, *supra*. At this point no sharp distinction is necessary between the various species of real privileges and the species of commonly personal privileges, nor between real and commonly personal privileges.

[69]Particular beneficiary is used generically so as to include subjects of commonly personal, real, and local privileges. However, it does not include subjects of purely personal privileges. Hence, particular beneficiary might refer to a particular community, a particular place, or a particular locality.

[70]Rodericus, E., *Quaestiones Regulares et Canonicae*, I, q. 55, n. 18; Tamburini, *De Iure Abbatum*, I, disp. 17, q. 11, claus. 1.

[71]Antonius a Spiritu Sancto, *Directorium Regularium* disp. 1, n. 44; Reiffenstuel, *Directorium Regularium op. cit.*, lib. V, tit. 33, nn. 61, 62; Pignatelli, *Consultationes Canonicae*, vol. X, consult. 1, n. 32.

[72]Van Hove states that Schmalzgrueber sponsored the opinion that privileges granted to a particular place for no special reason were considered incommunicable.—*De Privilegiis*, n. 145, note 5. This assertion is incorrect for Schmalzgrueber implies that a privilege granted to a certain place is excluded from communication only when it is restricted to a certain place. "Excipi tamen debet (a communicatione) . . . privilegia localia, ut quae censentur ad certum locum restricta . . . "—*Op. cit.*, lib. V, tit. 33, n. 83.

a formal similarity between the beneficiary to whom the privilege is originally granted and the beneficiary for whom the privilege is claimed by virtue of communication.[73]

Just as canonists do not admit an unrestricted interpretations of the phrase *"de fratribus privatis ad fratres privatos"*, so too, they do not subscribe to a literal interpretation of the phrases *"de conventibus ad conventos"*, *"de festivitatibus ad festivitates"*, which, of their nature, permit the acquisition of all commonly personal and real privileges given to a particular convent and, at least, some real privileges vested in a particular thing. Hence, with these doctrinal restrictions, communication of privileges, as enjoyed by religious institutes, is considered ineffective as a source for (1) purely personal privileges, regardless of the reason for which they are granted; (2) privileges granted for special reasons to particular communities (commonly personal), to particular places (local), to particular things (properly real).

In view of the fact that these restrictions exclude only those privileges which are granted to particular beneficiaries within a religious order, it would seem that all privileges given to the whole religious order are considered within the scope of communication. If the efficacy of communication as a source of privileges for religious orders before the Code were to be judged solely in the light of the restrictions already mentioned, such an inference would be correct. However, not only certain privileges given to particular beneficiaries within a religious order are considered incommunicable, but there are also some privileges which are excluded from communication even when they were granted for the benefit of all the places, persons, or things of the whole order. Thus, all privileges, whether

[73]Alphonsus M. de Ligouri, St. *Theologia Moralis* (4 vols., Romae: 1905-1912), I, tract. 2, Appendix 2, n. 11; Suarez, *De Legibus*, lib. 8, c. 17, n. 7.

they are granted to particular beneficiaries within a religious institute or to the institute as a whole, are considered incommunicable (1) if they are granted for special motives;[74] (2) if they are classed as exorbitant or extraordinary;[75] (3) if they are expressly declared incommunicable;[76] (4) if they would be burdensome or detrimental to the party favored with communication;[77] (5) if they preju-

[74]Schmalzgrueber, *op. cit.*, lib. V, tit. 33, n. 83; Reiffenstuel, *op. cit.*, lib. V, tit. 33, n. 62; Donatus considers the privilege given to the Jesuits of not singing office in choir as one which was granted for special reasons. *Rerum Regularium Praxis Resolutoria* (4 vols., Coloniae: 1675), I, pars 1, tract. 7, quest. 14, n. 9.

[75]Cf. Petra, V., *Commentaria ad Constitutiones Apostolicas*, V, 45; Tatjer gives a partial list of such privileges in *Apollinaris*, V (1932), 464.

[76]E.g., Pope Benedict XIV forbade Congregations enjoying communication of privileges with Regulars to acquire the privilege given to the Regulars of receiving orders from any Catholic bishop. Benedictus XIV, Const. *Impositi nobis*, 27 Feb., 1747—*Opera Omnia* (16 vols., Prati: 1846), II, 164. Privileges which are expressly excluded from communication can be acquired through communication if the clause forbidding communication is expressly derogated.—Suarez, *De Legibus*, lib. 8, c. 17, n. 8. Some canonists maintain that the clause forbidding communication is implicitly derogated if communication is permitted with comprehensive terminology (in terminis praegnantibus). Reiffenstuel, *Ius Canonicum Universum*, lib. V, tit. 33, n. 64; Rodericus, E., *Quaestiones Regulares et Canonicae*, I, quest. 55, n. 17; Didacus ab Aragonia, *Dilucidatio Privilegiorum*, I, q. 8, n. 8.

[77]Among such privileges are those which contain penalties and those which contradict the rules and constitutions of a particular order. "Privilegia repugnantia observantiae religionis, cui fit communicatio, non veniunt communicanda . . . etiamsi id non exprimitur in bulla communicationis, semper enim intelligitur appositum et expressum, alias cederet non in favorem, sed in odium, non in aedificationem, sed destructionem, et dissipationem religionum, quod est maxime alienum a mente Pontificum."—Rodericus, H., *Quaestiones Regulares et Canonicae Enucleatae*, p. 837, n. 54; Cf. also Suarez, *De Legibus*, lib. 8, c. 17, n. 54. Some canonists exclude penal and odious privileges unequivocally, maintaining that a favor (i.e., communication) should never be turned into a burden.—Salsmans, "De Religiosis et Missionariis supplementa et monumenta, continuans De Religiosis II, ed. 2," *Periodica de Re Canonica et Morali utili praesertim Religiosis et Missionariis* (Brugis: 1905—; ab anno 1927, *Periodica de Re Morali, Canonica, Liturgica*), V (1913), 41; Tatjer, *art. cit.*, Apollinaris, V (1932),

dice the rights of third parties;[78] (6) if they have been revoked by the Council of Trent,[79] or by a decree of the Sovereign Pontiff.[80]

By prescribing that communicable privileges must be granted to a primary grantee without special relation to a certain person, place, or thing the Code expressly incorporates only that part of the pre-Code doctrine on communication according to which it was held that, under certain circumstances, privileges granted to a religious order in favor of particular beneficiaries were excluded from communication.[81] When pre-Code canonists insisted upon the exclusion of privileges granted to particular persons, places, or things they were expressly concerned with a proper interpretation of the terminology of those papal documents which implied that privileges granted to particular persons, places, or things within a religious order

464. Other canonists maintain more correctly that penal privileges can be acquired through communication if they bring a favor to the religious institute as such (e.g., the improvement of religious discipline) even though they do entail a penalty for particular religious. Cf. Salmanticenses, *Cursus Theologiae Moralis*, II, tract. 18, c. 1, punct. 7, n. 101. Though penal privileges can be acquired under these 'circumstances, privileges which contradict the discipline of a particular organization can never be acquired through communication.

78Pignatelli, *Consultationes Canonicae*, X, consult. 1, n. 34; D'Annibale, *Summula Theologiae Moralis*, I, n. 104, note 21; *Analecta Iuris Pontificii*, IX (1867), col. 385. Privileges prejudicial to the rights of third parties are excluded from communication only when communication of privileges is permitted without express mention of such privileges. Cf. *supra*, pages 78, 79.

79Some canonists maintain that only those privileges which were expressly revoked by the Council of Trent cannot be acquired through communication. Cf. Tamburini, *De Iure Abbatum*, disp. 18, claus. 1, n. 3; Rodericus, E., *op. cit.*, I, quest. 8, art. 6. Others maintain that not only those which were expressly revoked by the Council of Trent, but also those which were contrary to any laws of the Council were considered incommunicable. Petra, *p. cit.*, III, 11; IV, 16; Rodericus, H. *Op. cit.*, 818, n. 14.

80Vasto, *De Communicatione Privilegiorum*, p. 56.

81Cf. *supra*, pages 154-156.

were subject to communication. Obviously, the provisions of the clause "granted to a primary grantee without special relation to a certain place, thing, or person" are fundamentally the same as the teaching of pre-Code canonists. However, instead of referring to a religious order as the subject whose privileges are made accessible to others, the Code refers to an indeterminate primary grantee in order to accommodate the provisions of this Canon to the operation of the institute of communication for all persons who might be favored by the benefits of this source.

Although the Code refers to an indeterminate primary grantee in Canon 64, undoubtedly it is mindful of the actual operation of the institute in favor of religious orders in the old law as well as the instances in which it is permitted in the new law.[82] In all of these instances it is presupposed that the primary grantee is a moral person, capable of receiving privileges in favor of all its personnel, places, or things. Unless the composition of the clause "granted to a primary grantee without special relation to a certain place, thing, or person" is understood in this sense, it is difficult to explain the distinction which is implied between the primary grantee and the particular beneficiaries in relation to whom privileges are given. Thus by virtue of pre-Code teaching as well as the express provision of the above-mentioned clause in Canon 64, only those privileges are included within the scope of communication which are granted to a primary grantee in favor of all places (e.g. territory of all monasteries of an order), things (e. g. all churches), or persons. There is no doubt that the Code foresees the actual operation of the institute as permitted by the law of the Code when it arranges the wording of the clause, which is being discussed at this point. Anticipating the benefits of this source of privileges especially in favor of the nuns and aggregated lay so-

[82]Canons 613, § 2; 713, § 1, 722, § 2.

cieties,[83] the Code intends to forestall any attempt on the part of these beneficiaries to claim those privileges which are granted to the primary grantee in favor of certain persons, places, or things. Keeping in mind the relationship obviously implied by the Code between the primary grantee and particular beneficiaries and applying the principles proposed by pre-Code canonists, not only those privileges which are granted to the primary grantee in favor of all persons, places, or things connected with it but also those privileges which are granted to particular places, things, or communities would be subject to communication as long as they are not granted with special relation to those particular beneficiaries. Thus, according to the more common pre-Code opinion, privileges granted to a particular community within a religious order were liable to communication as long as they were not granted for special reasons. If the pre-Code opinion on this question still prevails, then privileges given to a particular community within a religious order of men can be acquired by the corresponding order of women to whom communication of privileges is permitted by Canon 613, § 2. Since it was generally admitted by pre-Code canonists that privileges granted to particular beneficiaries, excepting private individuals, within a religious order were not excluded from communication by others when no special reason on the part of the grantor or special circumstances on the part of the grantee motivated the concession to particular beneficiaries, it is lawful to use the same interpretation for the phrase "without special relation to a particular person, place, or thing" as prescribed by Canon 64.

According to pre-Code doctrine, which is accepted

83Canons 613, § 2, 722, § 2. There is no room for the application of these norms in regard to communication of privileges as permitted by Canon 713, § 1. In this instance only those favors can be communicated which are specifically declared communicable by the Holy See.

unequivocally by modern canonists,[84] privileges are given to a primary grantee with special relation to a particular person, place, or thing when their concession is motivated by a special reason whether the special reason exists with the beneficiary or in the mind of the grantor. Thus, for example, a privilege is given to a religious order with special relation to a particular thing if it is granted to favor a church which contains the relics of some saint. It can also be maintained that privileges are given to a primary grantee with special relation to a certain person, place, or thing merely because it is granted in favor of a particular beneficiary. However, in view of the fact that the Code demands that a privilege be granted to a primary privileged party "without special relation" to a particular beneficiary, it implies that a privilege can be given to a primary grantee with such a relation to a particular beneficiary which is ordinary or common. Thus, if a privilege is granted to a religious order in favor of a particular community for no special reason whatsoever, it is granted without special relation to that particular community. Such a privilege can be acquired through communication because it is not intended to remain exclusively in possession of the primary grantee either by virtue of the fact that it is granted for some exclusive reason or by virtue of the fact that the grantor intends to restrict it to the beneficiary in relation to which it was granted. Hence, by stating that a privilege must be granted "without special relation," the Code sanctions the teaching of pre-Code canonists who maintained that privileges granted to particular beneficiaries within a religious order could be acquired by other religious orders through communication.[85] Thus, applying this

[84]Cf. Van Hove, *De Privilegiis*, nn. 145, 146; Vasto, *De Communicatione Privilegiorum*, p. 59, n. 88; Tatjer, "De Communicatione privilegiorum inter religiones,"—*Apollinaris*, V (1932), 465; Michiels, *Normae Generales*, II, 362.

[85]Cf. *supra*, page 159.

provision to communication as permitted by Canon 613, § 2, nuns can acquire the privileges of the corresponding order of men when privileges are given to the latter in favor of particular beneficiaries, excepting private individuals, provided there is a formal similarity between the beneficiary in whose favor the privilege is granted and the beneficiary for whom it is claimed.

Since the clause "given to a primary grantee without special relation to a certain place, thing, or person" is undoubtedly based on the teaching of pre-Code canonists, it is fitting that it be interpreted in accord with their teaching. However, if their teaching be followed without any qualification, it would be necessary to maintain that, in reference to personal privileges, the Code only demands as a requisite for communicability that they be granted to a primary grantee without special relation to a private individual. It would be necessary to apply such an interpretation to the phrase "without special relation to a certain person" because pre-Code canonists expressly excluded from communication only those privileges which are given to private individuals.[86] It could not be inferred that these canonists implicitly excluded commonly personal privileges or those granted to a particular moral person because in referring to privileges granted to particular persons they expressly mentioned those privileges which are given to private individuals. They left no room for the inference because they referred to purely personal privileges as distinct from those which a private individual enjoys through the office or dignity in which they are vested. Some modern canonists[87] accept the opinion proposed by pre-Code canonists and apply it to the

[86]Cf. Schmalzgrueber, *Ius Ecclesiasticum Universum,* lib. V, tit. 33, n. 92; Antonius a Spiritu Sancto, *Directorium Regularium,* disp. 1, n. 42; Piatus Montensis, *Praelectiones Iuris Regularis,* II, q. 143.

[87]Vasto, *op. cit.* p. 59, n. 88; Tatjer, *op. cit.,* p. 465; Van Hove, op. *cit.* n. 146.

provision of Canon 64 demanding only that privileges be granted without special relation to a certain person in order that they may be subject to communication. However, it is more correct to interpret it as implying that, to be communicable, privileges must be granted without special relation either to a moral person or to a private individual.[88]

If the above mentioned explanation of the phraseology of the clause "given to a primary grantee without special relation to a certain place, thing, or person" is accepted at face value, it must be admitted that the Code does not demand that communicable privileges must be granted without special relation to the primary grantee. However, as acceptable as the explanation of the phraseology might be, this is by no means its implication; for the Code hardly intends to imply that all privileges given to the primary grantee without special relation to certain persons, places, or things are subject to communication. On the contrary, it is certain that the Code intends to proscribe the communication of privileges given with special relation to the primary grantee as much as those which are given with special relation to persons, places, or things connected with the primary grantee. That it intends to do this is evident from the fact the legislator is more intent on restricting the efficacy of communication in the new law, rather than on increasing it.[89] Moreover, it was the unanimous opinion among pre-Code authors that all privileges given to any beneficiary for special reasons are not subject to communi-

[88]"Excluduntur a qualibet communicatione . . . privilegia . . . alicui personae morali aut physicae aut coetui personarum concessa; aut concessa personae physicae qua tali seu privilegia singulariter personalia."—Coronata, *Institutiones,* I, n. 92; cf. also Cicognani, *Canon Law,* p. 793.

[89]Canon 64 itself introduces a new restriction by demanding that privileges must be granted directly. Canon 613, § 1 prohibits future communication of privileges between religious orders. Canons 713, § 1 and 722, § 2 permit communication of those privileges only which are specifically declared communicable by the Holy See.

cation. For these reasons, it cannot be maintained—even though the wording of Canon 64 would permit such an inference— that privileges given with special relation to the primary grantee are included within the scope of communication. In view of the fact that the wording of Canon 64 is slightly ambiguous, the following is suggested to remove all doubt concerning the implications attached to the clause which has been analyzed in the foregoing pages: Only those privileges can be acquired through communication which have been given to a primary grantee without a special reason and without special relation to a certain person, place, or thing.

In order to explain why privileges granted for special reasons or with special relation to certain persons, places, or things are excluded from communication, most authors[90] state that their exclusion is demanded by the very nature of the subject because the reason for which the privilege is granted is not verified in the case of those who enjoy communication of privileges with the one to whom the privilege is given for special reasons. The explanation is acceptable but it is not adequate, because it implies that such privileges can be acquired by the person favored with communication if the reason is verified in his case. It is true that the reason for which a privilege is given to the primary grantee cannot be reproduced materially in the case of the one favored with communication; but the very nature of the institute of communication would permit the acquisition of an otherwise communicable privilege by the latter beneficiary if the reason is reproduced with a formal similarity.[91] Privileges given for special reasons are considered incommunicable especially because they are generally classed as those privileges which require special

[90]Cf. Cicognani, *op. cit.*, 793; Roelker, *Principles of Privilege*, 50; Van Hove, *De Privilegiis*, n. 145.

[91]Cf. Suarez, *De Legibus*, lib. 8, c. 17, n. 7; Alphonsus, St., *Theologia Moralis*, I, tract. 2, Appendix 2, n. 11.

mention in order that they may be acquired validly.[92]

In order to determine when a privilege is given for a special reason or with special relation to a certain beneficiary, the following principles might be helpful. Privileges are granted with special relation to a beneficiary; and consequently, they are not liable to communication when their concession is motivated by characteristics or merits which exist exclusively with the beneficiary to whom the privileges are granted. Thus, for example, a privilege is given with special relation to a religious order when it is given to honor some outstanding and distinctive contribution made by that order in the service of the church. A privilege is given to a religious order (primary grantee) with special relation to a particular person when it is given to a particular community to provide for some unusual circumstance of place or time.

It is not absolutely necessary that the beneficiary of a privilege possess some distinctive characteristics as the motive cause of a concession in order that a privilege might be classified as one which is given with special relation to the beneficiary. A privilege is also classified as one which is given with special relation to a beneficary when it is the grantor's intention that the privilege remain exclusively in the possession of the beneficiary. Such an intention on the grantor's part can be easily presumed when an exorbitant privilege is granted. The intention is made manifest when the grantor expressly declares that a privilege is not subject to communication.

92"In generali concessione non veniunt ea, quae quis non esset verisimiliter in specie concessurus." Regula 81, *De Regulis Iuris* in VI°

D. *The Subject of Communication Must Be Capable of Receiving a Privilege through Communication.*

". . . HABITA ETIAM RATIONE CAPACITATIS SUBIECTI, cui fit communicatio."

After enumerating the characteristics that are required of a communicable privilege, Canon 64 prescribes, as a final condition for communication of privileges, that the capacity of the subject favored with communication must be considered. This means that persons who are permitted to acquire the privileges of another must possess the qualifications that are necessary prerequisites for the enjoyment of certain privileges. Some privileges are adaptable to all beneficiaries. Others, however, are restricted to those beneficiaries who possess the qualifications in consideration of which the privileges are originally given. If it is evident that privileges are given in consideration of certain qualities or a special juridic condition, communication is obviously of no avail to a subject who does not possess the presupposed qualities or who is not constituted in that juridic condition which is the foundation of the privilege.[93] It might be objected that the grantor's benevolence is thus unduly nullified because in granting communication he is supposed to have wished that the person favored should acquire the privileges of another without any qualification. The grantor's benevolence is not nullified by demanding that a subject favored with communication possess the qualifications that are presupposed for the enjoyment of some privileges. Since it is presumed that the grantor always acts in accord with reason and not contrary to it, it is presumed in this case that he does

[93] "Excipi tamen debet (a communicatione) . . . item illa (privilegia) quae in eos, quibus fit communicatio, propter defectum certae qualitatis non quadrant." Schmalzgrueber, *Ius Ecclesiasticum Universum,* lib. V, tit. 33, n. 83.

not intend to permit a person to acquire a privilege where the very foundation of the privilege does not exist.

The following examples, which are hardly necessary, will serve to illustrate the practical application of the last requisite prescribe by Canon 64 for the acquisition of privileges through communication.

Lay people cannot acquire those privileges which are granted in consideration of religious profession.[94] Persons lacking the power of jurisdiction cannot acquire those privileges which presuppose that power. The same holds true for the power of orders.[95] Obviously, nuns, who are permitted to acquire the privileges of the corresponding first order of nuns,[96] cannot acquire those privileges which belong exclusively to men, nor can they acquire any privileges which presuppose the power of orders or jurisdiction.[97]

ARTICLE 4. THE CODE IMPLICITLY RETAINS THE PRE-CODE DOCTRINAL RESTRICTIONS IN CANON 64

Although the Code does not expressly proscribe the communication of other privileges which were considered incommunicable before the Code,[98] there is no doubt that it does so implicitly. This may be deduced from the fact that it is the obvious policy of the Code to diminish the efficacy of communication. However, not only the policy of the Code, but more especially the very nature of these

[94]Vermeersch—Creusen, *Epitome Iuris Canonici* I, 181. In the year 1519 Leo X branded as erroneous the practice of those lay people who claimed those favors which had been given to the religious orders "*intuitu religionis.*"—Const. *Dudum per nos,* 10 dec. 1519—*BRT,* V, 732.

[95]Van Hove, *De Privilegiis,* n. 145.

[96]Canon 613, § 2.

[97]Van Hove, *loc. cit.*

[98]Cf. list given on pages 155-157, *supra.*

privileges, argues against their inclusion within the scope of communication. If it were maintained that exorbitant, prejudicial, burdensome, detrimental, and other privileges could be acquired through communication merely because the Code does not mention such privileges explicitly, special rights could be acquired in contradiction to time-tried juridic principles,[99] in contradiction to principles which safeguard good order within society,[100] and even in direct contradiction to the wishes of the grantor.[101] In short, it can be said that Canon 64 implicitly retains those restrictions commonly accepted before the Code because the very nature of the subject and the principles of law demand their retention.[102]

99Thus, it has always been maintained that exorbitant privileges or those which are rarely conceded cannot be acquired by anyone unless they are explicitly defined and granted to a definite person, place or thing. Cf. *Reg.* 81, R.J., in VI°; Pignatelli, *Consultationes Canonicae*, X, consult. 1, n. 13. Penal and burdensome privileges are generally incommunicable by virtue of the fact that a favor should not become a burden. Cf. Salsmans, "De Religiosis et Missionariis Supplementa et Monumenta, Continuans De Religiosis II, ed. 2," *Periodica de Re Canonica et Morali Utili praesertim Religiosis et Missionariis*, V (1913), 41; Reiffenstuel, *Ius Canonicum Universum*, lib. V, tit. 33, n. 66.

100Order within society would be disrupted completely if, for example, religious institutes could claim communication as a source for privileges which would contradict the rule or constitutions of their institute. This principle is especially applicable today as to the communication of privileges which is permitted by Canon 613, § 2.

101It is self evident that privileges which are expressly declared incommunicable by the grantor cannot be acquired through communication even though the Code does not proscribe the communicability of such privileges.

102"Ex ipsa natura rei et ex dispositionibus iuris superioris a communicatione excluduntur . . . "—Van Hove, *De Privilegiis*, n. 148.

CHAPTER VIII

COMMENTARY ON CANON 65

After the Code has prescribed the characteristics that a privilege must possess in order that it might be acquired through communication, it next considers the relationship between the privileges of the primary grantee and those which are acquired by a person to whom the privileges of the former are made available through communication. In taking up the question of the status of a privilege acquired through communication, the Code must necessarily consider its status in relation to the privileges of another because communication is a source through which a person is permitted to acquire the privileges of another. The privileges of the latter are an essential element of communication for they serve as the mediate cause for the actualization of the grantor's benevolence, and, consequently, for the production and specification of the privileges to be acquired through communication. Hence, since at least the origin and nature of a privilege acquired through communication depends upon the privileges of another, it is evident that a privilege acquired through this source cannot but be considered in relation to the privileges of another, who is technically called the primary grantee.

Assuming that a privilege has already been acquired through communication and thus necessarily presupposing that it received its essence and existence[1] from the privi-

[1]Regardless of the source of acquisition the existence of a privilege depends upon the will of the superior. This same holds true when communication serves as a source of privileges. Thus, both the essence and existence of a privilege acquired through communication ultimately depend upon the will of the superior. Proximately, however, a privilege to be acquired through communication depends for its essence and existence on another's privilege. Cf. *supra*, page 5 and *infra*, pages 131 ff.

leges of the primary grantee, the Code is primarily concerned with the influence that a primary grantee's privileges have upon the privileges of the person to whom the former's privileges have been made available through communication. The Code takes up this question in Canon 65, wherein it incorporates the traditional teaching of canonists[2] with a slight accidental variation which pertains only to the external form of presentation. Thus, Canon 65 expressly states that privileges acquired through accessory communication are automatically increased, diminished, or lost with the increase, diminution, or loss of the primary grantee's privileges.[3] The opposite, it states, occurs when a privilege is acquired through equal communication.[4] Although the Code does not expressly state what effects takes place when a privilege is acquired through equal communication, it implies very clearly that a privilege acquired through equal communication is not affected by the change or loss of the privilege which served as its proximate cause. In spite of the fact that the legislator leaves no doubt about the fact that a privilege acquired through equal communication is not in any way affected by the increase, loss, or diminution of the primary grantee's privilege,[5] the decree to which reference is made in the footnote to this part of Canon 65, is, strange to say, diametrically opposed to the norms which are clearly, though only implicitly, contained in the Canon. The footnote to this part of the Canon refers to an answer given by the Sacred Congregation of Indulgences which branded

[2]"His canonizata est communis doctrina canonistarum . . . " Coronata, *Institutiones*, I, p. 102, n. 92.

[3]"Cum privilegia acquiruntur per communicationem in forma accessoria, augentur, imminuuntur, vel amittuntur ipso facto, si forte augeantur, imminuantur vel cessent in principali privilegiario; . . . "—Canon 65.

[4]" . . . secus si acquirantur per communicationem in forma aeque principali."—Canon 65.

[5]"Normas de communicatione in forma aeque principali Codex indirecte statuit, illas opponendo regulis statutis pro communicatione in forma accessoria.—Van Hove, *De Privilegiis*, n. 141.

as false the opinion favoring the non-revocation of indulgences acquired through equal communication when those indulgences were expressly revoked only for the primary grantee.[6] The citation has influenced one author to conclude that the pre-Code theory concerning the effects of equal communication can no longer be upheld.[7] Hence, according to this conclusion, privileges acquired through equal communication are automatically revoked when the primary grantee's privileges are revoked. Furthermore, if they are thus affected by the revocation of the primary grantee's privileges, much more so would they be affected by the increase or diminution of those privileges. This conclusion, however, is incorrect because it is based on a particular answer given by one of the Sacred Congregations, which are not wont to give a general answer in a particular case. Obviously such a particular answer cannot be used to interpret the general law of the Code, which is done by the author who draws the above mentioned conclusion from a specific answer given by the Sacred Congregation of Indulgences.[8] Moreover, anyone who maintains that a privilege acquired through equal communication is subject to the increase, decrease, or loss of the primary grantee's privilege flatly contradicts the very wording of Canon 65, which does not admit such an interpretation. By introducing the clause pertaining to privileges acquired through equal communication with the word *"secus"*, the Code clearly implies that privileges acquired through equal

[6]"Utrum tuta sit opinio, quae docet indulgentiis pro Ordine communicante per revocationem pontificiam sublatis, ceteri quibus illae per communicationem factae sunt propriae, iis frui nihilominus pergant, nisi revocatio expresse etiam ad eos dirigatur. Resp. ad XVII: Negative, imo falsa." —S. C. Indulg. *Tertii Ordinis S. Francisci*, 31 ian. 1893—*AAS*, XXV, 506.

[7]"Ex C. ergo C.I.C. collata responsione S. C. Ind. clare apparet hodie doctrina ab AA. passim tradita niti supra falsum fundamentum. Diximus hodie tantum quia iurisprudentia AA. veterum satis fundata apparet et revera est."—Vasto, *De Communicatione Privilegiorum*, p. 48, n. 78.

[8]*Loc. cit.*

communication are not increased, diminished, or lost when these modifications affect only the privileges of the primary grantee.[9] If the word *"secus"* and the clause which it introduces is interpreted in the light of the context which precedes it, it must necessarily receive this interpretation, which is an exact reproduction of the constant teaching of pre-Code canonists,[10] and not the doctrine contained in a particular citation, which is not exactly apropos.

ARTICLE 1. STATUS OF A PRIVILEGE ACQUIRED THROUGH ACCESSORY COMMUNICATION

In order to indicate to what extent a privilege acquired through communication is affected by the modifications which affect the privileges of the primary grantee, the Code gives accessory communication first and explicit consideration in spite of the fact that it is the less perfect of the two

[9]Vasto denies that such an interpretation can be attributed to this part of the Canon by questioning the force of the word "secus." Thus, he states: "Difficultas facit illud 'secus' ". After making this statement, he adds that the wording the Canon has its origin in the above mentioned response of the Sacred Congregation of Indulgences.—Vasto, *De Communicatione Privilegiorum*, p. 48, n. 78. Both statements are erroneous. If the word "secus" is interpreted in the light of the context of the law, which is the first rule of correct interpretation (cf. Canon 18), it offers no difficulty whatsoever. It cannot be maintained, as Vasto does, that the law of Canon 65 derives its origin, and, consequently, its interpretation from the answer of the S. C. of Ind. which is cited in the footnote. It is true that the sources which are cited for the various canons of the Code are oftentimes exactly the same as the law of the Code. In many instances, however, as in this one, the sources which are cited differ materially as well as formally. If Vasto's line of reasoning were applied to all of the Canons of the Code, it would be necessary to admit that the interpretation demanded by the text and context of Code laws is not always correct.

[10]Cf. Salmanticenses, *Cursus Theologiae Moralis*, II, tract. 18, c. 1, punct. 7, § 1, nn. 95-99; Suarez, *De Legibus*, lib. 8, c. 16, n. 12; Gregory van Etten, *Compendium privilegiorum Regularium* (Romae, 1900), p. 17; Bouix, *Tractatus de Iure Regularium*, II, pars 5, p. 77, n. 5; Parma, *Collectio Indulgentiarum*, p. 625, n. 26.

species of communication.[11] Undoubtedly accessory communication is given this primacy of place in Canon 65 because the Code itself favors persons with the benefits of this source of privileges,[12] whereas equal communication is only a potential source of privileges today.

Privileges acquired by means of accessory communication are automatically increased, diminished, or lost with the increase, diminution, or loss of the primary grantee's privileges.[13] That privileges acquired through this form of communication should be subject to the change or loss which directly affects the privileges of the primary grantee[14] is a logical consequence of this form of communication, whose nature is clearly revealed by its title, namely "*communicatio in forma accessoria.*" According to accepted juridic-philosophic principles, anything of an accessory nature is subject to the same consequences as those which affect the principal in which the accessory inheres, to which it is attached, or from which it derives its nature.[15] Thus, persons, places, or things are implicitly subject to the same provisions which explicitly affect only the principal when persons, places, or things are considered accessory of their nature or are declared such by provision of law.[16] Although provisions which directly affect the principal automatically

[11]"Communicatio fieri potest . . . imperfecte, seu accessorie . . . " Reiffenstuel, *Ius Canonicum Universum*, lib. 5, tit. 33, n. 54; cf. also Parma, *loc. cit.*

[12]Cf. Canons 613, § 2, 713, § 1, 722, § 2.

[13]Canon 65.

[14]"Privilegia communicata (per formam accessoriam) vices seu fata participant privilegiorum directe concessorum . . . "—Vermeersch—Creusen, *Epitome Iuris Canonici*, I, p. 157, n. 182.

[15]"Tanta est dependentia accessorii a principali, ut, regulariter loquendo, inducto, concesso, prohibito, annullato, sublato, vel confirmato principali, inductum, concessum, prohibitum, annulatum, sublatum, vel confirmatum etiam censeatur accessorium."—Reiffenstuel, *Ius Canonicum Universum*, vol. VI, *Tractatus de Regulis Iuris* (Romae: 1834), p. 73, Reg. 42, n. 5.

[16]"Accessorium . . . vel ex natura rei vel ex dispositione legis . . . " Reiffenstuel, *op. cit.*, p. 73, Reg. 42, n. 2.

affect the accessory, the opposite is not true. "It is fitting that the accessory follow the nature of the principal",[17] and not that the principal follow the accessory.[18] It would be incongruous for that which is dependent upon another for its essence and existence to affect the more eminent item on which it depends.[19]

In order to explain why a privilege acquired in accessory form should be affected by the same consequences as those which affect the principal, all canonists, without exception, have recourse to Rule 42 of the Rules of Law, which states: "*Accessorium naturam sequi congruit principalis.*" However, since every rule of law admits of exceptions,[20] it might be argued that a privilege acquired through accessory communication is not always subject to the increase, decrease, or loss of the primary grantee's privileges. It is true enough that all the rules of law admit of exceptions; but it must be remembered that exceptions cannot be alleged when the law itself forbids them[21] or when the very nature of the subject precludes the introduction of such exceptions. The rule of law which is quoted in support of the complete dependence of privileges acquired in accessory form upon the principal admits of no exceptions for both the above mentioned reasons. First of all, the terminology of Canon 65 admits no exceptions to the rule. Secondly, the very nature of accessory communication excludes the introduction of any exception because the rule in question suffers an exception only

[17]Reg. 42, R. J., in VI°.

[18]Schmalzgrueber, *Ius Ecclesiasticum Universum*, lib. V, tit. 33, n. 77; Suarez, *De Legibus*, lib. 8, c. 16, n. 12.

[19]Reiffenstuel, *op. cit.*, p. 72, Reg. 42, n. 5.

[20]" . . . nihil enim est tam generaliter dictum quod non recipit exceptionem."—Bernardus Papiensis, *Summa Decretalium*, lib. V, tit. 33, *De Reg. Iuris*, pars 2; "Ut vero omnes aliae Regulae suas exceptiones patiuntur, et in nonnullis casibus fallunt, ita et Regulae Iuris . . . "—Pirhing, *Synopsis Pirhingiana seu Compendiaria SS. Canonum Doctrina* (2. ed. Augustae Vindelicorum et Dilingae: 1695), ad. lib. V, tit. 41; cf. also, Reh, *Rules of Law and Canon Law*, pp. 54-63.

[21]Wernz, *Ius Decretalium* (6 vols., Romae et Prati, 1898-1905), I, n. 134.

when the accessory is divisible from the principal and can exist without the principal.[22] A privilege which is acquired in accessory form, however, is not divisible from the principal, even though the persons favored with a privilege through this source are distinct and even independent of the primary grantee. It must be remembered that it is the privilege which is accessory and not the persons who enjoy the privilege.[23] A privilege acquired through accessory communication is not separable from the privilege which is communicated; and consequently it cannot escape the consequences which affect it, because, in an efficient sense, accessory communication is nothing else but the extension of one and the same privilege to others besides the beneficiaries to whom it was first given.[24] As an indivisible juridic entity, difficult as it might be to imagine it as such, it remains the property of the primary grantee, who retains full control over the privilege to the extent that his privilege is affected only by those acts which are directed immediately to him[25] or by those acts which he himself posits.[26] When and if the primary grantee's privilege is affected by any of these acts, they automatically affect the same privilege which is enjoyed by persons favored with

[22]"Fallit in accessorio quod se solo, et independenter a principali potest subsistere, sicque ab eo divisibile est . . . " Reiffenstuel, *Tractatus de Regulis Iuris*, p. 74, Reg. 42, n. 13.

[23]"Accessorium has reference only to the privileges. It does not consider the dignity of the person who benefits by this method of communication. It may occur that the second grantee may be even more worthy of a privilege than the first . . . "—Roelker, *Principles of Privilege*, p. 51.

[24]" . . . privilegium communicatum accessorie . . . est extensio quaedam eiusdem privilegii."—Suarez, *De Legibus*, lib. 8, c. 16, n. 12; "Communicatio autem imperfecta operatur . . . quando privilegia unius religionis ad familares . . . extenduntur."—Didacus ab Aragonia, *Dilucidatio Privilegiorum Ordinum Regularium*, tr. 1, c. 8, n. 1.

[25]Thus, for example, the primary grantee must be expressly informed of the increase, decrease, or revocation of the privilege.

[26]Thus, the primary grantee can lose his privilege by a legitimate renunciation on his part. Cf. Canon 72. He can be deprived of it because of abuse only when he himself is responsible for the abuse. Canon 78.

accessory communication. Thus, for example, the beneficiary who is favored with accessory communication might not be guilty in the least for abusing a privilege which is the object of accessory communication, while the primary grantee alone is fully and directly responsible for the abuse which eventually prompted the grantor to take the privilege away from him.[27] Nevertheless, in spite of the fact that the person favored with accessory communication is in no way responsible for the recall of the privilege, he is still deprived of the privilege by virtue of the fact that the principal which is its foundation and upon which it depends is destroyed. Although many other examples can be presented to illustrate how the primary grantee retains full and complete control over the privilege which is acquired through accessory communication, only one more will be offered to complete this discussion. Suppose that a real privilege is acquired in accessory form in favor of a church. Now, if the church in which the original principal privilege is vested should suffer destruction it would automatically be deprived of its privilege.[28] So too, the other church would suffer the loss of its privilege despite the fact that the church itself still stands.

Although the principles governing those privileges which are acquired through accessory communication need no further explanation, it is highly important to offer some explanation as to how accessory communication might be identified. Privileges acquired through communication are necessarily acquired in accessory form when they are communicated to beneficiaries in virtue of their accessory juridic condition in relation to the primary grantee. Thus, privileges are acquired accessorily when they are communicated to others because of their association with or dependence upon a primary grantee. Hence, even if the specific nature of communication is not mentioned by the grantor,

[27]Cf. Canon 78.

[28]Canon 75.

there cannot be the slightest doubt that accessory communication takes place when beneficiaries are permitted to acquire the privileges of the primary grantee merely because of their affiliation with or dependence upon the latter.[29] Much more is accessory communication implicitly effected when communication is permitted to beneficiaries, who together with affiliation or dependence upon the primary grantee, are dissimilar from the primary grantee insofar as their juridic condition is concerned. Accessory communication must necessarily serve as the source of communication of privileges for any beneficiaries whose circumstances correspond to the above mentioned condition, because the privileges are given in consideration of the merits or juridic condition of the primary grantee, to whom other beneficiaries, who of their nature cannot partake of the privileges, are assimilated by a fiction of law in order that they may partake of the privileges.[30] Moreover, when communication is permitted in favor of beneficiaries who are assimilated to the primary grantee by a fiction of law in order that they may enjoy privileges which could not otherwise be acquired by them through communication, not only the acquisition and subsequent status of the privilege depends upon the privileges of the primary grantee, but its use is also controlled by the primary grantee.[31]

When the above mentioned characteristics are not realized by a beneficiary favored with communication of privileges, accessory communication can be identified only when

[29] "Communicatio fieri potest . . . accessorie tantum propter connexionem, quomodo privilegia religiosorum communicantur eorum familiaribus, domesticis . . ." Pichler, *Epitome Iuris Canonici iuxta Decretalium Libros Gregorianae Collectionis Explanati*, lib. V, tit. 33, *de privilegiis*, II, p. 665. Cf. also Suarez, *De Legibus*, lib. 8, c. 16, n. 11.

[30] " . . . sic enim hoc privilegium [i. e., communicatum in forma accessoria] dum extenditur ad familiares religionis, aestimare illos videtur tanquam religiosos fictione iuris, vel per quandam habitudinem et analogiam."—Suarez, *De Legibus*, lib. 8, c. 16, n. 12.

[31] " . . . a quo omnino pendet in illorum usu et fructu."—Suarez, *De Legibus*, lib. 8, c. 16, n. 11.

the grantor clearly states that this form of communication is to be enjoyed by a beneficiary in a given instance. Thus, in view of the fact that similarity of juridic condition and juridic independence of beneficiaries are characteristics which favor equal communication,[32] it would be necessary for the grantor to state expressly that accessory communication is intended when beneficiaries possessing these characteristics are permitted to enjoy communication of privileges. In such instances the relation between the accessory and principal and the absolute dependence of the former upon the latter would pertain exclusively to the privileges and not to the beneficiaries who enjoy the privileges. Whether the use of the privilege which is thus acquired through accessory communication is in any way subject to the primary grantee remains to be seen.

It was mentioned above[33] that not only the acquisition but also the use of a privilege acquired in accessory form depends upon the primary grantee. However, the primary grantee's right to control the use of the privilege is not as unconditional as Suarez implies.[34] It is easy to understand why the primary grantee should have such an absolute right when the primary grantee and the subject favored with accessory communication are so closely allied that the unrestricted use of the privilege by the latter would endanger uniformity of discipline. Hence, undoubtedly a religious community had full and complete control over the use of a privilege by novices, who, in the old law, were permitted to enjoy communication of privileges through the religious order in which they were enrolled.[35] So too, it is reasonable that the primary grantee should control the use of privileges which are acquired in accessory form by those who are subject to the jurisdiction of the primary grantee

[32]Cf. *supra,* pages 69-73.

[33]Cf. *supra,* pages 20-22.

[34]Cf. *supra,* page 176, note 31.

[35]Cf. Rodericus, E., *Quaestiones Regulares et Canonicae,* III, q. 52, art. 12.

in disciplinary and administrative matters, as nuns and third orders of seculars were in the former discipline. Thus, it would seem that religious orders, through their superiors or general chapters, could control the use of privileges acquired in accessory form by those beneficiaries who were subject to the jurisdiction of the religious order of men. It seems only reasonable that the primary grantee should have some control over the use of privileges acquired in accessory form under the above mentioned circumstances. However, in view of the fact that this question is not contemplated by documents of communication nor by canonists, except Suarez, who mentions this point only casually, it would be extremely difficult to determine the limits of the primary grantee's right to control the use of a privilege acquired in accessory form. In any event, this much is certain. First of all, the beneficiary favored with a privilege through accessory communication must necessarily use it in exactly the same way as it is used by the primary grantee, nor can he ever use it in such a way that it would bring any harm to the primary grantee. The observance of these regulations by subjects of accessory communication is especially necessary in those instances when the basis of communication is founded on a formal as well as a material association between the primary grantee and the subject of accessory communication, as is the case between members of a religious order and the lay servants who might enjoy a communication of privileges through the former. Hence, if the primary grantee (the religious order in the example given above) were to acquire privileges which are later communicated to the accessory (lay servants), the latter could not arbitrarily refuse to use those privileges if such a refusal would in any way prejudice the primary grantee. Failure to use a privilege by subjects of accessory communication under the above mentioned conditions would be very reprehensible. If failure to use a privilege by subjects of accessory communication would entail no harm or prejudice to the primary grantee, there is no reason why the former subjects could not exercise the option of using or not using the privilege acquired through accessory communication. However, even if the subjects of accessory communication would refrain from using a privilege acquired through communication, the failure to use such a privilege would never effect the cessation of the privilege.[36] Subjects of accessory communication might lose their right of enjoying a certain privilege as a result of non-use; but the privilege itself must necessarily remain intact because accessory communication implies that there is only one privilege which remains under the control of the primary grantee. Non-use of a privilege on the part of subjects of accessory communication might restrict the scope of a privilege as far as subjects of a privilege are concerned, but non-use on the part of subjects of accessory communication cannot destroy the privilege. If the privilege which is the object of accessory communication cannot be destroyed by mere non-use on the part of the beneficiaries of such a communication, much less would these same beneficiaries enjoy the right of renouncing a privilege.[37] Subjects of accessory communication can never renounce a privilege acquired through communication which is based on dependence or affiliation with a primary grantee.[38] The right of renouncing a privilege must be denied to the subjects of accessory communication because they do not acquire a distinct normative right over which they might exercise full control independently of the primary grantee. As will be observed shortly, the right to renounce the privilege which is the object of accessory communication belongs exclusively to the primary grantee.

Secondly, the primary grantee exercises complete control

[36]Cf. Canon 76 to determine how a privilege might pass out of existence as a result of non-use.

[37]Renunciation of a privilege signifies the destruction of a privilege. The rules for renunciation are presented in Canon 72.

[38]Castro Palao, *Opus Morale*, tract. 3, disp. 4, punct. 17, n. 1; Reiffenstuel, *Ius Canonicum Universum*, V, 33, n. 194; Schmalzgrueber, *Ius Ecclesiasticum Universum*, V, 33, n. 178; Van Hove, *De Privilegiis*, n. 245.

over the privilege, which is the object of accessory communication, for himself as well as for the person favored with the benefits of accessory communication. The primary grantee exercises such control in so far as he alone, apart from revocation by competent authority, can bring about the cessation of a privilege by non-use, contrary use,[39] or by legitimate renunciation.[40]

It certainly is reasonable that the primary grantee should have some right to control the use of a privilege acquired in accessory form by beneficiaries who are subject to the jurisdiction of the primary grantee or are so closely associated with him that an uncontrolled use of the privilege acquired through this form of communication would disrupt good order in society. However, even though that right cannot be denied to the primary grantee in the above mentioned circumstances, it can be questioned whether the primary grantee has any right to decide how and when a privilege should be used by a beneficiary favored with privileges in accessory form when that beneficiary is juridically independent of the primary grantee, not affiliated with the primary grantee by any juridic bond, nor associated with him by reason of material proximity. In so far as it can be determined, there is no doctrinal opinion, nor even any speculation among canonists, on this point. Moreover, it is certain that there is no express general legal provision concerning this question. However, despite this deficiency, two arguments can be adduced to show that the primary grantee has no right, under the specified circumstances, to control the use of a privilege acquired in accessory form. First of all, justice demands that duly acquired rights be

[39]"Per non usum vel per usum contrarium privilegia aliis haud onerosa non cessant; quae vero in aliorum gravamen cedunt, amittuntur, si accedat legitima praescriptio vel tacita renuntiatio."—Canon 76. Obviously a privilege can be lost through non-use or contrary use when the conditions stipulated in the latter part of the canon are fulfilled.

[40]Canon 72, § 1, § 3, § 4. § 2 of this Canon is excluded because, in practice, communication never served as a source of privileges for private individuals.

respected by others.[41] It might be objected that recourse to an argument from justice is just as applicable to those circumstances in which primary grantee and subject of accessory communication are closely united by a bond of formal and material unity as it would be in this instance. If such an objection were raised it would lead to the inference that all subjects of accessory communication, regardless of their juridic condition, would be free from the control of the primary grantee in regard to the use of a privilege acquired through accessory communication. Such an objection and the logical deduction therefrom is not a valid one because the higher good of uniform discipline and well regulated order in society demands that subjects of accessory communication, which is based on close affiliation or dependence, yield to the supremacy of the primary grantee in this matter. Moreover, since these subjects of accessory communication enjoy the privileges of the primary grantee merely because of their close affiliation with the latter, it is only reasonable that the latter would have the full right of interpreting the scope of the privilege as well as the conditions under which the subject of accessory communication might use the privilege. Secondly, Canon 722, by means of which aggregated confraternities are permitted to acquire the privileges of the aggregating confraternity or primary union,[42] stipulates that the latter

[41] "Haec obligatio . . . oritur . . . ex ipsa natura rerum ex facto quod aliquis legitime gaudet aliqua praerogativa ex concessione principis."—Van Hove, *De Privilegiis*, p. 29, n. 25.

[42] "Per aggregationem communicantur omnes indulgentiae, privilegia et àliae gratiaę spirituales communicabiles quae associationi aggreganti directe et nominatim a Sede Apostolica concessae fuerint vel in posterum concedantur, nisi aliud in indulto apostolico caveatur."—Canon 722, § 1. Although the Code does not expressly state through what form of communication the aggregated association acquires the privileges of the aggregating association, it is generally deduced that communication in accessory form is implied. Cf. Van Hove, *De Privilegiis*, p. 144, n. 149; Vasto, *De Communicatione Privilegiorum*, p. 53, n. 84. Cicognani does not commit himself on this point. He implies that it is different from communication in accessory form

associations acquire no right over the former by virtue of the communication of privileges which is permitted to the former.[43]

As sound as these reasons might seem to be, they do not offer a final solution to the problem about the primary grantee's right to control the use of the privileges acquired in accessory form by a beneficiary who is juridically independent of the primary grantee. In so far as the first reason is concerned, it must be remembered that accessory communication never gives rise to an independent privilege over which the beneficiary of this form of communication acquires an absolute right.[44] It is the primary grantee who retains that absolute unconditional right by means of which he alone, independently of the beneficiary of accessory communication, can decide the fate of the privilege not only for himself but also for the one who acquires the privilege through accessory communication. Furthermore, the absolute mastery which the primary grantee always retains over the privilege acquired by another in accessory form is in no way conditioned by the juridic status of the latter. Nor is that right shared by the latter, who can

but does not state that it is either accessory or equal communication.—*Canon Law*, p. 788. That accessory communication is intended may be deduced from the fact that the aggregating association enjoys the greater dignity of the two associations. The aggregated society not only acquires its privileges through the aggregating society, but also its existence as a juridic person. In view of this it is only reasonable that the former should acquire the privileges in accessory form and not through equal communication. It cannot be inferred that privileges are acquired through equal communication because the Code deprives the aggregating society of all rights over the aggregated society. By depriving the aggregating society of its right to control the aggregated society, the Code denies it the right which would belong to it by nature. However, it is unlikely that it intends to permit the aggregated society to acquire privileges which would be independent of the primary grantee's privileges.

[43]"Ex hac communicatione nullum ius associatio aggregans acquirit supra aggregatam."—Canon 722, § 2.

[44]Cf. *supra*, page 23. " . . . there is *one* privilege."—Cicognani, *Canon Law*, p. 704.

never decide the fate of the privilege for the primary grantee. The juridic status of the beneficiary of accessory communication has no bearing on the status of the privilege acquired in accessory form and its absolute dependence upon the principal. Thus, if the primary grantee exercises his right of renouncing a certain privilege, in so far as this is permitted by law,[45] the beneficiary of accessory communication is automatically deprived of that privilege whether he approves of the renunciation or not.[46] In view of the fact that the primary grantee has such an absolute and exclusive right[47] over the fate of the privilege, it might be argued that he always has the right to control its use, which right is assuredly less than the right to cause its destruction. If the primary grantee were to determine how and when a privilege should be used by a beneficiary of accessory communication, he would not be interfering with the rights of another; but he would merely be controlling the use of a privilege, which, strictly speaking, is exclusively his, and is enjoyed by others only in his name.[48] In the face of these arguments favoring the primary grantee's right to control the use of privileges acquired in accessory form even by those beneficiaries who are juridically independent of the primary grantee, it would be somewhat difficult to determine whether religious orders of men can in any way control the use of privileges acquired by nuns in accessory form[49] by virtue of Canon 613, § 2. However, in spite of the fact that the provisions of Canon 722 pertain specifically to confraternities, it seems plausible to use the

[45]Cf. Canon 72.

[46]Cf. Suarez, *De Legibus*, lib. 8, c. 16, n. 12.

[47]Naturally, this right is conditioned by the will of the grantor, and by the provisions of law. Thus, under some circumstances, he could not renounce the privilege. Cf. Canon 72, § 4.

[48]" . . . non in propriis personis censeatur illis concessum privilegium sed in alio."—Suarez, *De Legibus*, lib. 8, c. 16, n. 11.

[49]Van Hove, *De Privilegiis*, p. 144, n. 149; Roelker, *Principles of Privilege*, p. 52; Vermeersch—Creusen, *Epitome Iuris Canonici*, I, n. 181.

provisions of this canon to solve the problem.[50] Hence, it can be maintained in practice that the primary grantee has no right to control the use of privileges acquired in accessory form, neither in this instance nor in others where the beneficiary of this form of communication is juridically independent of the primary grantee. However, the application of these provisions must necessarily preserve the primary grantee's right to control the use of a privilege acquired in accessory form by juridically independent beneficiaries when its use by the latter would endanger good order in society or when its use would conflict with the privileges enjoyed by the primary grantee. In both instances, the primary grantee would have the right to restrict the use of a privilege by the beneficiary of accessory communication on the strength of the juridic pre-eminence usually enjoyed by the primary grantee when accessory communication of privileges is permitted.[51] However, even though there is perfect juridic similarity between the primary grantee and the beneficiary of accessory communication, the former's privilege would generally have the stronger right[52] because his privilege is always acquired

[50]"Leges ecclesiasticae . . . quae dubia et obscura manserit, ad locos Codicis parallelos, si qui sint . . . est recurrendum."—Canon 18.

[51]When accessory communication is permitted to beneficiaries because of their affiliation or dependence upon the primary grantee, the beneficiary of accessory communication is juridically inferior by virtue of the fact that he could not acquire the privileges of the primary grantee except on the basis of his affiliation with him. In such cases there is an obvious accessory and principal relationship between the beneficiaries. Such a relationship does not actually exist when privileges are communicated in accessory form to a beneficiary who is juridically similar to and independent of the primary grantee, but because the privilege is communicated in accessory form, there is at least a fictional accessory to principal relationship, which makes the primary grantee juridically more eminent than the beneficiary of accessory communication.

[52]Cf. *supra*, page 16 to see when the beneficiary of equal communication can defend himself against the primary grantee's use of the privilege which is acquired by the former through communication. All canonists without exception agree that the beneficiary of accessory communication cannot use

first. On the strength of this priority in time, the primary grantee's right to control the use of privileges in the above-mentioned eventualities should be justified. However, notwithstanding any right which the primary grantee might have in controlling the use of a privilege by the beneficiary of accessory communication, the privilege itself is always automatically subject to the same consequences as those which affect the privileges for the primary grantee.[53]

Article 2. Relationship Between a Primary Grantee's Privilege and a Privilege Acquired Through Equal Communication

The last part of Canon 65 is devoted to a statement of the relationship which exists between the primary grantee's privileges and those same privileges which are acquired by another through equal communication. Although the provisions contained in Canon 65 regarding this form of communication are indirect,[54] they cannot be misunderstood when they are interpreted in the light of the provisions which precede it.[55] Hence, if the concluding part of Canon 65 were transposed into a direct statement, it would read as follows: When privileges are acquired through equal communication they are not automatically increased, diminished, or lost with the increase, diminution, or loss of the primary grantee's privileges.

Although enough has already been said about the nature

a privilege acquired through accessory communication against the primary grantee. Cf. Rodericus, H., *Quaestiones Regulares et Canonicae Enucleatae,* p. 836, n. 53; Salmanticeness, *Cursus Theologiae Moralis,* II, tract. 18, c. 1, punct. 7, § II, n. 102.

[53]Canon 65.

[54]" . . . secus si acquirantur per communicationem in forma aeque principali."

[55]"Cum privilegia acquiruntur per communicationem in forma accessoria, augentur, imminuuntur vel amittuntur ipso facto, si forte augeantur, imminuantur vel cessent in principali privilegiario . . . "—Canon 65.

of equal communication,[56] it is not amiss to review, in summary fashion, the distinctive features of equal communication, comparing these with the characteristics of accessory communication. Such a summary review will serve as a helpful foundation for the proper understanding of the provisions contained in the concluding part of Canon 65.

Just as communication in accessory form implies that a beneficiary of communication acquires a privilege which is first acquired by another, so equal communication is necessarily characterized by this same feature. However, except for this characteristic which is common to both forms of communication, equal communication differs widely from communication in accessory form. Like accessory communication, equal communication favors another with a privilege which is formally the same as that which is made the object of communication through the benevolence of the grantor. Unlike accessory communication, however, it favors a beneficiary with a privilege which is numerically distinct from the object of communication.[57] The privilege which is thus materially reproduced through equal communication becomes equally principal with the object of communication, as is indicated by the official title of this species of communication. Thus, both the object of communication and the privilege which it fashions are self-subsisting entities,[58] in no way subject to the modifications which affect either the privilege acquired through equal communication or the primary grantee's privilege which served as its model. Finally, the beneficiary to whom a privilege accrues through equal communication acquires absolute ownership, subject, of course, to the will of the grantor, of a privilege in the same way as he would if the

[56]Cf. *supra*, pages 13-22.

[57]Suarez, *De Legibus*, lib. 8, c. 16, n. 12.

[58]"Principale est quod per se stat, seu propria sua virtute subsistit."—Reiffenstuel, *Tractatus de Regulis Iuris*, VI, 73, Reg. 42, n. 2; cf. also Cicognani, *Canon Law*, p. 704.

privilege were granted directly.[59] Hence, in view of the fact that a beneficiary of equal communication acquires a privilege which is numerically distinct and independent of the model privilege and in view of the fact that the privilege acquired through equal communication is juridically the same as one which is acquired through direct concession,[60] it is easy to understand why the increase, diminution, or loss of the primary grantee's privilege cannot affect that which is acquired through equal communication.[61] Conversely, the increase, diminution, or loss of the privilege which is acquired through equal communication does not affect the primary grantee's privilege. Thus, if the privileges of the Benedictine Order were acquired through equal communication by the Dominican Order, each Order possesses an independent privilege, which can be increased, diminished, or lost only when the respective beneficiaries are expressly notified of the increase, diminution, or revocation of its privilege. Obviously, in so far as the privileges of these beneficiaries are concerned they can be extended, limited, or revoked when any such changes or revocations are directed to the regulars in general. What is important, however, is the fact that a particular privilege which was acquired through equal communication is not affected for both orders if the increase, diminution, or revocation is applied only to one or the other. Moreover, a beneficiary of equal communication, or, conversely, the primary grantee does not suffer the loss of a privilege which is the object of equal communication when it is lost by only one of the

[59]It has already been pointed out that equal communication, in an efficient sense, is essentially the same as direct concession, from which it differs only accidentally. This accidental difference is constituted by the manner in which the nature of a privilege is specified. The nature of a privilege acquired through equal communication is determined by the privilege of another; the nature of a privilege acquired through direct concession is specified by the grantor. Cf. *supra*, pages 16 and 17.

[60]" . . . perinde ac si specialiter et expresse concessa fuissent . . . "—Pius VI, Const. *Inter multiplices*, 14 dec. 1792—*BRC*, VI, 2569.

[61]Cf. Canon 65.

parties through legitimate renunciation,[62] non-use or contrary use.[63] In order to suffer the loss of a privilege which is the object of equal communication, either the primary grantee or the beneficiary of equal communication must be directly responsible for the acts which lead to its loss. In view of the fact that a beneficiary of equal communication becomes the owner of an independent privilege, it is obvious that his privilege cannot be renounced by another who has no control over that privilege. Similarly, his privilege cannot be abused and subsequently taken away from him because another abused a similar privilege.

Despite the fact that the provisions of Canon 65 seem to demand no further elaboration, one point, however, needs to be clarified. Thus, it cannot be maintained as unequivocally as Canon 65 seems to imply, that a privilege acquired through equal communication is never affected by the increase of the primary grantee's privilege. In regard to the possible increase of a privilege acquired through equal communication, it must be noted whether the beneficiary favored with the advantages of this source is permitted to acquire those privileges which will be granted to the primary grantee in the future. It has already been pointed out that a beneficiary to whom communication is made available can acquire only those privileges which had been granted to the primary grantee,[64] unless it is expressly mentioned by the grantor that privileges which will be given to the primary grantee after communication is permitted are also included within the scope of this source.[65]

[62]Canon 72.

[63]Canon 76.

[64]Cf. *supra*, page 145. Consult also Castro Palao, *Opus Morale*, tr. 3, disp. 4, punct. 2, n. 9.

[65]" . . . ubi princeps vult largiorem facere communicationem, addit specialia verba quibus expresse declarat, non tantum communicare privilegia concessa, sed etiam concedenda . . . "—Cf. Suarez, *De Legibus*, lib. 8, c. 16, n. 16.

Such was the force of communication of privileges as enjoyed by religious orders before the promulgation of the Code,[66] which prescribes that religious institutes can no longer acquire privileges through this source.[67] However, despite the fact that this comprehensive communication is no longer available to religious institutes, equal communication is a potential source of privileges for them[68] and an actual source of privileges for other beneficiaries.[69] Hence, if equal communication is made available to any beneficiaries to serve as a source of not only of privileges already acquired by the primary grantee but also of those which will be acquired by him, the privileges acquired by the beneficiary of equal communication would enjoy the same increase as the primary grantee's privileges which served as the model for the acquisition.[70] There is no doubt that the beneficiary of equal communication can profit by the increase of the primary grantee's privileges when the former is favored with communication which extends to future privileges. However, when the beneficiary of equal communication profits by such an increase, the privilege which is acquired through equal communication is not increased because it is dependent upon the primary grantee's privilege. Equal communication abolishes that dependence. It is increased under the above-mentioned circumstances because such an extension[71] of a privilege is comparable to a

[66]Consult, for example, Leo X, Const. *Dudum per nos,* 10 dec. 1509—*BRT,* V, 732; Pius V, Const. *Ex Supernae,* 16, aug. 1567—*BRT,* VII, 584.

[67]Cf. Canon 613, § 1.

[68]"The Roman Pontiff is well able to grant this in future to some religious organization, or to several, or even to all . . . "—Cicognani, *Canon Law,* p. 704.

[69]Thus, since the promulgation of the Code privileges have been communicated through equal communication from one church to another. Consult, *AAS,* XI, (1919), 68, 457; XIV (1922), 5.

[70]Cf. Salmanticenses, *Cursus Theologiae Moralis,* II, tract. 18, c. 1. punct. 7, § 1, n. 95; Suarez, *De Legibus,* lib. 8, c. 16, n. 8.

[71]Extension here signifies the augmenting of the object of a privilege.

new concession. Since the beneficiary of equal communication is permitted to acquire all of the primary grantee's privileges, without regard to time of concession, it is only logical that he should profit by the increase of a primary grantee's privilege, which increase, in reality, is a new privilege. However, because the increase of a privilege is substantially the same as a new concession, the beneficiary of equal communication can profit by such an increase provided that its acquisition is not proscribed implicitly or explicitly. Thus, for example, the increase of a primary grantee's privilege would be of no avail to the beneficiary of equal communication if the grantor extends its scope for a special reason or for a determined length of time. Such increases would not profit the beneficiary of equal communication because privileges granted for special reasons[72] or temporarily are not liable to communication.[73]

Since Canon 65 makes no provision for the possible increase of a privilege acquired through equal communication, it might be inferred that its provisions are inadequate. This, however, is not the case because Canon 65 is only concerned with a statement of the logical consequences of equal communication, which produces a separate and independent privilege that can never be affected by the increase, diminution, or loss of a privilege which is numerically distinct. The increase of a privilege acquired through equal communication under the circumstances described above is no exception to this inflexible rule. In the strict sense, the privilege acquired through equal communication is not increased. Only the primary grantee's privilege is increased. If it favors the beneficiary of equal communication, it comes to him as a new privilege, which he is permitted to acquire by virtue of communication which extends to all privileges, irrespective of the time at which they are granted.

[72]Cf. *supra*, page 156, note 74.

[73]Canon 64.

Article 3. Confirmation of the Primary Grantee's Privileges and Its Effects upon Privileges Acquired Through Equal Communication

Another important corollary flowing from the theory of equal communication is the one which concerns the possible effects of a confirmation[74] of the primary grantee's privileges upon the privileges acquired through equal communication. Those canonists who discuss this specific point[75]

[74]Confirmation of a privilege is an authoritative corroboration or approval of already acquired privileges. There are two species of confirmation: (a) confirmation "*in forma specifica*" or "*ex certa scientia*"; (b) confirmation "*in forma communi.*" The former, which is equivalent to a new concession, is capable of sanating all defective or invalidly acquired privileges, unless their invalidity is due to subreption or obreption. It was the common pre-Code opinion, to which all modern canonists, except Michiels (cf. *Normae Generales,* II, p. 352, note 4 and 353, note 1), subscribe, that privileges acquired surreptitiously or obreptitiously are not sanated by a specific confirmation because the grantor is presumed to have no knowledge of such privileges. Other privileges, which are validly acquired but later lost through non-use or contrary use, or those which are revoked by common law or by a special act of the competent superior are sanated by a specific confirmation. (b) Confirmation '*in forma communi*' or simple confirmation is nothing other than a mere approval of existing privileges. Such an approval or confirmation gives added force to the privileges, which might be questioned by others, but it is not considered a new concession, nor does it have the far-reaching effects which are attached to a specific confirmation. Before the time of Suarez, there was no uniform opinion about the identification of either form of confirmation especially when significant words were not used. Since his time, however, it has been the accepted teaching that privileges are presumed to be confirmed by a simple confirmation, when the confirmation is not qualified by any significant terminology, such as "*ex certa scientia,*" "*de plenitudine potestatis,*" "*non obstante lege disponente in contrarium,*" etc. For fuller details concerning the theory of confirmation of privileges, the reader is referred to Suarez, *De Legibus*, lib. 8, c. 18; Castro Palao, *Opus Morale*, tract. 3, disp. 4, punct. 2; Reiffenstuel, *Ius Canonicum Universum*, lib. 2, tit. 30; Salmanticenses, *Cursus Theologiae Moralis*, tract. 18, c. 1, punct. 4; Michiels, *Normae Generales*, II, p. 352-355; Van Hove, *De Privilegiis*, pp. 56-61.

[75]Suarez, *De Legibus*, lib. 8, c. 19, nn. 8-14; Salmanticenses, *Cursus Theologiae Moralis*, tract. 18, c. 2; Van Hove, *De Privilegiis*, pp. 142-143, n. 147; Vasto, *De Communicatione Privilegiorum*, p. 66, n. 94.

maintain that equal communication, through which a beneficiary is permitted to acquire all of the primary grantee's privileges, (i.e. those that have been granted and those that will be granted) makes it possible for a beneficiary of this source to profit by a specific confirmation which corroborates the primary grantee's privilege. Basing their argument on the premise that a specific confirmation is juridically equivalent to a new concession,[76] these canonists conclude that a beneficiary of equal communication[77] must necessarily profit by a specific confirmation even though it is issued expressly in favor of the primary grantee. Suarez reports that it was the probable opinion among his predecessors that a beneficiary of equal communication could claim the benefits of any specific confirmation approving the primary grantee's privileges.[78] The proponents of this opinion based their arguments on the purpose of equal communication, which they claimed was instituted in order to establish an equality between the beneficiary of equal communication and the primary grantee. If a specific confirmation is equivalent to a new privilege —which fact has never been questioned— they argued that it would be contrary to the mind of the grantor to proscribe the communication of any specific confirmation because the equality which the grantor intended to establish between the primary grantee and the beneficiary of equal communication would not be preserved.[79] Suarez admits the soundness of

[76]" . . . subinde concessioni aequivalet, vel reipsa est concessio, licet verbum sit confirmandi . . . " Suarez, *De Legibus*, lib. 8, c. 19, n. 12; Van Hove, *De Privilegiis*, p. 56, n. 55.

[77]It must be remembered that this discussion concerns only equal communication which can serve as a source for the primary grantee's future privileges. It does not apply to equal communication through which a beneficiary is permitted to acquire only those privileges which had been previously granted to the primary grantee.

[78]"Praedicta sententia probabilis . . . "—Suarez, *De Legibus*, lib. 8, c. 19, n. 11.

[79]" . . . alias non manerent illae duae . . . aequales, quod est contra mentem pontificis."—Suarez, *De Legibus*, lib. 8, c. 19, n. 11.

the premises on which the above mentioned conclusion is based but he discredits the validity of their conclusion, which maintains that every specific confirmation, regardless of the privileges which it confirms, is liable to communication. The fallacy of such a conclusion consists in this that it considers a specific confirmation as a distinct entity, thus separating it from the pre-existing privileges to which it is directed and without which it has no separate existence. Such a conclusion is directly opposed to the mind of the grantor, who, in issuing a specific confirmation to a specific grantee, is presupposed to have a knowledge of those privileges alone, which were acquired by the grantee in whose favor the confirmation is issued.[80] It cannot be argued that the purpose of equal communication —i.e., equality between the beneficiaries— is voided by such a restriction. If it were admitted that such a restriction contradicts the purpose of equal communication, then, it must also be admitted that its purpose is nullified when it is taught that certain privileges cannot be acquired through this source.

Although Suarez discredits the conclusion reached by his predecessors, he does not discard it entirely. It was he who proposed the opinion, common since his time, that a specific confirmation issued in favor of the primary grantee is advantageous to a beneficiary of equal communication when that confirmation is directed to the privileges which are made the object of equal communication. However, Suarez does not teach, as some imply,[81] that the specific confirmation as such is acquired through equal communication. The confirmation as such is not acquired through equal communication, because it is intrinsically impossible to acquire an

[80]"Maximeque urget haec ratio in confirmatione ex certa scientia quia Papa non habet vel praesumitur habere scientiam aliorum privilegiorum, sed eorum tantum quae directe ac expresse ex tali scientia confirmat; ergo illa confirmatio non potest per communicationem transire ad alia privilegia dissimilia."—Suarez, *De Legibus*, lib. 8, c. 19, n. 12.

[81]Salmanticenses. *Cursus Theologiae Moralis*, II, tract. 18, c. 2; Van Hove, *De Privilegiis*, n. 147, note 2.

entity which cannot exist without a foundation. Confirmation always presupposes a pre-existing privilege in consideration of which it is issued. The confirmation, as such, cannot be acquired by the beneficiary of equal communication because his privilege is distinct from the primary grantee's privilege, which alone the grantor intends to approve. The one favored with the benefits of equal communication profits by a specific confirmation of the primary grantee's privilege only indirectly without acquiring the confirmation as such. Let it be supposed that a privilege acquired through direct concession by the primary grantee is communicated to another through equal communication. Let it be supposed further that the former privilege is revoked by the grantor, and the latter is lost through renunciation. Later, the grantor specifically confirms the privileges of the primary grantee. If no reason, such as contrary law or express prohibition, obviates the restoration of the privilege previously revoked, the privilege in question is revived through a specific confirmation.[82] Although only the primary grantee's privilege is restored by such a confirmation, it indirectly favors the beneficiary of equal communication by permitting him to acquire that same privilege (formally only) which was lost by renunciation. Proceeding further with his theory of the effects of a confirmation on privileges acquired through equal communication, Suarez maintains that a simple confirmation (*confirmatio in forma communi*) also favors a beneficiary of equal communication in an indirect way.[83] However, in view of the fact that a simple confirmation has no revalidating effects, it is hard to imagine what practical advantage a beneficiary of equal communication would derive from such a confirmation except to know that the privilege which served as the model for his has the grantor's approval.

[82]Cf. Reiffenstuel, *Ius Canonicum Universum*, lib. V, tit. 33, n. 78.

[83]*De Legibus*, lib. 8, c. 19, n. 10.

With this discussion concerning the effects of a confirmation on privileges acquired through equal communication, the commentary on Canon 65 as well as the analysis of the theory of communication of privileges is brought to a close.

CONCLUSIONS

From the foregoing analysis of the theory of communication of privileges, the following conclusions are drawn:

A. Conclusions drawn from the study of the history of the institute:

1. All canonists admit that the institute of communication is an adaptation from the Roman Law concession *ad instar*, but its introduction into the Church's system of privileges can be traced to Pope Gregory IX, who first used this method of granting privileges in 1233.

2. Neither the word "communication" itself, nor any of its derivatives, was used in reference to this source of privileges before the reign of Pope Leo X (1513-1521), who first used these terms in 1519. Other technical terms, associated with communication, such as *aeque-principaliter*, *pariformiter*, etc. were previously used by Pope Pius II (1458-1464) in 1462.

3. Reciprocal communication, which implies that privileges given to either party favored with the benefits of this source are automatically acquired by the other, is a distinctively ecclesiastical source of privileges. It was introduced by Pope Sixtus IV (1471-1484) in the year 1474.

B. Conclusions drawn from the study of the theory of the institute of communication.

1. The institute of communication cannot be styled a law or a privilege any more than direct concession, custom, or prescription may be styled as such. Like these institutes, communication is a legal source of privileges established by the legislator to serve as the instrumental cause of privileges.

2. Neither the word "communication," nor any of its derivatives, need be used by the grantor to reveal the operation of this source. As long as it is evident that a beneficiary depends upon the privileges of another for the specification of his own, communication serves as the source for those privileges.

3. Of all the technical terms used in conjunction with this source of privileges—e.g., *aeque-principaliter, pariformiter, sine ulla differentia, ad instar,* etc.,—*aeque-principaliter* alone reveals that an equal communication is effected by virtue of its inherent signification. According to the consensus of canonists, the term *ad instar* connotes the effects of an equal communication. No doctrinal meaning is attached to the terms *pariformiter* and *sine ulla differentia.* Their connotation in regard to the species of communication must be determined from the nature of the subjects who are permitted to enjoy the benefits of this source of privileges.

4. In the absence of any significant terminology in conjunction with this source, an equal communication can be presumed in favor of juridically similar and juridically independent beneficiaries.

5. Accessory communication is implied by the grantor, even if such terms as *pariformiter* or *sine ulla differentia* are used by him, when beneficiaries, favored with communication of privileges, are dependent upon or closely affiliated with the primary grantee and for that reason are permitted to acquire the privileges of the primary grantee. The technical phrase "*in forma accessoria*" does not appear in any of the papal documents which were studied.

6. The identification of a privilege with other favorable concessions, which are intrinsically different from a privilege, and hence, the inference that they are included within the scope of communication of privileges, are unwarranted in present law, even though it was quite generally assumed that they were included within the scope of communication in the pre-Code era. Advanced juridic opinion, and the Code of Canon Law, which acknowledges a sharp distinction between various favorable concessions, do not admit the inclusion of dispensations, indulgences, rescripts, and favors within the scope of communication. These items must be expressly mentioned in order that they may be claimed through communication; but in that case there is not pres-

ent any communication of privileges, but rather a communication of whatever specific concession has been granted, as, for example, communication of indulgences, rescripts, etc.

6. By prescribing that communicable privileges must be conceded directly, the Code does not exclude those privileges which have been acquired through custom or prescription.

7. The Code also implies that incommunicable, exorbitant, detrimental, prejudicial, and revoked privileges cannot be acquired through communication.

8. Privileges prejudicial to the rights of another cannot be acquired through communication when communication of privileges is permitted only in general. When specific prejudicial privileges are mentioned by the grantor as subject to communication, their acquisition through this source cannot be proscribed.

9. Beneficiaries of an accessory communication who are juridically related to the primary grantee as accessory to the principal depend upon the latter for the acquisition as well as the use of the privilege. Beneficiaries of an accessory communication who are juridically independent of the primary grantee are free from the primary grantee's control of their privilege except when its use would endanger the primary grantee's rights or infringe upon a required uniformity of discipline.

BIBLIOGRAPHY

SOURCES

Acta Apostolicae Sedis, Commentarium Officiale, Romae, 1909-.

Acta Sanctae Sedis, 41 vols., Romae, 1865-1908.

Bullarum Diplomatum et Privilegiorum Sanctorum Romanorum Pontificum Taurinensis Editio, auspicante Cardinali Francisco Gaude, 25 vols., Augustae Taurinorum, 1857-1872.

Bullarii Romani Continuatio Summorum Pontificum, 19 vols., Prato, 1756-1883.

Bullarium Ordinis Praedicatorum, editum a Th. Ripoli, 8 vols., Romae, 1729-1883.

Canones et Decreta Sacrosancti Oecumenici Concilii Tridentini, Romae, ex typographis polyglotta S. C. de Propaganda Fidei, 1882.

Codex Iuris Canonici Pii X Pontificis Maximi iussu digestus Benedicti Papae XV auctoritate promulgatus, Romae, Typis Polyglottis Vaticanis, 1917.

Codicis Iuris Canonici Fontes, cura Emi. Petri Card. Gasparri Editi, 9 vols., Romae (later Civitate Vaticana) : Typis Polyglottis Vaticanis, 1923-1939. (Vols. VII-IX ed. *cura et studio Emi Iustiniani Card. Seredi*.)

Collectanea in usum Secretariae Sacrae Congregationis Episcoporum et Regularium, ed. A. Bizzarri, Romae, 1885.

Corpus Iuris Canonici, Editio Lipsiensis II (Richter-Friedberg), 2 vols., Lipsiae, 1879-1881. Editio anastatice repetita, Lipsiae, 1922.

Corpus Iuris Civilis, 3 vols., Berolini: apud Weidmannos, 1928-1929;
Vol. I, ed. stereotypa quinta decima, *Institutiones*,—Paul Krueger;
Digesta,—Theodorum Mommsen, retractavit Paulus Krueger;
Vol. II, ed. stereot. decima, *Codex Iustinianus*,—Paul Krueger.
Vol. III, ed. stereot. quinta, *Novellae*,—Rudolphus Schoell; opus Schoelli morte interceptum absolvit Guilielmus Kroll.

Decreta Authentica Congregationis Sacrorum Rituum, 6 vols., Romae, 1898-1927.

Decreta Authentica Sacrae Congregationis Indulgentiis Sacrisque Reliquiis ab Anno 1668 ad Annum 1882, edita iussu et auctoritate Sanctissimi D. N. Leonis P. P. XIII, Ratisbonae, Neo-Eboraci, Cincinattis, 1883.

Denziger, H., et Bannwart, C., et Umberg, J., *Enchiridion Symbolorum, Definitionum, et Declarationum de Rebus Fidei et Morum*, 21-23 ed., Friburgi Brisgoviae: Herder, 1937.

Hardouin, Jean, *Acta Conciliorum et Epistolae Decretales ac Constitutiones Summorum Pontificum*, 12 vols., Parisiis, 1715.

Jaffé, P., *Regesta Pontificum Romanorum ab condita ecclesia ad annum 1198*, 2 ed., cura Wattenbach, Loewenfeld, Kaltenbrunner, Ewald, 2 vols. in 1, Lipsiae, 1885-1888.

Leonis XIII Pontificis Maximi Acta, 22 vols., Romae: ex typographia Vaticana, 1881-1903.

Liber Sextus Decretalium, una cum Clementinis et Extravagantibus earumque glossis restitutis, Romae, 1582.

Mansi, Ioannes, *Sacrorum Conciliorum Nova et Amplissima Collectio*, 53 vols. in 59, Parisiis, 1901-1927.

Migne, J. P., *Patrologiae Cursus Completus*, Series Latina, 221 vols., Parisiis, 1844-1864.

Potthast, *Regesta Pontificum Romanorum inde ab anno post Christum natum MCXCVIII ad annum MCCCIV*, Berolini, 1874.

Quinque Collectiones Antiquae, ed., Friedbreg, Leipsic, 1882.

Reference Works

Alphonsus M., de Ligouri, St., *Theologia Moralis*, ed. L. Guadé, 4 vols., Romae, 1905-1912.

Amydenius, Th., *Tractatus de Officio et Iurisdictione Datariae et de Stylo Datariae*, 2 vols., Venetiis, 1654.

André, Abbe Michel, *Cours Alphabétique et Méthodique de Droit Canon*, 2 vols. in 1, Paris, 1844.

Antonius a Spiritu Sancto, *Directorium Regularium*, Lugduni, 1661.

(Bachofen), Charles Augustine, *A Commentary on the New Code of Canon Law*, 8 vols., St. Louis: Herder; Vol. III, Religious, 5 ed. 1938.

(Bachofen), Charles Augustine, *Compendium Iuris Regularium*, Neo-Eboracensis: Benziger, 1903.

Baldus de Ubaldis, *Commentaria in XI Codicis Libros*, 3 vols., Venetiis, 1572.

Barbosa, A., *Iuris Ecclesiastici Universi Libri III*, Lugduni, 1660.

——— *Variae Tractationes Iuris*, 5 vols. in 1, Lugduni, 1631.

Benedictus XIV, *Opera Omnia*, 16 vols., Prati, 1846.

Berutti, Ch., *Institutiones Iuris Canonici*, 6 vols., Taurini—Romae: Marietti, 1936-1938.

Beste, U., *Introductio in Codicem*, Collegeville, Minnesota: St. John's Abbey Press, 1938.

Billuart, *Cursus Theologiae iuxta Mentem Divi Thomae, Parisiis*, 1878.

Bonacina, M., *Opus de Morali Theologia*, 2 vols., Venetiis, 1687.

Bollandists, *Examen Historicum et Canonicum Libri R. D. Verhoeven*, Bruxellis, 1847.

Bouix, D., *De Principiis Iuris Canonici*, Parisiis, 1882.

——— *Tractatus de Iure Regularium*, 3 ed., 2 vols., Parisiis, 1883.

Brys, J., *De Dispensatione in Iure Canonico*, Brugis: Beyaert, 1925.

Cappello, F., *Summa Iuris Canonici*, 3 vols., Romae: apud Aedes Universitatis Gregorianae; Vols. I and II, 2 ed., 1932-1934; Vol. III, 1933.

Castro—Palao, F., *Opus Morale*, 2 vols., Lugduni, 1682.

Chapman, J., *St. Benedict and the Sixth Century*, New York: Longmans, 1929.

Cicognani, A. G., *Canon Law*, authorized English version by J. O'Hara and F. Brennan, Philadelphia: Dolphin Press, 1934.

Cocchi, G., *Commentarium in Codicem Iuris Canonici ad usum scholarum*, 5 vols. in 8, Taurinorum Augustae: Marietti, 1922-1930; Vol. I, 3 ed. 1925.

Coronata, Mattheus Conte a, *Institutiones Iuris Canonici ad Usum Utriusque Cleri ac Scholarum*, 5 vols., Taurini (Italia): Marietti, 1928-1936; Vol. I, 2 ed. 1939.

—————— *Ius Publicum Ecclesiasticum*, 2 ed. Taurini: Marietti, 1934.

Corazza, *Sacrae Romanae Rotae Decisiones coram Rev. J. Molines*, 6 vols. in 5, Romae, 1728.

Creusen, J., *Religious Men and Women in the Code*, 3 ed., by Adam Ellis, translated by Edward Garesche, Milwaukee: Bruce Publishing Co., 1939.

De Angelis, P., *Praelectiones Iuris Canonici*, 6 vols., Romae, 1877-1891.

D'Annibale, J., *Summula Theologiae Moralis*, 5 ed., 3 vols., Romae: Desclee, Lefebvre, et Soc., 1908.

De Luca, I., *Theatrum Veritatis et Iustitiae*, 16 vols. in 9, Coloniae Agrippinae, 1706.

Didacus ab Aragonia, *Dilucidatio Privilegiorum Ordinum Regularium*, Bononiae, 1765.

Donatus, H., *Rerum Regularium Praxis Resolutoria*, 4 vols., Coloniae, 1675.

Du Cange, C., *Glossarium Mediae et Infimae Latinitatis conditum a Carolo du Fresne Domino du Cange Auctum a Monachis Ordinis S. Benedicti*, editio nova a Leopold Favre, 10 vols., Paris, 1937.

Fagnanus, P., *Commentaria in Libros Decretalium*, 3 vols., Coloniae, 1704-1705.

Ferraris, F., *Prompta Bibliotheca, Canonica, Iuridica, Moralis, Theologica, necnon Ascetica, Polemica, Rubristica, Historica*, ed. Migne, 8 vols., Parisiis, 1860-1863.

Hefele, C., and Leclerq, H., *Histoire des Conciles*, 10 vols. in 18, Paris, 1907-1921.

Herincx, *Summa Theologica Scholastica*, Antwerpiae, 1680.

Hinschius, P., *Das Kirchenrecht der Katholiken und Protestanten in Deutschland*, 6 vols., Berlin, 1869-1897.—Vols. I-IV, *System des katholischen Kirchenrechts*, Berlin, 1869-1888.

Hostiensis, Cardinalis (Henricus de Segusio), *Summa Aurea*, Venetiis, 1570.

Lehmkuhl, *Theologia Moralis*, Friburgi Brisgoviae, 1897.

Lewis, C., and Short, C., *A New Latin Dictionary*, founded on the translation of Freund's Latin German Lexicon, American Book Company, 1927.

Maroto, P., *Institutiones Iuris Canonici ad Norman Novi Codicis*, 2 vols. Romae, 1919; Vol. I, 3 ed., 1921.

Michiels, P. G., *Normae Generales Iuris Canonici*, 2 vols., Lublin, Poloniae: Universitas Catholica, 1929.

Mocchegiani, P., *Iurisprudentia Ecclesiastica ad Usum et Commoditatem Utriusque Cleri*, 3 vols., Ad Claras Aquas, 1904-1905.

Murray, J., *A New English Dictionary on Historical Principles*, 9 vols., Oxford Clarendon Press, 1893.

Navarrus (Martinus de Azpilcueta), *Opera Omnia*, 6 vols., Venetiis: apud Ioannem Guerilum, 1618.

Ottaviani, A., *Institutiones Iuris Publici Ecclesiastici*, 2 vols., Typis Polyglottis Vaticanis, 1935.

Ojetti, B., *Commentarium in Codicem Iuris Canonici*, 4 vols., Romae, 1927-1931.

O'Neill, W., *Papal Rescripts of Favor*, The Catholic University of America Canon Law Studies, n. 57, Washington: The Catholic University of America, 1930.

Papiensis, Bernardus, *Summa Decretalium*, ed. E. Th. Laspeyeres, Ratisbonae, 1860.

Parma, A., *Collectio Indulgentiarum Theologica, Canonice, ac Historice Digesta*, Ad Claras Aquas, 1897.

Parsons, A., *Canonical Elections*, The Catholic University of America Canon Law Studies, n. 118, Washington: The Catholic University of America Press, 1939.

Pastor, L., *The History of the Popes from the Close of the Middle Ages*, 29 vols., translation, Vols. I-VI, ed. by Frederick Antrobus; Vols. VII-XXIV, ed. by Ralph Kerr; Vols. XXV-XXIX, ed. by Dom Ernest Graf, St. Louis: Herder, 1906-1938.

Petra, V., *Commentarium ad Constitutiones Apostolicas*, 5 vols. in 2, Venetiis, 1729.

Phillips, G., *Kirchenrecht*, 7 vols., Regensburg, 1845-1872.

Piatus Montensis, *Praelectiones Iuris Regularis*, 3 ed., 2 vols., Tornaci: Casterman, 1906.

Pichler, V., *Epitome Iuris Canonici iuxta Decretalium Libros Gregorianae Collectionis Explanati*, 2 vols., Venetiis, 1741.

Pignatelli, I., *Consultationes Canonicae*, 11 vols. in 4, Coloniae Allobrogum, 1700.

Pirhing, E., *Synopsis Pirhingiana seu Compendiaria SS. Canonum Doctrina*, 2 ed., Augustae Vindelicorum et Dilingae, 1695.

Reh, F., *The Rules of Law and Canon Law*, Romae: apud Pont. Universitatis Gregorianae, 1939.

Reiffenstuel, A., *Ius Canonicum Universum*, 5 vols. in 7, Parisiis, 1864-1870.

Reilly, E., *The General Norms of Dispensation*, The Catholic University of America Canon Law Studies, n. 119, Washington: The Catholic University of America Press, 1939.

Rodericus, E., *Quaestiones Regulares et Canonicae Enucleatae, sive Resolutiones Quaestionum Regularium*, 3 vols. in 1, Antwerpiae, 1628.

Rodericus, H., *Quaestiones Regulares et Canonicae Enucleatae*, Lugduni, 1634.

Roelker, E., *Principles of Privilege according to the Code of Canon Law*, The Catholic University of America Canon Law Studies, n. 35; Washington: The Catholic University of America, 1926.

Sanchez, T., *De Sancto Matrimonii Sacramento Disputationum Libri Decem, in Tres Tomos Distributi*, Venetiis, 1712.

Sinistrari, L., (Maria de Ameno), *De Delictis et Poenis*, 3 vols., Romae: 1754.

Sagmüeller, J., *Lehrbuch des katholischen Kirchenrechts*, Freiburg im Breisgau, 1900.

Salmanticenses, *Cursus Theologiae Moralis*, 4 vols. in 2, Venetiis, 1728.

Schmalzgrueber, F., *Ius Ecclesiasticum Universum*, 5 vols. in 12, Romae, 1843-1845.

Schreiber, G., *Kurie und Kloster im 12 Jahrhundert*, Kirchenrechtliche Abhandlungen von Dr. Ulrich Stutz, Heft. 65-68, 2 vols., Stuttgart, 1910.

Schroeder, H. J., *Disciplinary Decrees of the General Councils, Text, Translation, and Commentary*, St. Louis: Herder, 1937.

Schulte, J. F., *Das katholische Kirchenrecht*, Giessen, 1860.

Sipos, S., *Enchiridion Iuris Canonici*, 3 ed., Pecs, 1936.

Suarez, F., *Opera Omnia*, 26 vols., Parisiis, 1856-1866.

Tamburini, A., *De Iure Abbatum et Aliorum Praelatorum, tam Regularium quam Saecularium Episcopis Inferiorum*, 3 vols. in 1, Coloniae Agrippinae, 1691.

Thesaurus Linguae Latinae, editus auctoritate et consilio Academiarum Quinque Germanicarum, Berolinsis, Gottingensis, Lipsiensis, Monacensis, Vindobonensis, 6 vols., 1906-1912.

Thomas Aquinas, St., *Summa Theologica*, 6 vols., Parisiis: Vives, 1895.

Thomassinus, L., *Vetus et Nova Ecclesiae Disciplina circa Beneficia et Beneficiarios*, 10 vols., Moguntiae, 1787.

Toso, A., *Ad Codicem Iuris Canonici Commentaria Minora*, 5 vols., Romae: Marietti, 1920-1934; Vol. I, 2 ed., 1921.

Vermeersch, A., *De Religiosis Institutis et Personis, Tractatus Canonico-Moralis*, 2 vols., Brugis, vol. I, 2 ed., 1907; vol. II, 4 ed., 1909.

Vermeersch, A.—Creusen, J., *Epitome Iuris Canonici*, 3 vols., Mechliniae: Dessain, vol. I, 6 ed., 1937; vol. II, 5 ed., 1934; vol. III, 5 ed. 1936.

Van Etten, G., *Compendium Privilegiorum Regularium*, Romae, 1900.

Van Hove, A., *Commentarium Lovaniense in Codicem Iuris Canonici*, 1 vol. in 5 tom., Mechliniae—Romae: H. Dessain, 1928-1939. Tom. IV, *De Rescriptis*, 1936; tom. V, *De Privilegiis, De Dispensationibus*; 1939.

Vasto, B., *De Communicatione Privilegiorum praesertim inter Religiones*, Aquilae in Vestinis, Italia, 1936.

Vecchiotti, S., *Institutiones Canonicae ad Usum Seminariorum Accomodatae*, 5 vols., 10 ed., Augustae Taurinorum, 1886.

Vromant, G., *De Fidelium Associationibus*, Louvain, 1932.

Wernz, F., *Ius Decretalium*, 6 vols., Romae et Prati, 1898-1905.

Wernz, F.,—Vidal, P., *Ius Canonicum*, 7 vols. in 8, Romae: Universitas Gregoriana, 1923-1938.

Woywod, S., *A Practical Commentary on the Code of Canon Law*, 5 ed., 2 vols., New York, 1939.

Zallinger, J., *Institutiones Iuris Ecclesiastici*, 5 vols., Romae, 1823.

Periodicals

Apollinaris, Romae, 1928-

Analecta Iuris Pontificii, Rome, 1855-1868; Paris, 1869-1890.

Commentarium pro Religiosis, Romae, 1920-; after 1935, *Commentarium pro Religiosis et Missionariis*.

Perfice Munus, Turin, 1926-

Periodica de Re Canonica et Morali utili Praesertim Religiosis et Missionariis, Brugis, 1905-

Revue des Communautés Religieuses, Louvain, 1925-

Articles

Creusen, J., "Privileges par Communication."—*Revues des Communautés Religieuses*, IX (1933), 113.

Darmanin, "Consuetudine e portio paroecialis,"—*Perfice Munus*, XII (1937), 152-154.

Goyeneche, "Commentarium in Responsum P.C.I. ad Can. 613, § 1," *Apollinaris*, XI (1938), 178-180.

Larraona, A., "Questio Canonica," *Commentarium pro Religiosis*, III (1922), 205-213.

Salsmans, "De Religiosis et Missionariis supplementa et monumenta, continuans De Religiosis II, ed. 2," *Periodica de Re Canonica et Morali utili praesertim Religiosis et Missionariis*, V (1913), 41.

Tatjer, "De Communicatione Privilegiorum inter Religiones," *Apollinaris*, V (1932), 458-486.

ABBREVIATIONS

AAS—Acta Apostolicae Sedis.
ASS—Acta Sanctae Sedis.
BRC—Bullarii Romani Continuatio Summorum Pontificum.
BRT—Bullarum Diplomatum et Privilegiorum Sanctorum Romanorum Pontificum Taurinensis Editio.
CpR—Commentarium pro Religiosis.
CpRM—Commentarium pro Religiosis et Missionariis.
Hardouin—Acta Conciliorum, etc.
PCI—Pontificia Commissio Interpretationis.

ALPHABETICAL INDEX

Index of Papal Documents

BIOGRAPHICAL NOTE

Raymond Anthony Matulenas was born on May 29, 1915, in Waukegan, Illinois. After completing his elementary education at St. Bartholomew's School in Waukegan, he entered Pio Nono Academy, Milwaukee, Wisconsin, where he completed his high school education. Then, in the fall of 1931 he began his college course at St. Bede College, Peru, Illinois. After two years of college training, he entered the novitiate of the Order of St. Benedict, at Latrobe, Pennsylvania, where he made his religious profession as a member of St. Bede Abbey on July 2, 1934. In the fall of that year he was enrolled in the Seminary at St. Bede Abbey, where he completed his philosophical and theological course. He made his solemn profession on July 2, 1937, and was ordained to the priesthood on June 2, 1940. In September of that year his superior offered him the opportunity of taking an advanced course in the School of Canon Law at the Catholic University of America. In June of 1941 he received the degree of the Baccalaureate in Canon Law and in May of the following year he received the degree of Licentiate in Canon Law.

CANON LAW STUDIES*

1. Freriks, Rev. Celestine A., C.PP.S., J.C.D., Religious Congregations in Their External Relations, 121 pp., 1916.
2. Galliher, Rev. Daniel M., O.P., J.C.D., Canonical Elections, 117 pp., 1917.
3. Borkowski, Rev. Áurelius L., O.F.M., J.C.D., De Confraternitatibus Ecclesiasticis, 136 pp., 1918.
4. Castillo, Rev. Cayo, J.C.D., Disertacion Historico-Canonica sobre la Potestad del Cabildo en Sede Vacante o Impedida del Vicario Capitular, 99 pp., 1919 (1918).
5. Kubelbeck, Rev. William J., S.T.B., J.C.D., The Sacred Penitentiaria and Its Relation to Faculties of Ordinaries and Priests, 129 pp., 1918.
6. Petrovits, Rev. Joseph, J.C., S.T.D., J.C.D., The New Church Law on Matrimony, X-461 pp., 1919.
7. Hickey, Rev. John J., S.T.B., J.C.D., Irregularities and Simple Impediments in the New Code of Canon Law, 100 pp., 1920.
8. Klekotka, Rev. Peter J., S.T.B., J.C.D., Diocesan Consultors, 179 pp., 1920.
9. Wanenmacher, Rev. Francis, J.C.D., The Evidence in Ecclesiastical Procedure Affecting the Marriage Bond, 1920 (Printed 1935).
10. Golden, Rev. Henry Francis, J.C.D., Parochial Benefices in the New Code, IV-119 pp., 1921 (Printed 1925).
11. Koudelka, Rev. Charles J., J.C.D., Pastors, Their Rights and Duties According to the New Code of Canon Law, 211 pp., 1921.
12. Melo, Rev. Antonius, O.F.M., J.C.D., De Exemptione Regularium, X-188 pp., 1921.
13. Schaaf, Rev. Valentine Theodore, O.F.M., S.T.B., J.C.D., The Cloister, X-180 pp., 1921.
14. Burke, Rev. Thomas Joseph, S.T.D., J.C.D., Competence in Ecclesiastical Tribunals, IV-117 pp., 1922.
15. Leech, Rev. George Leo, J.C.D., A Comparative Study of the Constitution "Apostolicae Sedis" and the "Codex Juris Canonici," 179 pp., 1922.
16. Motry, Rev. Hubert Louis, S.T.D., J.C.D., Diocesan Faculties According to the Code of Canon Law, II-167, pp., 1922.
17. Murphy, Rev. George Lawrence, J.C.D., Delinquencies and Penalties in the Administration and the Reception of the Sacraments, IV-121 pp., 1923.
18. O'Reilly, Rev. John Anthony, S.T.B., J.C.D., Ecclesiastical Sepulture in the New Code of Canon Law, II-129 pp., 1923.

*Below n. 100 only the following numbers are still available: Nn. 3, 4, 9, 25, 34, 57 and 75. Beginning with n. 100 only the following are unavailable: Nn. 100, 101, 102, 104, 105, 107, 108, 109, 111 and 113.

19. Michalicka, Rev. Wenceslas Cyril, O.S.B., J.C.D., Judicial Procedure in Dismissal of Clerical Exempt Religious, 107 pp., 1923.
20. Dargin, Rev. Edward Vincent, S.T.B., J.C.D., Reserved Cases According to the Code of Canon Law, IV-103 pp., 1924.
21. Godfrey, Rev. John A., S.T.B., J.C.D., The Right of Patronage According to the Code of Canon Law, 153 pp., 1924.
22. Hagedorn, Rev. Francis Edward, J.C.D., General Legislation of Indulgences, II-154 pp., 1924.
23. King, Rev. James Ignatius, J.C.D., The Administration of the Sacraments to Dying Non-Catholics, V-141 pp., 1924.
24. Winslow, Rev. Francis Joseph, O.F.M., J.C.D., Vicars and Prefects Apostolic, IV-149 pp., 1924.
25. Correa, Rev. Jose Servelion, S.T.L., J.C.D., La Potestad Legislativa de la Iglesia Catolica, IV-127 pp., 1925.
26. Dugan, Rev. Henry Francis, A.M., J.C.D., The Judiciary Department of the Diocesan Curia, 87 pp., 1925.
27. Keller, Rev. Charles Frederick, S.T.B., J.C.D., Mass Stipends, 167 pp., 1925.
28. Paschang, Rev. John Linus, J.C.D., The Sacramentals According to the Code of Canon Law, 129 pp., 1925.
29. Piontek, Rev. Cyrillus, O.F.M., S.T.B., J.C.D., De Indulto Exclaustrationis necnon Saecularizationis, XIII-289 pp., 1925.
30. Kearney, Rev. Richard Joseph, S.T.B., J.C.D., Sponsors at Baptism According to the Code of Canon Law, IV-127 pp., 1925.
31. Bartlett, Rev. Chester Joseph, A.M., LL.B., J.C.D., The Tenure of Parochial Property in the United States of America, V-108 pp., 1926.
32. Kilker, Rev. Adrian Jerome, J.C.D., Extreme Unction, V-425 pp., 1926.
33. McCormick, Rev. Robert Emmett, J.C.D., Confessors of Religious, VIII-266 pp., 1926.
34. Miller, Rev. Newton Thomas, J.C.D., Founded Masses According to the Code of Canon Law, VII-93 pp., 1926.
35. Roelker, Rev. Edward G., S.T.D., J.C.D., Principles of Privilege According to the Code of Canon Law, XI-166 pp., 1926.
36. Bakalarczyk, Rev. Richardus, M.I.C., J.U.D., De Novitiatu, VIII-208 pp., 1927.
37. Pizzuti, Rev. Lawrence, O.F.M., J.U.L., De Parochis Religiosis, 1927. (Not Printed.)
38. Bliley, Rev. Nicholas Martin, O.S.B., J.C.D., Altars According to the Code of Canon Law, XIX-132 pp., 1927.
39. Brown, Mr. Brendan Francis, A.B., LL.M., J.U.D., The Canonical Juristic Personality with Special Reference to its Status in the United States of America, V-212 pp., 1927.

40. Cavanaugh, Rev. William Thomas, C.P., J.U.D., The Reservation of the Blessed Sacrament, VIII-101 pp., 1927.
41. Doheny, Rev. William J., C.S.C., A.B., J.U.D., Church Property: Modes of Acquisition, X-118 pp., 1927.
42. Feldhaus, Rev. Aloysius H., C.PP.S., J.C.D., Oratories, IX-141 pp., 1927.
43. Kelly, Rev. James Patrick, A.B., J.C.D., The Jurisdiction of the Simple Confessor, X-208 pp., 1927.
44. Neuberger, Rev. Nicholas J., J.C.D., Canon 6 or the Relation of the Codex Juris Canonici to the Preceding Legislation, V-95 pp., 1927.
45. O'Keefe, Rev. Gerald Michael, J.C.D., Matrimonial Dispensations, Powers of Bishops, Priests, and Confessors, VIII-232 pp., 1927.
46. Quigley, Rev. Joseph A. M., A.B., J.C.D., Condemned Societies, 139 pp., 1927.
47. Zaplotnik, Rev. Johannes Leo, J.C.D., De Vicariis Foraneis, X-142 pp., 1927.
48. Duskie, Rev. John Aloysius, A.B., J.C.D., The Canonical Status of the Orientals in the United States, VIII-196 pp., 1928.
49. Hyland, Rev. Francis Edward, J.C.D., Excommunication, Its Nature, Historical Development and Effects. VIII-181 pp., 1928.
50. Reinmann, Rev. Gerald Joseph, O.M.C., J.C.D., The Third Order Secular of Saint Francis, 201 pp., 1928.
51. Schenk, Rev. Francis, J., J.C.D., The Matrimonial Impediments of Mixed Religion and Disparity of Cult, XVI-318 pp., 1929.
52. Coady, Rev. John Joseph, S.T.D., J.U.D., A.M., The Appointment of Pastors, VIII-150 pp., 1929.
53. Kay, Rev. Thomas Henry, J.C.D., Competence in Matrimonial Procedure, VIII-164 pp.; 1929.
54. Turner, Rev. Sidney Joseph, C.P., J.U.D., The Vow of Poverty, XLIX-217 pp., 1929.
55. Kearney, Rev. Raymond A., A.B., S.T.D., J.C.D., The Principles of Delegation, VII-149 pp., 1929.
56. Conran, Rev. Edward James, A.B., J.C.D., The Interdict, V-163 pp., 1930.
57. O'Neill, Rev William H., J.C.D., Papal Rescripts of Favor, VII-218 pp., 1930.
58. Bastnagel, Rev. Clement Vincent, J.U.D., The Appointment of Parochial Adjutants and Assistants, XV-257 pp., 1930.
59. Ferry, Rev. William A., A.B., J.C.D., Stole Fees, V-136 pp., 1930.
60. Costello, Rev. John Michael, A.B., J.C.D., Domicile and Quasi-Domicile, VII-201 pp., 1930.
61. Kremer, Rev. Michael Nicholas, A.B., S.T.B., J.C.D., Church Support in the United States, VI-136 pp., 1930.

62. Angulo, Rev. Luis, C.M., J.C.D., Legislation de la Iglesia sobre la intencion en la application de la Santa Misa, VII-104 pp., 1931.
63. Frey, Rev. Wolfgang Norbert, O.S.B., A.B., J.C.D., The Act of Religious Profession, VIII-174 pp., 1931.
64. Roberts, Rev. James Brendan, A.B., J.C.D., The Banns of Marriage, XIV-140 pp., 1931.
65. Ryder, Rev. Raymond Aloysius, A.B., J.C.D., Simony, IX-151 pp., 1931.
66. Campagna, Rev. Angelo, Ph.D., J.U.D., Il Vicario Generale del Vescovo, VII-205 pp., 1931.
67. Cox, Rev. Joseph Godfrey, A.B., J.C.D., The Administration of Seminaries, VI-124 pp., 1931.
68. Gregory, Rev. Donald J., J.U.D., The Pauline Privilege, XV-165 pp., 1931.
69. Donohue, Rev. John F., J.C.D., The Impediment of Crime, VII-110 pp., 1931.
70. Dooley, Rev. Eugene A., O.M.I., J.C.D., Church Law on Sacred Relics, IX-143 pp., 1931.
71. Orth, Rev. Clement Raymond, O.M.C., J.C.D., The Approbation of Religious Institutes, 171 pp., 1931.
72. Pernicone, Rev. Joseph M., A.B., J.C.D., The Ecclesiastical Prohibition of Books, XII-267 pp., 1932.
73. Clinton, Rev. Connell, A.B., J.C.D., The Paschal Precept, IX-108 pp., 1932.
74. Donnelly, Rev. Francis B., A.M., S.T.L., J.C.D., The Diocesan Synod, VIII-125 pp., 1932.
75. Torrente, Rev. Camilo, C.M.F., J.C.D., Las Processiones Sagradas, V-145 pp., 1932.
76. Murphy, Rev. Edwin J., C.PP.S., J.C.D., Suspension Ex Informata Conscientia, XI-122 pp., 1932.
77. MacKenzie, Rev. Eric F., A.M., S.T.L., J.C.D., The Delict of Heresy in its Commission, Penalization, Absolution, VII-124 pp., 1932.
78. Lyons, Rev. Avitus E., S.T.B., J.C.D., The Collegiate Tribunal of First Instance, XI-147 pp., 1932.
79. Connolly, Rev. Thomas A., J.C.D., Appeals, XI-195 pp., 1932.
80. Sangmeister, Rev. Joseph V., A.B., J.C.D., Force and Fear as Precluding Matrimonial Consent, V-211 pp., 1932.
81. Jaeger, Rev. Leo A., A.B., J.C.D., The Administration of Vacant and Quasi-Vacant Episcopal Sees in the United States, IX-229 pp., 1932.
82. Rimlinger, Rev. Herbert T., J.C.D., Error Invalidating Matrimonial Consent, VII-79 pp., 1932.
83. Barrett, Rev. John D. M., S.S., J.C.D., A Comparative Study of the Third Plenary Council of Baltimore and the Code, IX-221 pp., 1932.

84. Carberry, Rev. John J., Ph.D., S.T.D., J.C.D., The Juridical Form of Marriage, X-177 pp., 1934.
85. Dolan, Rev. John L., A.B., J.C.D., The Defensor Vinculi, XII-157 pp., 1934.
86. Hannan, Rev. Jerome D., A.M., S.T.D., LL.B., J.C.D., The Canon Law of Wills, IX-157 pp., 1934.
87. Lemieux, Rev. Delise A., A.M., J.C.D., The Sentence in Ecclesiastical Procedure, IX-131 pp., 1934.
88. O'Rourke, Rev. James J., A.B., J.C.D., Parish Registers, VII-109 pp., 1934.
89. Timlin, Rev. Bartholomew, O.F.M., A.M., J.C.D., Conditional Matrimonial Consent, X-381 pp., 1934.
90. Wahl, Rev. Francis X., A.B., J.C.D., The Matrimonial Impediments of Consanguinity and Affinity, VI-125 pp., 1934.
91. White, Rev. Robert J., A.B., LL.B., S.T.B., J.C.D., Canonical Ante-Nuptial Promises and the Civil Law, VI-152 pp., 1934.
92. Herrera, Rev. Antonio Parra, O.C.D., J.C.D., Legislacion Ecclesiastica sobra el Ayuno y la Abstinencia, XI-191 pp., 1935.
93. Kennedy, Rev. Edwin J., J.C.D., The Special Matrimonial Process in Cases of Evident Nullity, X-165 pp., 1935.
94. Manning, Rev. John J., A.B., J.C.D., Presumption of Law in Matrimonial Procedure, XI-111 pp., 1935.
95. Moeder, Rev. John M., J.C.D., The Proper Bishop for Ordination and Dimissorial Letters, VII-135 pp., 1935.
96. O'Mara, Rev. William A., A.B., J.C.D., Canonical Causes for Matrimonial Dispensations, IX-155 pp., 1935.
97. Reilly, Rev. Peter, J.C.D., Residence of Pastors, IX-81 pp., 1935.
98. Smith, Rev. Mariner T., O.P., S.T.Lr., J.C.D., The Penal Law for Religious, VII-169 pp., 1935.
99. Whalen, Rev. Donald W., A.M., J.C.D., The Value of Testimonial Evidence in Matrimonial Procedure, XIII-297 pp., 1935.
100. Cleary, Rev. Joseph F., J.C.D., Canonical Limitations on the Alienation of Church Property, VIII-141 pp., 1936.
101. Glynn, Rev. John C., J.C.D., The Promoter of Justice, XX-337 pp., 1936.
102. Brennan, Rev. James H., S.S., M.A., S.T.B., J.C.D., The Simple Convalidation of Marriage, VI-135 pp., 1937.
103. Brunini, Rev. Joseph Bernard, J.C.D., The Clerical Obligations of Canons 139 and 142, X-121 pp., 1937.
104. Connor, Rev. Maurice, A.B., J.C.D., The Administrative Removal of Pastors, VIII-159 pp., 1937.
105. Guilfoyle, Rev. Merlin Joseph, J.C.D., Custom, XI-144 pp., 1937.
106. Hughes, Rev. James Austin, A.B., A.M., J.C.D., Witnesses in Criminal Trials of Clerics, IX-140 pp., 1937.

107. Jansen, Rev. Raymond, J., A.B., S.T.L., J.C.D., Canonical Provisions for Catechetical Instruction, VII-153 pp., 1937.

108. Kealy, Rev. John James, A.B., J.C.D., The Introductory Libellus in Church Court Procedure, XI-121 pp., 1937.

109. McManus, Rev. James Edward, C.SS.R., J.C.D., The Administration of Temporal Goods in Religious Institutes, XVI-196 pp., 1937.

110. Moriarty, Rev. Eugene James, J.C.D., Oaths in Ecclesiastical Courts, X-115 pp., 1937.

111. Rainer, Rev. Eligius George, C.SSR., J.C.D., Suspension of Clerics, XVII-249 pp., 1937.

112. Reilly, Rev. Thomas F., C.SS.R., J.C.D., Visitation of Religious, VI-195 pp., 1938.

113. Moriarty, Rev. Francis E., C.SS.R., J.C.D., The Extraordinary Absolution from Censures, XV-334 pp., 1938.

114. Connolly, Rev. Nicholas P., J.C.D., The Canonical Erection of Parishes, X-132 pp., 1938.

115. Donovan, Rev. James Joseph, J.C.D., The Pastor's Obligation in Prenuptial Investigation, XII-322 pp., 1938.

116. Harrigan, Rev. Robert J., M.A., S.T.B., J.C.D., The Radical Sanation of Invalid Marriages, VIII-208 pp., 1938.

117. Boffa, Rev. Conrad Humbert, J.C.D., Canonical Provisions for Catholic Schools, VII-211 pp., 1939.

118. Parsons, Rev. Anscar John, O.M.Cap., J.C.D., Canonical Elections, XII-236 pp., 1939.

119. Reilly, Rev. Edward Michael, A.B., J.C.D., The General Norms of Dispensation, XII-156 pp., 1939.

120. Ryan, Rev. Gerald Aloysius, A.B., J.C.D., Principles of Episcopal Jurisdiction, XII-172 pp., 1939.

121. Burton, Rev. Francis James, C.S.C., A.B., J.C.D., A Commentary on Canon 1125, X-222 pp., 1940.

122. Miaskiewicz, Rev. Francis Sigismund, J.C.D., Supplied Jurisdiction According to Canon 209, XII-340 pp., 1940.

123. Rice, Rev. Patrick William, A.B., J.C.D., Proof of Death in Prenuptial Investigation, VIII-156 pp., 1940.

124. Anglin, Rev. Thomas Francis, M.S., J.C.D., The Eucharistic Fast, VIII-183 pp., 1941.

125. Coleman, Rev. John Jerome, J.C.D., The Minister of Confirmation, VI-153 pp., 1941.

126. Downs, Rev. Joseph Emmanuel, A.B., J.C.D., The Concept of Clerical Immunity, XI-163 pp., 1941.

127. Esswein, Rev. Anthony Albert, J.C.D., Extrajudicial Coercive Powers of Ecclesiastical Superiors, X-144 pp., 1941.

128. Farrell, Rev. Benjamin Francis, M.A., S.T.L., J.C.D., The Rights and Duties of the Local Ordinary Regarding Congregations of Women Religious of Pontifical Approval, V-195 pp., 1941.
129. Feeney, Rev. Thomas John, A.B., S.T.L., J.C.D., Restitutio in Integrum, VI-169 pp., 1941.
130. Findlay, Rev. Stephen William, O.S.B., A.B., J.C.D., Canonical Norms Governing the Deposition and Degradation of Clerics, XVII-279 pp., 1941.
131. Goodwine, Rev. John, A.B., S.T.L., J.C.D., The Right of the Church to Acquire Property, VIII-119 pp., 1941.
132. Heston, Rev. Edward Louis, C.S.C., Ph.D., S.T.D., J.C.D., The Alienation of Church Property in the United States, XII-222 pp., 1941.
133. Hogan, Rev. James John, A.B., S.T.L., J.C.D., Judicial Advocates and Procurators, XIII-200 pp., 1941.
134. Kealy, Rev. Thomas M., A.B., Litt.B., J.C.D., Dowry of Women Religious, IX-152 pp., 1941.
135. Keene, Rev. Michael James, O.S.B., J.C.D., Religious Ordinaries and Canon 198, V-164 pp., 1942.
136. Kerin, Rev. Charles A., S.S., M.A., S.T.B., J.C.D., The Privation of Christian Burial, XVI-279 pp., 1941.
137. Louis, Rev. William Francis, M.A., J.C.D., Diocesan Archives, X-101 pp., 1941.
138. McDevitt, Rev. Gilbert Joseph, A.B., J.C.D., Legitimacy and Legitimation, X-247 pp., 1941.
139. McDonough, Rev. Thomas Joseph, A.B., J.C.D., Apostolic Administrators, X-217 pp., 1941.
140. Meier, Rev. Carl Anthony, A.B., J.C.D., Penal Administrative Procedure Against Negligent Pastors, XI-240 pp., 1941.
141. Schmidt, Rev. John Rogg, A.B., J.C.D., The Principles of Authentic Interpretation in Canon 17 of the Code of Canon Law, XII-331 pp., 1941.
142. Slafkosy, Rev. Anderew Leonard, A.B., J.C.D., The Canonical Episcopal Visitation of the Diocese, X-197 pp., 1941.
143. Swoboda, Rev. Innocent Robert, O.F.M., J.C.D., Ignorance in Relation to the Imputability of Delicts, IX-271 pp., 1941.
144. Dubé, Rev. Arthur Joseph, A.B., J.C.D., The General Principles for the Reckoning of Time in Canon Law, VIII-299 pp., 1941.
145. McBride, Rev. James T., A.B., J.C.D., Incardination and Excardination of Seculars, XX-585 pp., 1941.
146. Krol, Rev. John T., J.C.D., The Defendant in Ecclesiastical Trials, XII-207 pp., 1942.
147. Comyns, Rev. Joseph J., C.SS.R., A.B., J.C.D., Papal and Episcopal Administration of Church Property, XIV-155 pp., 1942.

148. Barry, Rev. Garrett Francis O.M.I., J.J.D., Violation of the Cloister, XII-260 pp., 1942.
149. Bolduc, Rev. Gatien, C.S.V., A.B., S.T.L., J.C.L., Les Etudes dans les Religions Cléricales.
150. Boyle, Rev. David John, M.A., J.C.D., The Juridic Effects of Moral Certitude on Pre-Nuptial Guarantees, XII-188 pp., 1942.
151. Canavan, Rev. Walter Joseph, M.A., Litt.D., J.C.D., The Profession of Faith, XII-143 pp., 1942.
152. Desrochers, Rev. Bruno, A.B., Ph.L., S.T.B., J.C.D., Le Premier Concile Plénier de Québec et le Code de Droit Canonique, XIV-186 pp., 1942.
153. Dillon, Rev. Robert Edward, A.B., J.C.D., Common Law Marriage, X-148 pp., 1942.
154. Dodwell, Rev. Edward John, Ph.D., S.T.B., J.C.L., The Time and Place for the Celebration of Marriage.
155. Donnellan, Rev. Thomas Andrew, A.B., J.C.D., The Obligation of the Missa pro Populo, VII-131 pp., 1942.
156. Eltz, Rev. Louis Anthony, A.B., J.C.L., Cooperation in Crime.
157. Gass, Rev. Sylvester Francis, M.A., J.C.D., Ecclesiastical Pensions, XI-206 pp., 1942.
158. Guiniven, Rev. John Joseph, C.SS.R., J.C.D., The Precept of Hearing Mass, XIV-188 pp., 1942.
159. Gulczynski, Rev. John Theophilus, J.C.L., The Desecration and Violation of Churches.
160. Hammill, Rev. John Leo, M.A., J.C.D., The Obligations of the Traveler According to Canon 14, VIII-204 pp., 1942.
161. Haydt, Rev. John Joseph, A.B., J.C.D., Reserved Benefices, XI-148 pp., 1942.
162. Huser, Rev. Roger John, O.F.M., A.B., J.C.L., The Crime of Abortion in Canon Law.
163. Kearney, Rev. Francis Patrick, A.B., S.T.L., J.C.L., The Principles of Canon 1127.
164. Linahen, Rev. Leo James, S.T.L., J.C.D., De Absolutione Complicis In Peccato Turpi, 114 pp., 1942.
165. McCloskey, Rev. Joseph Aloysius, A.B., J.C.D., The Subject of Ecclesiastical Law According to Canon 12, XVII-246 pp., 1942.
166. O'Neill, Rev. Francis Joseph, C.SS.R., J.C.D., The Dismissal of Religious in Temporary Vows, XIII-220 pp., 1942.
167. Prince, Rev. John Edward, A.B., S.T.B., J.C.D., The Diocesan Chancellor, X-136 pp., 1942.
168. Riesner, Rev. Albert Joseph, C.SS.R., J.C.D., Apostates and Fugitives from Religious Institutes, IX-168 pp., 1942.
169. Stenger, Rev. Joseph Bernard, J.C.D., The Mortgaging of Church Property, 186 pp., 1942.

170. Waldron, Rev. Joseph Francis, A.B., J.C.D., The Minister of Baptism, XII-197 pp., 1942.
171. Willett, Rev. Robert Albert, J.C.D., The Probative Value of Documents in Ecclesiastical Trials, X-124 pp., 1942.
172. Woeber, Rev. Edward Martin, M.A., J.C.D., The Interpellations, XII-161 pp., 1942.
173. Benko, Rev. Matthew Aloysius, O.S.B., M.A., J.C.L., The Abbot *Nullius*.
174. Christ, Rev. Joseph James, M.A., S.T.L., J.C.L., Dispensation from Vindicative Penalties.
175. Clancy, Rev. Patrick M. J., O.P., A.B., S.T.Lr., J.C.L., The Local Religious Superior.
176. Clarke, Rev. Thomas James, J.C.L., Parish Societies.
177. Connolly, Rev. John Patrick, S.T.L., J.C.L., Synodal Examiners and Parish Priest Consultors.
178. Drumm, Rev. William Martin, A.B., J.C.L., Hospital Chaplains.
179. Flanagan, Rev. Bernard Joseph, A.B., S.T.L., J.C.L., The Canonical Erection of Religious Houses.
180. Kelleher, Rev. Stephen Joseph, A.B., S.T.B., J.C.L., Discussions with non-Catholics: Canonical Legislation.
181. Lewis, Rev. Gordian, C.P., J.C.L., Chapters in Religious Institutes.
182. Marx, Rev. Adolph, J.C.L., The Declaration of Nullity of Marriages Contracted Outside the Church.
183. Matulenas, Rev. Raymond Anthony, O.S.B., A.B., J.C.L., Communication, a Source of Privileges.
184. O'Leary, Rev. Charles Gerard, C.SS.R., Religious Dismissed After Perpetual Profession.
185. Power, Rev. Cornelius Michael, J.C.L., The Blessing of Cemeteries.
186. Shuhler, Rev. Ralph Vincent, O.S.A., J.C.L., Privileges of Religious to Absolve and Dispense.
187. Ziolkowski, Rev. Thaddeus Stanislaus, A.B., J.C.L., The Consecration and Blessing of Churches.

www.ingramcontent.com/pod-product-compliance
Lightning Source LLC
LaVergne TN
LVHW050248080826
844660LV00012B/611

* 9 7 8 0 8 1 3 2 2 3 7 2 8 *